SIR DAVID LYNDSAY

Dauid Lyndsay herauld to ye soverain lord

SIR DAVID LYNDSAY

*Poet, and Satirist of the Old Church
in Scotland*

BY

W. MURISON

CAMBRIDGE
AT THE UNIVERSITY PRESS
1938

CAMBRIDGE
UNIVERSITY PRESS

University Printing House, Cambridge CB2 8BS, United Kingdom

Cambridge University Press is part of the University of Cambridge.

It furthers the University's mission by disseminating knowledge in the pursuit of education, learning and research at the highest international levels of excellence.

www.cambridge.org
Information on this title: www.cambridge.org/9781107505346

© Cambridge University Press 1938

First published 1938
First paperback edition 2015

A catalogue record for this publication is available from the British Library

ISBN 978-1-107-50534-6 Paperback

CONTENTS

[1] Reproduced from an engraving in Chalmers' *Lyndsay*. The original is in the first edition of Bullein's *Dialogue* (see below, p. xi). The signature, also reproduced from Chalmers, is from the Antwerp letter (see below, pp. ix note, 10).

PREFACE

I SHOULD like to make clear at the outset what precisely is my aim in this book. For there are several points which have been intentionally omitted or merely glanced at. For example, I have not discussed how far Lyndsay departed from the Roman faith and progressed towards Lutheran or Genevan doctrines. In this connexion it is interesting to learn that a list of his belongings, drawn up after his death, includes both a rosary of silver with "gaudees" of gold and a bible in English. Again, I have not tried to analyse the language of his works. To do this satisfactorily would lay on one the hard preliminary task of settling how much of the language—vocabulary, accidence, syntax—belonged to Lyndsay himself, how much to his editors or printers. I have also left unexplored the question why he escaped punishment for his utterances against the clergy while Buchanan was imprisoned and had to flee the country. Did Lyndsay owe his safety to the jester's cap and bells? Nor have I attempted an estimate of his influence in promoting the Reformation. Material for this is difficult to lay hold of. We are not greatly helped by such stories as that recorded by Row sixty odd years after the event —the story of hundreds of Perth schoolboys stirred by *The Monarche* to hiss a friar denouncing "heretical" preachers.

What, then, is my aim? After some account of Lyndsay and his poems, I set forth in detail his charges against the Scottish clergy, and then I produce evidence to prove that the charges rest on a solid foundation of truth. The evidence comes, not from sources hostile to the Roman Church, but from official records of the Church, from state documents, and from writers loyal to the Church.

It was Professor A. A. Jack, of the Chalmers Chair of English in the University of Aberdeen, who suggested that the material I had gathered about Lyndsay should be put into book form. To him and to Professor J. B. Black, of the Burnett-Fletcher Chair of History, I am deeply indebted for advice and encouragement. I wish also to record my sincere thanks to the Carnegie Trustees for their promise of financial assistance towards publication; to Mr J. F. Walker, of the Aberdeen Grammar School, for great patience and ceaseless care in reading proofs; and to the University Press readers for their unremitting vigilance.

W. MURISON

ABERDEEN
March 1938

INTRODUCTION

In the story of the events leading to the collapse of the old Scottish Church in 1560, one outstanding figure is that of Sir David Lyndsay, whose name is now to the majority of his countrymen either quite unknown or known only in the haziest way. And yet for many years after the Reformation the name of Lyndsay was among the most familiar in Scotland. His poetry was very popular, and was used, we are told, in schools, alongside of Blind Harry's *Wallace*. "Out o' Davie Lyndsay into *Wallace*" denoted a pupil's promotion.[1] Portions were committed to memory. Describing an evening in a country cottage, Pennecuik writes:

> My Aunt, whom nane dare say has no Grace,
> Was reading on the *Pilgrim's Progress*:
> The meikle Tasker, Davie Dallas,
> Was telling Blads of *William Wallace*:
> My Mither bad her second Son say,
> What he'd by heart of Davie Lindsay.[2]

Robert Heron, in his *Observations made in a Journey...in the Autumn of* MDCCXCII, says:

Almost within my remembrance, Davie Lindsay was esteemed little less necessary in every family than the Bible. It is common to have, by memory, great part of his poetry.

---

[1] Kelly's *Proverbs* (1721). One would like fuller and more precise information (dates and localities) for the use of Lyndsay in schools.

[2] *Streams from Helicon*, p. 75 (1720). Pennecuik's spelling "Lindsay" is one of several variants. The signature of the Antwerp letter (see below, p. 10), the only autograph we possess, is "Lyndsay".

Sir Walter Scott makes frequent use of this popularity. The Baron of Bradwardine in *Waverley* reads Barbour's *Bruce*, Blind Harry's *Wallace*, and Lyndsay's *Works*. Monkbarns in *The Antiquary* would listen a whole day to tales of Bruce, Wallace and Lyndsay. In *Rob Roy* Andrew Fairservice disposes of Frank Osbaldistone's claim to be a poet by exclaiming, "Gude help him! Two lines o' Davie Lindsay wad ding a' he ever clerkit." Lyndsay, however, is more than a criterion of poetic excellence to Andrew. When rebuked for finding fault with the Union of 1707, he protests, "What wad Sir William Wallace, or auld David Lindsay, hae said to the Union, or them that made it?" In *The Monastery* Dame Glendinning wonders why the Lady of Avenel is always reading a book of devotion. "An it were about Robin Hood, or some o' David Lindsay's ballants, ane wad ken better what to say to it." But it is *Redgauntlet* that has the most famous reference to Lyndsay in Scott's novels—in the blind fiddler's weird story. The night before the funeral of the Laird who had fiercely persecuted the Covenanters, two of his servants, Dougal and Hutcheon, were watching, with brandy to fortify their courage; for on the previous nights the Laird's silver whistle had blown exactly as when he was alive:

So down the carles sat ower a stoup of brandy, and Hutcheon, who was something of a clerk, would read a chapter of the Bible; but Dougal wad hear naething but a blaud of Davie Lindsay, whilk was the waur preparation.

Scott was here remembering the story of a man on his death-bed to whom a neighbour was reading from the Bible. "Hoot awa with your daft nonsense," said the dying man. "Gie me a blaud o' Davie Lyndsay."[1]

In *Marmion* Scott paints a fine portrait of Lyndsay, whom he apostrophizes:

> Still is thy name in high account
> And still thy verse has charms.

That was in 1808; but even then Lyndsay's popularity had been waning for a considerable time.[2] The records of printing throw light on the waning. Up to 1800 editions of his works were far more numerous than those of the greater poets, Henryson and Dunbar. They were most numerous in the century and a half after his death in 1555. Since the date of *Marmion* there have been only four editions of Lyndsay: two by the same editor, David Laing; and two for Societies—the Early English Text Society and the Scottish Text Society.

Lyndsay's reputation in London shortly after his death is manifest from Bullein's *Dialogue*, 1564. The narrator names several poets, and then proceeds:

Nexte theim in a blacke chaire of Gette stone, in a coat of armes, sate an aunciente knight in Orange Tawnie as one forsaken, bearyng upon his breast a white Lion, with a Croune of riche golde on his hedde. His name was sir Dauie

---

[1] Prynne, in *Histriomastix*, speaking of Kyd's *Spanish Tragedy*, tells of a dying woman who, instead of seeking the consolations of religion, cried

"Hieronimo! Hieronimo! O let me see Hieronimo acted!"

[2] In 1793 Malcolm Laing (Henry's *History of Great Britain*, VI 609) called Lyndsay "a Scottish poet, whose laurels are faded". Tennant's lines in *Anster Fair*, II lxv 1 sq.—

"Others upon the green, in open air,
Enact the best of Davie Lindsay's plays"—

are no proof of Lyndsay's popularity in 1812; for the events of *Anster Fair* belong to James V's reign.

Linse vppon the mounte, with a hammer of strong steele in his hande, breakyng a sonder the counterfeicte crosse kaies of Rome, forged by Antichriste. And thus this good knight of Scotlande saied to England the elder brother and Scotlande the younger:

> Habitare fratres in unum
> Is a blesfull thing,
> One God, one faith, one baptisme pure,
> One lawe, one lande, and one kyng.
> Clappe handes together, brethren dere,
> Unfained truce together make,
> And like frendes dooe euer acorde,
> But French and Romaine doe first forsake.
> You are without the continent,
> A sole lande of auncient fame,
> Ab origine a people olde
> Bolde Britaines ecleped by name.

> Sicut erat in principio.
> Graunt, oh God, it maie bee
> In saecula saeculorum,
> That we maie have peace in thee.
> Then we shall feare no forein power
> That againste vs shall advaunce,
> The Tartre cruell, the curse of Rome,
> Ne yet the power of Fraunce, etc.

These verses do not occur in Lyndsay's works, though his last poem prophesies no peace between Scotland and England till both are under one king. Bullein's verses are part of the English propaganda which had been going on for years.[1]

A recent writer places Lyndsay second only to Knox in bringing about the Reformation. An earlier writer is bolder:

[1] See Murray's Introduction to *The Complaynt of Scotlande*, pp. xv, xxxviii (E.E.T.S.).

Sir David Lindsay was more the Reformer of Scotland than John Knox; for he prepared the ground, and John only sowed the seed.

Similarly, Allan Ramsay:

> Sir David's satires helped our nation
> To carry on the reformation,
> And gave the scarlet dame a box
> Mair snell than all the pelts of Knox.[1]

The following pages are an attempt to tell something about Lyndsay and his works, and also to indicate and justify his attitude to the old Scottish Church.

[1] Compare what Melchior Adam said of Erasmus: "Pontifici Romano plus nocuit jocando quam Lutherus stomachando."

CHAPTER I

LYNDSAY'S LIFE[1]

SIR DAVID LYNDSAY was the eldest son of David
Lyndsay of the Mount. "The Mount is a conspicuous
hill...on the north side of the Howe of Fife, in the Vale of
Eden, about three miles from Cupar...the old mansion
stood on the south side of the hill, and overlooked a great
part of the valley of the Eden."[2] In addition, this branch
of the Lyndsays possessed Garmylton (now Garleton) in
East Lothian, two miles north of Haddington. It is not
known where David Lyndsay was born—whether in Fife
or in East Lothian; nor if he attended the Grammar
School of Cupar or the Grammar School of Haddington.
We may assume that his father obeyed the injunctions of
the Act of Parliament, 1496, that all barons and substantial free-holders should send their eldest sons and
heirs to the Grammar Schools from the age of eight or
nine, there to remain till they were competently grounded
and had "perfect" Latin. The youths had then to study
in the schools of arts and law for three years so as to be
able to administer the law in their districts. Following up
the tradition that Lyndsay studied at St Andrews, Chalmers discovered in the list of incorporated students in St
Salvator's College, 1508–9, the name "Da. Lindesay".[3]

[1] See *Lives of the Lindsays*, vol. I; D.N.B. article by Aeneas J. G.
Mackay; T. F. Henderson, *Scottish Vernacular History*, and *The Cambridge
History of English Literature*, vol. III; editions of Lyndsay by Chalmers,
Laing and Hamer.

[2] Laing, *The Poetical Works of Sir David Lyndsay*, I liii (1879). Referred
to as Laing.

[3] See *The Early Records of the University of St Andrews* (Scottish History
Society, 1926).

An "incorporatus" was one who had been three years in residence; and "Da. Lindesay" would thus have matriculated in 1505. Chalmers accordingly concluded that this was the poet and inferred that he was born about 1490.[1]

Mr Douglas Hamer refuses to accept this date, and says that Lyndsay "seems to have been born a little before October 19, 1486, for on that date twenty-one years later he received a grant...of the lands of Garmilton-Alexander, Haddingtonshire, as eldest son of David Lindsay of the Mount, Fifeshire. He must then have been of legal age."[2] Mr Hamer also calls it "sentiment" to regard "Da. Lindesay" of the St Andrews list as the poet, and thinks it "very probable" that the poet is to be identified with "one called Lyndesay" mentioned in the Exchequer Rolls for 1508,[3] as holding a post in the stable of the late prince, the baby who died in February 1508, just about twelve months old. Naturally the St Andrews "incorporatus" and the equerry (or groom of the stable) could not be one and the same person in 1508.

"Who shall decide, when Doctors disagree?" We can only keep an open mind, for "The truth is, that of the youth of Lyndsay nothing is known".[4]

When and in what capacity Lyndsay entered James IV's Court must remain undecided. The Treasurer's Accounts from August 1508 to September 1511 are lost.

[1] Chalmers, *The Poetical Works of Sir David Lyndsay*, 1 3 sq. (1806). Referred to as Chalmers.
[2] Hamer, *The Works of Sir David Lindsay*, iv ix (Scottish Text Society, 1931–36). Referred to as Hamer. The charter is quoted by Laing, 1 ix and by Hamer, iv 245 sq.
[3] Exchequer Rolls, xiii 127; Hamer, iv ix sq. and 246.
[4] Tytler, *Scottish Worthies*, iii 192.

But from the Accounts for 1511–12 we learn that Lyndsay had some office, for one entry records payment to him of forty pounds "fee and pension for Alhallowmes, Candilmes, Rudmes and Lammes bypast".[1] On 21 October 1511 he was provided with two and a half ells of blue taffeta and six quarters of yellow taffeta "to be a play coat for the play played in the king and queen's presence in the Abbey of Holyrood".[2] James IV was a merry monarch and his Court was thronged with makers of mirth.[3]

But it was not all merry-making. Some twenty years earlier Scotland had become of special importance in the politics of Europe; and strenuous efforts had been made to detach her from the French alliance and bring her into the league by which Spain hoped to crush the power of France.[4] Marriage with a Spanish princess had been a bait dangled before the eyes of James. The offer of Margaret Tudor came later. James's marriage with her, however, did not break the French alliance; and in 1513 he was seriously bent on war with England. It was at this time that he received the oft-described warning against the projected campaign. Few ghost-stories are better vouched for than this. Pitscottie and Buchanan tell it—both on the authority of David Lyndsay.

The King, says Pitscottie, was worshipping in the Church of Linlithgow and praying for success in his campaign when there entered a man about fifty years of age, with a pikestaff in his hand. He wore a blue gown belted with a roll of linen, high boots to the calf of his leg, and

---

[1] Treasurer's Accounts, IV 269. [2] Treasurer's Accounts, IV 313.
[3] Buchanan, *Historia*, XIII xxi.
[4] Gregory Smith, *The Days of James IV*. See also P. F. Tytler, J. Hill Burton and P. Hume Brown.

other clothes in keeping. He had nothing on his head but long reddish-yellow hair falling to his shoulders, with forehead bald and bare. He pushed quickly through the lords, asking for the King, whom he approached with little reverence. Leaning on the King's desk, he said:

Sir King, my mother[1] has sent me to thee, desiring thee not to pass at this time where thou art purposed, for if thou dost thou wilt not fare well in thy journey nor none that passes with thee; further she bade thee not meddle with no women nor use their counsel...for an thou do it thou wilt be confounded and brought to shame.

By this time evensong was nearly done, and while the King was considering what answer to give to the message, the man, before the King's face and in the presence of the lords, disappeared. He could not be seen or laid hold of, but vanished like a blink of the sun or a whip of the whirlwind. Pitscottie adds:

I heard tell that Sir David Lyndsay, Lyon Herald, and John Inglis, Marshal, at that time young men and special servants of the King, were standing near and thought to seize the man and question him. But in vain; they could not touch him, for he vanished between them and was no more seen.[2]

Buchanan's account is shorter. He says that he would have omitted the story as a myth spread abroad by empty rumours had he not received it from David Lyndsay of the Mount, who was present, a man of proved trustworthiness and integrity, a man of letters, a life-long speaker of the truth.[3]

[1] The Virgin Mary.
[2] Robert Lindesay of Pitscottie, *Historie*, 1 258 sq. (Scottish Text Society). Sir Walter Scott skilfully wove the story into *Marmion*, IV xv–xvii.
[3] *Historia*, XIII xxxi.

A ghost-like figure, representing the Apostle John, certainly entered the Church; but it was not supernatural. The peace-party contrived the affair to influence the superstitious King; and, if Lyndsay had a hand in the device, no wonder the figure disappeared so easily when it came near him. This apparition did not influence James; neither did that other attempt when, from the Market Cross of Edinburgh at midnight a herald from "Plotcock" (Pluto, or the Devil) summoned, in legal form, King, nobles, gentry and burgesses to appear before his master within forty days.[1] Soon after the army set out for Flodden.

Lyndsay did not go with the army. Eighteen months earlier, when on 12 April 1512 the prince was born, afterwards James V, Lyndsay had been appointed the baby's usher, an office involving close personal attendance. The curiously intimate relations of Prince and usher may be gathered from what Lyndsay wrote years later:

> Quhen thow wes young, I bure thee in myne arme
>   Full tenderlie, tyll thow begouth to gang;
> And in thy bed oft happit thee full warme,
>   With lute in hand, syne, sweitlie to thee sang:
>   Sumtyme, in dansing, feiralie I flang;
> And sumtyme, playand farsis on the flure;
> And sumtyme, on myne office takkand cure:
>
> And sumtyme, lyke ane feind, transfigurate,
>   And sumtyme, lyke the greislie gaist of Gye;
> In divers formis oft tymes disfigurate,
>   And sumtyme, dissagyist full plesandlye,
>   So, sen thy birth, I have continewalye
> Bene occupyit, and aye to thy plesoure,
> And sumtyme, Seware, Coppare, and Carvoure;

---

[1] Pitscottie, 1 260 sq. Scott, *Marmion*, v xxv, xxvi.

Thy purs maister and secreit Thesaurare,
  Thy Yschare, aye sen thy natyvitie,
And of thy chalmer cheiffe Cubiculare.
The Dreme, 8 sqq.[1]

Quhow, as ane chapman beris his pak,
I bure thy Grace upon my bak,
And sumtymes, strydlingis on my nek,
Dansand with mony bend and bek.
The first sillabis that thow did mute
Was PA, DA LYN.[2] Upon the lute
Than playit I twenty spryngis, perqueir,
Quhilk wes gret piete for to heir.
Fra play thow leit me never rest,
Bot Gynkartoun thow lufit ay best;
And ay, quhen thow come frome the scule
Than I behuffit to play the fule;
As I at lenth, in to my Dreme,
My sindry servyce did expreme.
The Complaynt, 87 sqq.

When James grew older and was keen to hear of
ancient days and warlike deeds, Lyndsay told him about
Hector, Alexander of Macedon, Pompey the Great,
Julius Caesar, King Arthur, Jason and Medea, Hercules,
Samson. He related stories of true lovers, as well as the
joy and sorrow of Troilus, and also the sieges of Tyre,
Thebes and Troy. He narrated the prophecies of Thomas
the Rhymer, of Bede and of Merlin; and such fables as
those of the Red Etin and the Gyre Carlin.[3] Lyndsay
continued in attendance upon James for twelve years.
He was not James's tutor. In 1516 Gawain Dunbar,
Dean of Moray (later Archbishop of Glasgow), was ap-
pointed the King's Master or chief instructor, with John
Bellenden (later Archdeacon of Moray) as his assistant.

---

  [1] For quotations and references the text of Laing's three-volume
edition (1869) is used, unless otherwise stated.
  [2] Play, Davie Lyndsay.   [3] *The Dreme*, 29 sqq.

About 1522 Lyndsay married Janet Douglas. No record of the marriage exists, but the Treasurer's Accounts name Janet Douglas as Lyndsay's wife and state her position in the King's household. She was the King's "semestair" and received a yearly fee of ten pounds, with the usual "livery" clothing. The earliest mention is to be found in the Accounts, 5 June 1522 to 15 April 1524:

Item, to Jenet Dowglas, spous to David Lindsay maister Ischare to the King for sewing of the Kingis lynnyng claithis de mandato domini gubernatoris: xxiiii li.[1]

Here are two from the 1527 accounts:

Item, to Jonet Dowglas, semestair of the Kingis lynnyng claithis for this instant yer, and for the yer bypast, be the Kingis precept, X ellis Parys blak, price el 1s̄; summa xxv li.[2]

Item, to Jonet Dowglas, takand yeirlie for hir fe X li., summa for this yeir and the yeir precedand, wantand unpayit in Maister Johne Cambellis tyme, and now payit be the Kingis precept: XX li.[3]

Numerous entries record supplies to Janet of holland cloth for sheets, shirts, pillow slips—one entry is cloth for a night "courchye"—ounces of sewing silk, hanks of gold and silver thread, ribbons for shirts.[4] The last time Janet Douglas is mentioned in the Accounts is June 1540, when she and her husband received £666. 13s. 4d.[5]

In 1524 Lyndsay ceased to have charge of James.[6] The Queen Mother and the Earl of Arran, Governor, had contrived the "Erection" of the boy, that is, his proclamation as de facto King of Scots. Margaret, however, was

---

[1] v 196. [2] v 314. [3] v 329.
[4] See Indexes to volumes v, vi, vii of Treasurer's Accounts.
[5] vii 315. She was alive in 1542. See charters quoted by Hamer, iv xiii and 265 sq. [6] Dunbar and Bellenden were also dismissed.

unable to keep her son in her power. In a few months her husband, the Earl of Angus, whom she now hated, with the Douglases had full control of James. Lyndsay thus describes the revolution:

> The Kyng was bot twelf yeris of aige
> Quhen new rewlaris come, in thair raige,
> For Commonweill makand no cair,
> Bot for thair proffeit singulair.
> Imprudentlie, lyk wytles fuilis,
> Thay tuke that young Prince frome the sciulis,
> Quhare he, under obedience,
> Was lernand vertew and science,
> And haistelie platt in his hand
> The governance of all Scotland;
>
> .   .   .   .   .
>
> I gyf thame to the Devyll of Hell
> Quhilk first devysit that counsell
> I wyll nocht say that it was treassoun.
> I pray God, lat me never se ryng,
> In to this realme, so young ane Kyng.
>
> *The Complaynt*, 127 sqq.

For four years, 1524–28, Lyndsay was debarred from the Court; but he received his pension. James insisted on that, though Lyndsay was slandered by his enemies.[1] He retired to Garmylton, there to lament that James was being led into vices by flatterers; to meditate on the sad welter in Church and State; to read and to write. In July 1528 the King escaped from the hands of Angus, and set about crushing the power of the Douglases. In November Angus had to flee to England:

> Thay culde nocht keip thair feit from slyding;
> Bot of thair lyffis thay had sic dreid,
> That thay war faine tyll trott ouer Tueid.
>
> *The Complaynt*, 370 sqq.

---

[1] *The Complaynt*, 263 sqq.

Lyndsay was recalled to Court and was soon busy with official duties. At this point we meet another obscurity in Lyndsay's life. When did he become Lyon King of Arms?

Chalmers admitted that he had searched the records in vain for Lyndsay's appointment as Lyon King, but nevertheless he stated that Lyndsay's inauguration to this office and his knighthood both belonged to 1530.[1] Chalmers was also indignant because Irving made 1542 the date of installation.[2] According to Laing, Lyndsay became "Chief Herald, or as it was called, Lyon King of Arms" in 1529.[3]

Mr Douglas Hamer, however, has amassed evidence[4] which shows clearly that Lyndsay, while acting from about 1530 as Lyon King (and several times so designated in English and French documents), is in Scottish documents, till eight years later, styled either simply herald, or chief herald, or Snowdon herald.[5] It is in the Treasurer's Accounts for 1538 that he is first called Lyon in Scottish records; and then in the *Register of the Privy Seal*, 3 October 1542, we read: "David Lindesay of the Mont, knycht, alias Lyoun King of Armes." Hamer also points out that from 1529 to 1542 there was a Lyon King by name Thomas Pettigrew. During that period, then, David Lyndsay was what we should call Lyon Depute, while, as doing the work of the Lyon King, he was naturally called Lyon King outside Scotland. His formal in-

[1] I 11 sq.
[2] *The Lives of the Scotish Poets*, II 79 (1804).
[3] I xxii.　　　　　　[4] IV 288 sqq.
[5] For example, James V's letter (25 May 1531) to the Emperor Charles V has "cum fedeli nostro heraldo, et eius ordinis primo, dauide Lyndesayo, snawdon vocato". Quoted by Hamer, IV 254.

auguration and his knighthood came in the autumn of
1542.

Let us now go back about a dozen years. We find
Lyndsay beginning then a series of embassies to Flanders,
France, Denmark and England.[1] In 1531 Sir John
Campbell of Lundy, accompanied by David Lyndsay
and David Panter, crossed to Flanders to renew the
century-old commercial treaty. They were welcomed
with great splendour in Brussels by the Governess of the
Netherlands, the Queen of Hungary, and her brother,
the Emperor Charles V. In a letter from Antwerp,[2] 23
August, Lyndsay announces the success of the mission
and refers to the "triumphs"—

that is to say the triwmphand justynis, the terribill turnements, the feychtyn on fut in barras, the naymis of lords and
knychts that war hurt the day of the gret towrnament;
quhais circumstans I haiff writtin at length, in articles, to
schaw the Kingis grace at my haym cumin.

What Lyndsay wrote for the King's eyes has disappeared.

Spain and England were again eager to detach Scotland from France. Within the space of a few years, James
received the Order of the Garter from Henry VIII and
the Order of the Golden Fleece from Charles V, while as
a counterpoise came from Francis I the French Order of
St Michael. Charles also suggested one relative of his

[1] From two passages, one in *Syde Taillis*, 37 sqq., the other in *The
Monarche*, 5417 sqq., some have inferred that Lyndsay had visited Italy.
The Monarche passage refers to the year 1510:
        "I saw Pape Julius manfullye
         Passe to the feild tryumphantlye,
         With ane rycht aufull ordinance,
         Contrar Lowis, the kyng of France."
[2] Given in facsimile by Laing, I xxiv. It is interesting as the only example extant of Lyndsay's handwriting.

after another as a wife for James. But James would not accept the suggestion. He was, in fact, seeking a marriage alliance with France; and Lyndsay was with the envoys sent to negotiate for the hand of Marie de Bourbon, daughter of the Duke of Vendôme. Annoyed by what seemed to him unnecessary delay, James sailed to France and went incognito to see Marie. His disguise was penetrated and he was sumptuously feasted. The lady, however, did not find favour in his sight; and he left, ostensibly to consult the French King. Francis advised the Vendôme marriage, but James became the importunate suitor for the King's eldest daughter, Magdalene. As she was of delicate constitution, her father was unwilling, but at last gave way to James's urgency. The wedding was celebrated in Paris on 1 January 1537. James and his bride landed at Leith on 19 May. Lyndsay was busy with preparations for the Queen's coronation when she died on 7 July; and he had now to compose an elegy, *The Deploratioun of the Deith of Quene Magdalene*.[1]

Reasons of state demanded that James should again marry, and the bride chosen was Mary of Lorraine, daughter of the Duke of Guise, and widow of the Duke of Longueville. She landed in the East of Fife on 10 June 1538, and was welcomed at St Andrews with great rejoicing. Part of the welcome consisted of pageants and plays, with the preparation of which Lyndsay had a great deal to do.

And first she was received at the New Abbey Gate. Upon the east side there was made to her a triumphal pageant by Sir David Lyndsay of the Mount, Lyon Herald, who caused a great cloud to come out of the heavens constructed

[1] See below, p. 28 sq.

above the gate where the Queen came in and to open in two halves instantly; and there appeared a fair lady most like an angel having the keys of all Scotland in her hands, delivering them unto the Queen's Grace in sign and token that all the hearts of Scotland were opened to the receiving of her Grace; with certain addresses and exhortations made by the said Sir David Lyndsay for the Queen's instruction, which taught her to serve her God, obey her husband, and keep her body clean according to God's will and commandment.[1]

About this time, or not long after, Lyndsay would be engaged on the first version of *Ane Satyre of the Three Estaitis*—more correctly we should call it the "interlude"—performed at Linlithgow on 6 January 1540 before the King and Queen, and the whole Council Spiritual and Temporal. According to Eure's account[2] (and he is our sole authority) James countenanced the performance for the express purpose of promoting Church reform. Parliament, not long after, registered the prevalent dissatisfaction with the state of the Church when it passed an Act calling attention to "the unhonestie and misreule of Kirkmen baith in witt, knawledge and maneris" as being in part "the mater and cause that the Kirk and Kirkmen are lychtlyit and contempnit";[3] and exhorting all clerics, each in his degree, to reform. But the Church was too powerful, and could claim to be the patriotic party opposed to England.

In August 1542, Scotland was invaded by an English army; and later, in November, came the shameful rout of Solway Moss, which, following other disasters, broke James's heart. He died on 14 December in the Palace of

---

[1] Pitscottie, I 379.   [2] See below, p. 38.
[3] Act. Parl. 14 Mai 1541, ii 370.

Falkland. Among those present was Lyndsay, the King's life-long friend and loyal servant.[1] He might have repeated then, with even greater truth, what he had written fourteen years earlier:

> I see rycht weill, that proverbe is full trew
> Wo to the realme that hes ouer young ane King.
>
> *The Dreme*, 1010 sq.

For now the heir to the throne was a baby girl, only a few days old. The usual results followed—English intrigues, quarrels of nobles and clergy.

Some time later Lyndsay visited three foreign rulers to return the Orders bestowed on James—the Golden Fleece to the Emperor Charles; the St Michael to Francis I; and the Garter to Henry VIII. In a letter of acknowledgment to the Earl of Arran, Regent, 24 May 1544, Henry gives high praise to Lyndsay:[2]

We have thought good by these our letters to signify the same unto you with this also, that the said Lyon in the delivery thereof hath used himself right discreetly and much to our content.

High praise indeed; for "King Henry knew a man when he saw him".

In May 1546, Cardinal Beaton was barbarously assassinated.[3] One view of the deed is expressed in a stanza which is found in several slightly varying forms. Wodrow in telling the story of Archbishop Sharp's assassination quotes as "not unapplicable" what he calls "the known stanza of that excellent man, and, for his time, good

---

[1] Pitscottie, I 407 sq. with notes.
[2] The National Manuscripts of Scotland, Part III, No. XXVII.
[3] Pitscottie, II 82 sqq.

poet Sir David Lindsay of the Mount, upon Cardinal
Beaton:

> As for the Cardinal, I grant
> He was a man we might well want,
>   God will forgive it soon;
> But of a truth, the sooth to say,
> Altho' the loon be well away,
>   The fact was foully done."[1]

It is very doubtful if the stanza should be attributed to
Lyndsay. What he did write on Beaton was *The Tragedie*
(i.e. *Tragic Tale*) *of the Cardinall*.[2]

It has been said that Lyndsay was one of those who for
various reasons sought refuge in the Castle of St Andrews
after the Cardinal's murder. This, however, is far from
the truth. He was present at the meeting of the Estates
when, on 4 August 1546, the summons for treason was
issued against the murderers; and ten days later he was
directed, as Lyon King, to execute the summons. On 17
December the Governor and Council sent him with a
trumpeter to ask for a conference with the "Castilians",
but they gave no answer.[3] In April 1547 John Knox
found rest from his wanderings in the Castle; and soon
after, in the Parish Church of St Andrews he was called
to undertake the public ministry by John Rough, Henry
Balnaves and others. One of the promoters of the call
was Sir David Lyndsay—bold action for a government
official.[4]

---

[1] *History of the Sufferings of the Church of Scotland* (1721–22), III 48 of Dr
Robert Burns's edition, 1839. Wodrow is apparently the earliest to
attribute these lines to Lyndsay. See Hay Fleming in A. F. Mitchell's
Scottish Reformation, p. 81.
[2] See below, p. 32.
[3] State Papers, Henry VIII, v 581.
[4] Laing's *Knox*, I 186 sqq.

In 1548 Lyndsay was on embassy to Christian III of
Denmark to ask for ships to defend the Scottish coasts from
English attacks, and to negotiate free trade with Denmark
for Scottish merchants. Naval assistance was refused,
but free trade was readily granted.[1] Scotland had other
than trade connexions with Denmark; and in Copen-
hagen Lyndsay met John Macalpine (Machabaeus, to
use his Latin designation), Professor of Theology in the
University. His name, by an easy fiction, appears on the
title-page of Lyndsay's *Monarche*, which is stated to be
printed at the command and expense of "Doctor
MACHABEVS In Copmāhouin."[2]

There is little to say about the last years of Lyndsay's
life. In January 1555 he presided over a Chapter of
Heralds in the Abbey of Holyrood-house. Soon after
this he died; when and where being unknown. It is certain, however, that he was dead before 18 April 1555.
For under that date the *Register of the Privy Seal* speaks of
the "deceis of vmquhile Sir David Lyndesay of the Mont
knyght", and names his successor, as heir of tailzie, to
be his younger brother Alexander. Alexander "stands
second in the deed of entail in 1542. As no mention is
made of his [David Lyndsay's] wife, who had the lands
by the same deed in conjunct-fee, there can be no doubt
that she predeceased her husband."[3]

No portrait of Lyndsay is known to exist. A woodcut
on the title-page of the Edinburgh Edition of 1634 bears
his name.[4] The Jascuy reprint of 1558 contains a figure
intended to represent the poet as Lyon King.[5]

---

[1] Treasurer's Accounts, December 1548, IX 259. Chalmers, I 36 sq.
[2] It was really printed in Scotland.   [3] Laing, I xlv.
[4] Laing, III 246.   [5] Laing, III 265 sqq.

What sort of man was Lyndsay? George Buchanan, as we have seen,[1] spoke of his trustworthiness and integrity, his love of letters, his abhorrence of falsehood; and Henry VIII praised his discretion when on embassy in England.[2] The friendship and affection between James and Lyndsay stood unshaken for many years. Yet Lyndsay's loyalty and love did not forbid advice and admonition. He exhorts the King to be just, to observe the laws, to choose good counsellors and drive away flatterers; to remember that he is but a man under authority and may be called to account by his subjects: again and again kings are blamed for allowing the oppression of the poor, for appointing incompetent clergy, for making war needlessly.[3]

Like James V, Lyndsay favoured the commons. He felt deeply for them and boldly voiced their grievances—the burden of high rents and Church exactions, unjust decisions by judges, the plague of idle vagabonds.[4] Lyndsay lets us hear the poor labourers' complaint that law is brother to oppression.[5] He also represents the Barons and Burgesses as embracing John the Commonweal when they agree to make perpetual "band" with him and to give him a place in parliament.[6]

A notable characteristic of Lyndsay was his kindliness, without which he would have been no suitable "usher"

---

[1] See above, p. 4.   [2] See above, p. 13.

[3] *The Dreme*, 1037 sqq., *The Complaynt*, 269 sqq., *Papyngo*, 279 sqq., *Tragedie*, 344 sqq., *Ane Satyre*, 578 sqq., 1045 sqq., 1580 sqq., 1612 sqq., 1882 sqq., 3155 sqq., 3738 sqq., 4561 sqq. Lyndsay is expressing the same view of the accountability of kings as Major, *Historia*, IV iii, xvii and xviii (Constable's Translation, 158, 213 sqq. and 219 sq.).

[4] *The Dreme*, 918 sqq., *Ane Satyre*, 1968 sqq., 2440 sqq., 2553 sqq., 2650 sqq., 2725 sqq., 3058 sqq., *The Monarche*, 4682 sqq., 5701 sqq.

[5] *The Monarche*, 4733.   [6] *Ane Satyre*, 2715 sqq., 3774 sqq.

for the baby prince. He was fond of dogs and birds. He was genial and merry-hearted, fond of music and dancing, story-telling, innocent games and recreations.[1]

Lyndsay was a lover of his country; but a patriot had no easy time in Scotland in those days. One burning question was whether the kingdom was to unite with England, or remain a puppet in the hands of France. And Lyndsay was nobly inconsistent. In 1537 he writes that the King's marriage with Magdalene of France had confirmed the ancient alliance, and that, though she was dead, her memory would always keep the two realms in peace and amity.[2] In Folly's Sermon we are told that had it not been for French support, Scotland would have suffered disaster.[3] On the other hand, Beaton's ghost bewails his deeds which broke the peace with England and brought calamity on Scotland.[4] In the dark days after Pinkie the Clerk tells the braggart Captain that it is such as he that have ruined the country.[5] They cry for war, while he himself (adds the Clerk) prays to God for peace:

Sa quhat ye will, I think seuer peax is best,
Quha wald haif weir, God send thame littill rest.

In the last years of his life Lyndsay shudders at the miseries of war.[6] He bids those who have the governance put their trust, not in mortal man, but in God Omnipotent. Then they need not depend on France for guns or galleys or other munitions.[7] Kings and peoples are

[1] *The Dreme*, 8 sqq., *The Complaynt*, 87 sqq., *Papyngo*, 80 sqq., *Bagsche, Ane Satyre*, 1840 sqq.
[2] *The Deploratioun*, 82 sqq., 197 sqq.
[3] *Ane Satyre*, 4577 sqq.
[4] *The Tragedie*, 99 sqq., 141 sqq., 180 sqq.
[5] *The Auld Man and his Wife*, 180 sqq.
[6] *The Monarche*, 1889 sqq., 5381 sqq.
[7] *The Monarche*, 91 sqq.

ever ready to fight with each other; and Lyndsay concludes that there will be no peace in Britain till the whole
island is under one rule:

> Betuix thir realmes of Albione,
> Quhare battellis hes bene mony one,
> Can be maid none affinitie,
> Nor yit no consanguinitie;
> Nor be no waye thay can consydder
> That thay may have lang peace togydder,
> I dreid that weir makis none endyng
> Tyll thay be boith onder ane kyng.
>
> *The Monarche*, 5399 sqq.[1]

Lyndsay lived in an age in which speech was often very
blunt and, to our ideas, even filthy; and when he is dealing with certain subjects his language is naturally outspoken, or coarse, if you will. How far this corresponded
to a similar strain in his nature would be hard to deter-
mine. From his *Answer to the Kingis Flyting*, some have
inferred that Lyndsay was stained with the immorality
of his age and environment; and one need not be sur-
prised if this were true, seeing the example set by bishops
and cardinals.[2] Whatever he may have been in his

---

[1] John Major (*Historia*, IV xviii, Constable's Translation, 217 sqq.)
says that any one, English or Scottish, who did not believe that the royal
families of England and Scotland should intermarry so that a monarch
with a just title to both might rule over a united country, had no eye to
the welfare of his country and the common good. So also I vii, IV xii
and V xvii.

[2] The sixteenth century, however, frequently showed grave discrepancy between life and writings; especially among the humanists. Sir
Thomas More's epigrams are often wanton in tone, and he has now been
canonized. Buchanan, author of a Latin version of the Hebrew Psalms,
turned into Latin ludicrous and indelicate stories (of the type of Bebel's
"Facetiae"), as *In Rusticum* and part of the second *Palinodia*. Ruddiman,
Buchanan's editor, puts forward the plea that it was the fault of the poet,
not of the man; and he cites the Roman poet's excuse: "Lasciva est
nobis pagina, vita proba est."

younger days, he became in later years thoughtful, serious, religious. In his last poem he refuses to write on coarse subjects; and, when speaking of the sinners in the antique world, he declares that they abounded in wickedness,

> Quhilk I abhor to put in vers,
> Or tell with toung I am nocht abyll;
> The suthe bene so abhominabyll.[1]

Nor was he without visions of the higher life. More than once he lays down, as the end and aim of man's existence, not pleasure nor power nor wealth, but to win a good name, to do one's duty, to live uprightly and fear God.[2]

[1] *The Monarche*, 1230 sqq., 3392 sqq.
[2] *Ane Satyre*, 4491 sqq., *Squire Meldrum*, 1632 sqq., *Papyngo*, 598 sqq., *The Monarche*, 480 sqq., 4969 sqq., 5035 sqq., 6265 sqq., 6295 sqq.

CHAPTER II

LYNDSAY'S POEMS

WE possess none of Lyndsay's poems in his own hand-writing, but the following manuscripts[1] exist:

1. The Lambeth MS. of *The Monarche*, which Mr Hamer regards as "in direct descent from the author's MS."

2. The Edinburgh MS., containing *The Monarche*, *The Dreme*, *The Complaynt*, *The Deploratioun*, *The Papyngo*, which seem taken from some of the printed editions.

3. *The Bannatyne MS.*,[2] containing parts of *Ane Satyre* transcribed from a manuscript source.

Of the poems which we have, *The Dreme* is the earliest.[3] Internal evidence shows that it belongs to the period of Lyndsay's retirement, 1524–28, most likely to the first half of 1528, when James was still in the hands of Angus. It consists of 1134 lines divided into "The Epistil to the Kingis Grace", "The Prolog", "The Dreme" and "Ane Exhortatioun to the Kingis Grace". The metre is the Chaucerian heptastich, except in "Ane Exhortatioun", where Lyndsay employs the nine-line stanza, rhyming

---

[1] Hamer, IV 5 sqq.

[2] Edited for the Scottish Text Society by W. Tod Ritchie (1928–34).

[3] *The Dreme* is not the work of a beginner. Lyndsay must have written other poems, which have not been preserved. Mr Douglas Hamer, in the Scottish Text Society's Edition, I 1 and III 12, is confident that Lyndsay had written poems on the subjects with which he amused the young Prince James (see above, p. 6); and declares positively (III 101) that Lyndsay "tells us that he has written" them. But this is a probability, not a certainty; especially as Lyndsay's word *descryve* (*The Dreme*, 33) does not necessarily mean "write poetry", but may be simply "tell stories".

a a b a a b b a b; as Chaucer in part of *Anelida and Arcyte* and Dunbar in *The Goldyn Targe*.

Lyndsay introduces himself as the King's old servant, who played with him when a child and later amused him with legends and stories. He has now a new story to tell. One January morning, after a sleepless night, he sets out for the sea shore. He meets Dame Flora, dressed in mourning weeds, and hears the birds lamenting the absence of summer with its sunshine and warmth:

> "Allace! Aurora," the syllie Larke can crye,
>   "Quhare hes thou left thy balmy liquour sweit,
> That us rejosit, we mounting in the skye?
>   Thy silver droppis ar turnit in to sleit.
>   O fair Phebus! quhare is thy hoilsum heit?
> Quhy tholis thow thy hevinlie plesand face
>   With mystie vapouris to be obscurit, allace!
>
>   "Quhar art thow May, with June thy syster schene,
>   Weill bordourit with dasyis of delyte?
>   And gentyll Julie, with thy mantyll grene,
>   Enamilit with rosis red and quhyte?
>   Now auld and cauld Januar, in dispyte,
>   Reiffis frome us all pastyme and plesour:
>   Allace! quhat gentyll hart may this endure?"

From the sands Lyndsay climbs to a little cave, and there falls asleep, lulled by the sound of winds and waves. In a marvellous dream, he imagines that Dame Remembrance conveys him down to Hell. He sees, lying in heaps, popes and other churchmen, kings and queens, lords and ladies, commoners in thousands; and he details the sins that brought them to that infernal furnace,

> Quhose reward is rew, without remede,
> Ever deyand and never to be dede.

After visiting Purgatory, *limbus infantum* and *limbus patrum*, they mount to the Earth and then to the Moon,

> Quene of the See and bewtie of the nycht.

Next they ascend through the other spheres, which Lyndsay describes with the long-drawn-out learning of mediaeval astronomy and astrology. They behold all the glories of Heaven; and as they look down on the Earth, Remembrance in very prosaic lines tells its size, its three[1] divisions and their sub-divisions. After viewing the Garden of Eden, Lyndsay asks to be shown Scotland. By nature, Scotland is good and fair: why is it so miserably poor? Though rich in natural resources and possessing a fine race of people, it has no strong ruler to enforce the laws, ensure peace and justice, and allow work to be done. Just then, a sad-faced, ragged wayfarer appears, John the Commonweal, who gives a woeful account of Scotland. In the South Border there is nothing but plunder and murder. In the Highlands the lazy sluggards would not let him stay. In the Isles and in Argyle is nothing but unthrift, laziness, falsehood, poverty and strife. In the Lowlands Singulare Profeit[2] ill-treated him. He fared no better among the clergy, who love simony, covetousness, pride and sensuality. The nobles also are degenerate:

> Thare is nocht ellis bot ilk man for hym self,
> That garris me go thus baneist lyke ane elf.

Lyndsay's only consolation is:

> Yit, efter the nycht, cumis the glaid morrow.

John has resolved not to return till the country is under

[1] America was not yet known to Lyndsay as a fourth division.

[2] In the *Diurnal of Occurrents*, 1544, we are told of a Secret Council appointed (earls, lords, bishops, abbots). Every lord acted "for his own particular profit and took no heed of the common weal".

a wise old king, who delights to do justice and punish traitors; for the proverb is true:

> Wo to the realme that hes ouer young a King.

John flies away over firth and fell; and Lyndsay is soon back in the cave, where he is wakened by the roar of a ship's guns and the shouting of the sailors.

Home he goes and, writing down the dream, he adds "Ane Exhortatioun". Let the King remember his high station and observe the laws; comfort his people; drive away flatterers; take the advice of his nobles; be just, prudent, virtuous; no miser, and neither covetous nor licentious. Finally, he tells the King:

> remember thow mon dee,
> And suddanlie pass of this mortall see.

The Complaynt is later than *The Dreme*, and belongs to 1529–30.[1] It contains 510 lines in octosyllabic couplets.

Lyndsay feels he must complain; for, while others have been richly rewarded, he has obtained nothing. And yet he served the King from his very birth. Perhaps he should have been importunate, for

> Ane dum man yit wan never land.

Still it is hard to see those rewarded who were

> full far to seik
> Quhen I lay nychtlie be thy cheik.

Lyndsay recalls his intimate service to the King; and, though better, as the proverb runs, luck at court than good service, yet all expected Lyndsay to be made a lord. But, when the King was twelve, new rulers took control in his name and led him into bad ways. Lyndsay was banished from Court. At last, however, the King escaped.

---

[1] Hamer, III 47 sqq.

Now there is justice in the land, and order in the Highlands and the Borders: prosperity returns, property is
safe:

> Jhone Upeland bene full blyith, I trow,
> Because the rysche bus kepis his kow.

Only churchmen are unreformed; and James is charged,
as he hopes for the bliss of Heaven, to make them do their
duty.

The King is rich, and will surely bestow a reward on
Lyndsay, or at least give him a loan. He will, in proper
legal form, bind himself to repay the loan when the Bass
Rock and the Isle of May are set on Mount Sinai; or

> Quhen kirkmen yairnis no dignitie,
> Nor wyffis no soveranitie;

or at some other impossible date. Otherwise, Lyndsay
will pray that the King's heart may be softened, or that
he himself may be content to live quietly on little and in
his old age retire to his ancestral estate.

*The Testament and Complaynt of Our Soverane Lordis
Papyngo*, according to one of the two colophons of the
1538 edition, was "compyled by Dauid Lyndesay of the
mount, and finysshed the xiiij of Decembre, in the yere of
our lorde. 1530."[1] The poem, of 1185 lines in all, is
divided into "The Prolog"; "The Complaynt of the
Papyngo"; "The First Epystyll of the Papyngo, Direct
till our Soverane Lord"; "The Secund Epistyl of the
Papyngo, Directit to her Brether of Courte"; "The Commonyng betuix the Papyngo and hir Holye Execu-
touris"; concluding with one stanza to the reader and

[1] Laing, III 259. This edition of the *Papyngo*, London, 1538, used to be
regarded as the earliest printed of Lyndsay's works. Hamer, however,
holds (I 55, III 65) that there was an edition in 1530, and that this
colophon refers not to completion of the writing of the poem but to its
first publication. The other colophon says "printed in 1538".

one to the book. "The Prolog" is in stanzas of nine five-foot lines, *a a b a a b b c c*, as in Douglas's *Palace of Honour* (Third Part). The rest of the poem is in the Chaucerian heptastich. The final stanza has its lines cut in two, with additional rhymes for the first half of each line.

Lyndsay begins with a lament that all themes have been written upon by the great poets of former days—Chaucer, Gower, Lydgate, Kennedie, Dunbar,

> quhilk language had at large,
> As may be sene in tyll his Goldin Terge,

Quintyn, Merser, Rowle, Henderson, Hay, Holland and Gawain Douglas. Still living are Sir James Inglis, Kyd, Stewart, "quhilk desyrith ane staitly style", Stewart of Lorne, Galbraith, Kinlouch and Ballendyne. Lyndsay has no "ingyne" and can find no better subject than this complaint of the Papyngo. He writes for rural folk; and, when "cunnyng men" despise his work,

> Then sall I sweir, I maid it bot in mowis
> To landwart lassis, quhilks kepith kye and yowis.

The incident with which *The Complaynt* opens, proves the truth of the proverb,

> Quho clymmis to hycht, perforce his feit mon faill.

Lyndsay had charge of the King's Papyngo, which he trained to speak and to whistle. She would, untaught,

> Syng lyke the merle, and crawe lyke to the cocke,
> Pew lyke the gled, and chant lyke the laverock,
> Bark lyk ane dog, and kekell lyke ane ka,
> Blait lyk ane hog, and buller lyke ane bull,
> Gaill lyke ane goik, and greit quhen scho wes wa;
> Clym on ane corde, syne lauch, and play the fule;
> Scho mycht have bene ane Menstrall agane Yule.[1]

[1] For a very elaborate enumeration of the cries of birds and beasts, see *The Complaynt of Scotland*, p. 39 (E.E.T.S.).

One day he carries her into his garden, where she begins
to climb to the top of a tree. A gust of wind breaks a
branch and down the Papyngo falls on a stub, which
pierces her breast. She cries for a priest. Instead of
hastening to help her, Lyndsay hides under a hawthorn;
for the plan of the poem demands that he shall overhear
what she says. She bewails fortune's fickleness and the
ambition which brought her to Court. Then she begins
her epistle to the King:

> Prepotent Prince, peirles of pulchritude,

and rolls off a goodly array of aureate terms. She proceeds to remind James that a king is merely God's
vassal;[1] and must render an account of his deeds. Her
advice to James is: "Learn to be a king. Rule your own
self, for only so can you rule others. Choose wise counsellors. Read history, and profit by the mistakes of your
predecessors. Trust your faithful barons. Curb op-
pressors, seasoning justice with mercy."

Her advice to the Courtiers is on the text,

> Quho sittith moist hie, sal fynd the sait moist slidder.

She draws some examples of downfall from the Scottish
Court, and others from France, Rome and England, re-
ferring in conclusion to Troy, to Alexander of Macedon,
to Julius Caesar and to Agamemnon. Courtiers should
fear God and seek to reach Heaven, the only true Court.
She bids farewell to Edinburgh, Stirling, Linlithgow and
Falkland.

At this point three birds swoop down, typifying three
kinds of ecclesiastics—a Pie, a Canon Regular; a Raven,
a Black Monk; a Kite, a Holy Friar. Each urges his

---

[1] In 1596 Andrew Melville told James VI that he was "but God's
sillie (=feeble) vassal".

claims to shrive the Papyngo and take charge of her property. The Papyngo objects to the Kite: she once saw him steal a chicken from the mother hen. "My teind", he promptly explains. The Papyngo, however, would prefer the merle, the mavis, the nightingale, the turtle dove, the jay, the peacock, the lark, the swallow. "Why", asks the Kite, "are we churchmen hated?" The Papyngo gives an elaborate account of clerical degeneration from the time of the Emperor Constantine.[1] At last she is shriven by the Kite and makes her will, leaving different parts of her body to different birds, and her heart to the King. When she dies, her three executors, disregarding her will, devour her body, while the Kite flies off with the heart.

Lyndsay ends by telling his book, since it is so rude, to keep away from the company of the learned.

An Answer quhilk Schir David Lyndesay maid to the Kingis Flyting[2] consists of seventy lines, in the Chaucerian heptastich, a metre quite out of keeping with the ribaldry of the piece. A reference to the King's approaching

---

[1] Constantine, according to a document—a forgery but believed in during the Middle Ages and all-important historically—granted Pope Silvester and his successors temporal power over Rome, Italy and the Western States. The Donation of Constantine, as it was called, was often referred to as a source of harm: in Dante, for example, *Inferno*, xix 115 sqq. To deny the authenticity of the Donation was counted heresy as late as 1533.

[2] James's *Flyting* has not been preserved. The name "Flyting", that is "scolding", denotes the type of poem found in various literatures—the Continental *desbat, estrif, disputoison* of older days. In Scotland it rose to an extraordinary height of personal vituperation in such writings as *The Flyting of Dunbar and Kennedie*, and *The Flyting betwixt Montgomerie and Hume*. See Dunbar, i cix sqq. (Scottish Text Society), and Montgomery, pp. xxxii sqq. (Scottish Text Society).

marriage suggests 1536 as the probable date of composition.

Lyndsay compliments James as *the* Prince of Poetry, and says that he is reluctant to reply. In very outspoken language he describes a ludicrous accident to James in his time of wild oats.

The Complaynt and Publict Confessioun of the Kingis Auld Hound callit Bagsche, 224 lines in length, may have been written in 1536 or a little earlier. Its metre is octo-syllabic octave, rhyming *a b a b b c b c*. The hound is a mouthpiece to satirize courtiers.

Bagsche, the former favourite, gives advice to his successor, Bawtie. Bagsche, proud in prosperity, acted wrongly; and would have been hanged; but, on account of his age, has been spared, to wander at large, kicked by those he formerly injured. He entreats Lanceman, Lyndsay's dog, to intercede so that he may share in a church appointment in Dunfermline, and, through royal influence, obtain collation to a benefice with fire and light. If he is to live, he must have leave to worry lambs in Lent. Let Bawtie be warned not to act oppressively in his time of prosperity. For the proverb is true:

Hiest in Court nixt the widdie.

The Deploratioun of the Deith of Quene Magdalene, written in 1537,[1] contains 203 lines, in the Chaucerian hepta-stich, eminently suitable for the lament.

Lyndsay begins with an invocation to Death, destroyer of all living—of emperors and kings, and now of the Flower of France. Adam, Nature, Venus, Cupid, Fortune are also, more or less, to blame for Magdalene's

---

[1] See above, p. 11.

LYNDSAY'S POEMS 29

death. Paris is praised for the reception given to James, and for the magnificent wedding ceremony:

> Thare selit was the confirmatioun
> Of the weill keipit ancient Alliance,
> Maid betuix Scotland and the realme of France.

Lyndsay then gives a glowing account of Magdalene's arrival in Scotland. He pictures the royal greeting that would have been hers in Edinburgh; he sees in his mind's eye the Queen herself in her raiment

> Of gold, and perle, and precious stonis brycht,
> Twinklyng lyke sterris, in ane frostie nycht;

and tells of the pageants, the orations in her honour, the coronation, the banquets, the tournaments. But alas! this was all turned *in Requiem Aeternam.* Yet, the memory of the Queen will keep Scotland and France in peace and amity for all time. For so Lyndsay apostrophizes Death:

> Thocht thow hes slane the hevinly Flour of France,
>   Quhilk impit was in to the Thrissil kene,
> Quhairin all Scotland saw thair haill plesance,
>   And maid the Lyoun rejoysit frome the splene:
>   Thocht rute be pullit frome the levis grene,
> The smell of it sall, in despyte of thee,
> Keip ay twa Realmes in peace, and amitie.[1]

The Justing betuix James Watsoun and Jhone Barbour Servitouris to King James the Fyft is a short burlesque account in heroic couplets of a jousting which, tradition says, was part of the festivities in 1538 when James married Mary of Lorraine. It may be of a slightly later date.

The champions, one a "medicinar", one a leech,

---

[1] Buchanan wrote this epigram on the marriage:

> "Quam bene cum fulvo sunt lilia juncta leone:
>   Floribus illa quidem praestat, at ille feris."

fought a ridiculous duel in ridiculous style, on horseback and on foot, with spears and swords and fists. Thank God! no blood was shed.

Ane Supplicatioun Directit to the Kingis Grace in Contemptioun of Syde Taillis consists of 176 lines, in octosyllabic couplets. Editors give different dates, 1538, 1539–41, for its composition. It was first printed in 1568.

The King has settled Highlands and Borders; but another matter calls for reform, not treasonable but certainly irrational—the long dresses of women, trailing through dust and mud three-quarters behind their heels. Bishops and queens may have trains, but why should every lady sweep "kirk and calsay" clean? The very images would curse the dust which rises. How pleasant in contrast are the Italian ladies, whose feet can be seen below their gowns. Lyndsay ridicules the clergy, their trains upborne to show their feet: how different were the saints and apostles. He laughs loudest to see a nun with gown uplifted to display her lily-white hose. He despises the ill-paid draggletails with two ells of cloth below her knee; the moorland ewe-milker in barn and byre with a long trailing kirtle; and the mere child who will imitate the Queen. Burgess wives contend who shall have the longest trains, bordered with fine velvet. In summer one cannot approach them for dust. He would "thae Borrowstounis barnis had breikkis". After rain their tucked-up tails, all bespattered, are disgusting. And what a waste of cloth! No good can result from trains longer than cover the ankles. Greater length than that comes of pride, and pride comes of the devil. Therefore, long tails proceed from evil.

Another fault is for ladies, when gentlemen salute them, to cover all the face except the eyes. Let the King make proclamation that ladies shall show their faces and cut their gowns.

Kitteis Confessioun consists of 140 lines of octosyllabic couplets. Its date is doubtful. If the mention of the King in line 25 refers to James V, it was written before December 1542. The poem first appears in Charteris's edition of 1568, with the note "compylit (as is beleuit) be Schir David Lyndesay of the Mount". There is no certainty that David Lyndsay was the author, yet the fact that the poem was ascribed to him shows the popular opinion that it was just what he might have written. The *Confessioun* speaks with two voices—in lines 1–94 the voice of the humorist and satirist attacking the immorality and the incompetence of the clergy; in the rest of the poem the voice of the serious thinker. One might consider the first part as a sketch for an episode in *Ane Satyre*, and the second as a fragment from *The Monarche*, inartistically stitched together. If Lyndsay was the author, the *Confessioun* must have been transmitted orally or in writing from sometime before the spring of 1555 till Charteris secured it.

The poem begins with an attack on auricular confession as affording the clergy an opportunity for immoral behaviour and a means to ferret out secrets. For this purpose, the author pictures Kittie at confession.[1] In the next part of the poem, friars are denounced for declaring that confession is necessary for salvation, whereas it is merely a dream of men. Confess to God alone: repent

[1] See below, p. 101, for a fuller account.

and trust in Christ. Any difficulty in faith or morals should be shown to a true preacher, who will give counsel and comfort. In the primitive church, confession was not compulsory, but voluntary.

The Tragedie[1] *of the Cardinall* contains 434 lines, in the Chaucerian heptastich. The date of composition is 1547.[2] The poem is divided into "The Prolog"; "The Tragedie"; "To the Prelats"; "To the Prencis".

As Lyndsay was musing over Boccaccio's *Fall of Princes*, a figure appeared and said that his tragedy was greater than any in Boccaccio. He, David Beaton, will narrate it for Lyndsay to write. The Cardinal sketches his career as ecclesiastic and as statesman: how he rose to supreme power in Scotland and how he purposed to destroy his adversaries, especially all who favoured the Old and the New Testament. Then he was suddenly assassinated.

> I lay unburyit seven monethis, and more,
>   Or I was borne to closter, kirk, or queir,
>
> .   .   .   .   .   .
>
>   All proud Prelatis at me may lessonis leir,
>   Quhilk rang so lang, and so tryumphantlie,
>   Syne, in the dust, doung doun so dulefullie.

Let these unprofitable hirelings, greedy and unlearned, amend their ways while they have time. Princes should choose bishops who know their duties. All churchmen should be competent, not ignorant and not vicious.

[1]   "Tragedie is to seyn a certeyn storie,

.   .   .   .   .

Of him that stood in great prosperitie
And is y-fallen out of heigh degree
Into miserie, and endeth wrecchedly."
                    Chaucer, *Canterbury Tales*, B. 3163 sqq.

[2] See Hamer, III 152.

Beaton counsels every Christian king to make reformation; else princes and prelates shall all be buried in Hell.

The Historie of Ane Nobill and Vailyeand Squyer, William Meldrum, umquhyle Laird of Cleische and Bynnis, 1594 lines in length, divides into two parts: "The Historie" and "The Testament". "The Historie" is in easy-flowing octosyllabic couplets; "The Testament" in the Chaucerian heptastich, except the concluding stanza, which is the octosyllabic octave, rhyming *a b a b b c b c*. The date of the poem is uncertain. The end of 1550 seems the likeliest date, at least for the Squire's death, though the first part of the poem may have been written earlier. Hamer discusses this at length, III 176 sqq.

Poets preserve the memory of notable men to be ensamples to others to follow virtue and eschew vice. Lyndsay will tell the story of a noble squire, William Meldrum, soldier and lover. He began his vassalage at twenty,

> Proportionat weill, of mid stature,
> Feirie and wicht .   .   .   .
> Blyith in countenance, richt fair of face,
> And stude weill ay in his ladies grace.

He was with the Scottish navy when a descent was made on Carrickfergus. Then he did valiant deeds in France, in particular he defeated the boastful English champion. After other conquests (over English *men* and French *ladies*), Meldrum set sail for Scotland, and on the way he overcame a famous English captain. At home he fell in love with a young widow, but they could not marry without a papal dispensation. They lived together; but a rival in love, with a band of men, attacked Meldrum and left him covered with many severe wounds. During his healing, he learned the art of surgery, which he used to help others. But his worst wound could not be healed —the loss of his lady; for she was forced to marry another. Meldrum became marshal to Lord Lyndsay. When dying he appointed three Lyndsays as executors:

That Surname failyeit never to the Croun.

He committed his soul to God and bequeathed his body to Mars, his tongue to Mercury, his heart to Venus. His friend, Sir David Lyndsay, was selected to arrange the funeral procession. No monks were to be there nor friars, but men of war: no weeds of black, but red, blue and green: no tolling of bells, but firing of guns, blare of trumpets, and sweet music: no priest, unless of Venus' profession. Bidding adieu to his friends and asking for the last rites of the Church, he commended his soul "In manus tuas, Domine".

Ane Dialog betuix Experience and Ane Courteour, commonly spoken of as *The Monarche*, a long poem of 6333 lines, was most likely finished in 1553, and printed in 1554, perhaps under Lyndsay's supervision.[1] It consists of "The Epistil to the Redar"; "The Prolog"; "The First Buke"; "The Secund Buke"; "The Thrid Buke"; "The Fourt Buke"; "Ane Exhortatioun".

The metre of "The Epistil" and of "Ane Exhortatioun" is the stanza of nine five-foot lines, rhyming *a a b a a b b c c*; of "The Prolog" and of other passages (e.g. 6101 sqq.) the Chaucerian heptastich; and of 2397 sqq. the decasyllabic octave, rhyming *a b a b b c b c*; but most of the poem (e.g. 300 sqq.) is in octosyllabic couplets.

[1] Laing, III 173 sqq., 264 sqq.; Hamer, I 197, III 237 sq. See above, p. 15.

Lyndsay announces his theme to be the miserable state of the world, and so his book should be clad in sable. Since Scotland has no King and since the Queen is in France, he dedicates the poem to the Regent, the Earl of Arran, and his brother, Archbishop Hamilton. If they, the Head of the State and the Head of the Church, approve, let the book go to the clergy and the nobility to show the world's misery and to tell how the woes of Scotland are the Lord's punishment for sins in Church and State. "Preach the sincere word: do justice. Trust in God and there is no need to depend on France."

"The Prolog" describes how Lyndsay, after a restless night, musing on the misery of mankind, went forth one May morning to hear the sweet birds sing, to smell the fragrant herbs and flowers, to see the glorious sun arise and pale the moon and stars. He would have written on these beauties, but that would be matter without edification. No Muse, no pagan deity will he invoke, but the God of David and Paul. He prays to Christ, for Calvary is his Parnassus.

In the beginning of Book I, Courtier (Lyndsay himself) sees a white-haired, white-bearded old man, Experience, in a mantle of sapphire blue. Experience answers questions and expatiates on topics asked and suggested by Courtier, who after his life at Court and after much travel wishes to find peace. "Fool!" says Experience, "this life has never-ending troubles, only after death is peace." Courtier would willingly hear of the woes of others; for

> Marrowis in trybulatioun
> Bene wracheis consolatioun.

Woe, says Experience, is the outcome of sin. Faith

in Christ (with Hope and Charity) brings salvation.
Charity is

> First, lufe thy God above all thyng,
> And thy nychtbour but fenzeyng;
> Do none injure nor villanie,
> Bot as thow wald wer done to thee.

Sin came through Adam, as Genesis tells, and Experience
will unfold the story. Lyndsay interposes a defence of his
paraphrasing scripture in the "vulgare and maternall
language". Latin works by "cunnyng Clerkis" may do
for the learned, but the unlearned know little of these.
But Lyndsay's rhyme is directed to colliers, carters and
cooks, to Jack and Tom. Those who have only their
mother tongue should not be left ignorant of God's
wonderful works. How ridiculous to repeat prayers in
Latin, without understanding.[1] Prayers, and the Creed,
and books necessary to salvation should be in the
vernacular; and also the laws of the land.

Book I concludes with an account of the Creation, the
Fall of Man, and the Deluge.

Book II begins with the building of Babel by Nimrod
and his introduction of fire-worship. A passage is inserted denouncing war and vividly describing its miseries.
We now hear of Ninus, who instituted monarchy and
invented image-worship. Then follows an exclamation
against idolatry and the misuse of images among
Christians, against processions of images, against pilgrimages and pretended miracles. Lyndsay wishes for
a speedy reformation. The narrative returns to Ninus,
builder of Nineveh, and then tells of Semiramis and
Sardanapalus.

[1] See below, p. 111.

Book III deals with Sodom; with the second, the third and the fourth monarchies; with the destruction of Jerusalem; with the sad end of tyrants; and with the first spiritual (i.e. the papal) monarchy. Next, Lyndsay gives a satiric account of Church and churchmen, degenerated and decayed: he wishes reform, not destruction.

Book IV tells of Death, Anti-Christ, and the End of the World. Now comes a digression on the decadence of the Spiritual Estate, and what results therefrom. Resuming the narrative, Experience describes the Last Judgment, Heaven and Hell.

Then follows an exhortation to Courtier: "Memento Mori: trust in Christ: be content in thy calling: God will provide."

> Dreid nocht to dee, for Deith is bot ane slummer:
> Leve ane just lyfe, and with ane joyous hart,
> And of thy guddis tak pleasandlye thy part.

The conclusion is a beautiful evening scene: the sun sets, the moon rises, the stars appear:

> The dew now donkis the rosis redolent:
> The mareguildis that all day wer rejosit
> Of Phebus heit, now craftelly ar closit.

> The blysfull byrdis bownis to the treis,
> And ceissis of thare hevinlye armoneis:
> The cornecraik in the crofte, I heir hir cry;
> The bak, the howlat, febyll of thare eis,
> For thair pastyme, now in the evenyng fleis;
> The nychtyngaill, with myrthfull melody,
> Hir naturall notis persith throw the sky,
> Tyll Synthea makand hir observance,
> Quhilk on the nycht dois tak hir dalyance.

Lyndsay parts from Experience, and goes home to write down what he has heard.

Pedder Coffeis is a poem of nine stanzas, written in the metre of *Bagsche*. David Laing was the first to include it among Lyndsay's works "on the somewhat", as he says himself, "doubtful or suspicious name—LINSDSAY—to whom it is attributed in George Bannatyne's MS. 1568".[1] The poem is a satire on seven types of rascally hucksters.

The attribution to David Lyndsay must remain doubtful. Though some phrases are akin to Lyndsay's, the general tone and style are not his. Its inclusion in his works, however, or its exclusion, makes no difference in any estimate we may form of his opinions or his poetic powers.

Ane Pleasant Satyre of the Three Estaitis was performed on at least three occasions—6 January 1540; 7 June 1552; and 12 August 1554.

A. There exists no text of the 1540 performance, but it is generally held that the play presented at the Feast of Epiphany of that year before the Court at Linlithgow was by David Lyndsay. Who else could have written it? A play was certainly performed; and what it was about we know from a letter of 26 January 1540, and from a summary of the play sent by Sir William Eure to Thomas, Lord Cromwell. Eure was at Coldstream as Commissioner for settling Border disputes and he relates a conversation with the Scottish Justice-Clerk, Thomas Bellenden, on the prospect of Church reformation in Scotland. Bellenden said that the King and the Lords Temporal were much inclined to the reformation of the

---

[1] Laing, I 300. See *The Bannatyne Manuscript*, III 84 (Scottish Text Society). The editor says, "*Linsdsay* is in more faded ink, as if written by a different hand".

misdemeanours of bishops, religious[1] and priests: so much indeed that by favour of the King an interlude was played at the Feast of Epiphany before the King and Queen and the whole Council, Spiritual and Temporal. The play dealt with the depravity in religion, the presumption of bishops, the collusion of the Consistory Courts, and the improper behaviour of priests. Eure encloses "a note of the effect", or summary, of the play given him by a Scot, of the English interest, who saw the play. Bellenden also told Eure that after the performance, the King exhorted the Archbishop of Glasgow and other prelates to reform their fashions and manners of living, else he would send six of the proudest of them to his uncle of England; and as Henry dealt with these, so would he himself deal with all the others who would not amend.[2]

Copy of the "note of effect" of the play:[3]

First came in Solace, whose part was simply to make merry, sing ballads with his fellows, and drink at the interludes of the play. He showed first to the audience the play to be played, which was a general thing, meaning nothing in special to displease anyone, praying therefore no one to be angry with it. Next entered a King, who passed to his throne, having no speech till the end, and then merely to ratify as in open parliament all things done by the rest of the players, who represented the Three Estates. With him came his

---

[1] That is, monks and nuns.

[2] According to Sir James Melville of Halhill (*Memoirs*, pp. 63 sqq., Bannatyne Club), once when James was displeased with his prelates, he asked: "Wherefore gave my predecessors so many lands and rents to the kirk? Was it to maintain hawks, dogs and whores to a number of idle priests? The King of England burns, the King of Denmark beheads you; but I shall stick you with this same whinger." Thereupon he drew his dagger, and they fled in great fear.

[3] The summary is here modernized completely in spelling and partly in language. Hamer (II 3 sqq.) gives letter and note in full. The originals are in the British Museum MSS. Reg. 7. c. xvi. folios 136–9.

courtiers—Placebo, Pickthank and Flattery—and a guard
of the same kind: one swearing he was the lustiest, starkest,
best-proportioned and most valiant man that ever was;
another swearing that he was the best with long bow, cross
bow, and culverin in the world; another swearing that he
was the best jouster and man of arms in the world; and so
forth during their parts. Thereafter came a man armed in
harness, with a drawn sword in his hand, a bishop, a
burgess man, and Experience, clad like a doctor, who set
them all down on the dais, under the King. After them
came a poor man, who went up and down the stage, making
a heavy complaint that he was harried by the courtiers
taking his feu in one place, and also his tacks in another.
Because of this he had broken up[1] his home, his wife and
children begging their bread; and the same was the case of
many thousands in Scotland, which would make the King's
Grace loss of men if his Grace stood in need; saying there
was no remedy to be got, for though he would make suit
to the King's Grace, he was neither acquainted with con-
troller nor treasurer, and without them might no man get
any boon from the King. Afterwards he asked for the King.
When he was conducted to the man who was King in the
play, he said he was no King. For there is but one King,
who made all and governeth all, who is eternal, to whom
he and all earthly Kings are but officers, of the which they
must take account; and much more to that effect. Then he
looked to the King and said he was not the King of Scotland,
for there was another King in Scotland that hanged John
Armstrong with his fellows, Sym the laird, and many more;
which had pacified the country and stanched theft, but
he had left one thing undone and which pertained as well
to his charge as this. When he was asked what that was,
he made a long narration of the oppression of the poor by
the taking of the corpse-present beasts, and of the harrying
of poor men by consistory laws, and of many other wrongs
done by the Spirituality and the Church, with many
long stories and authorities. Then the bishop rose and

---

[1] The Scottish Text Society edition (II 4, last line) has the form
strayled instead of *skayled*. See *skail* in Jamieson's *Dictionary*.

rebuked him, saying that it behoved not him to utter such things, commanding him silence, or else to suffer death for it, by their law. Thereafter rose the man of arms, alleging the contrary, and commanded the poor man to speak, saying their ill-treatment had been over long suffered, without any law. Then the poor man showed the great wrong-doing of bishops, prelates, abbots, reiving men's wives and daughters and holding them, and of the maintaining of their children, and of their over-buying of Lords' and Barons' eldest sons to their daughters, wherethrough the nobility of the blood of the realm was degenerate; and of the great superfluous rents that pertained to the Church by reason of overmuch temporal lands given to them, which they proved that the King might take both by the Canon Law and Civil Law; and of the great abominable vices that reign in monasteries, and of the common brothels that were kept in nunneries. All this was proved by Experience. The office of bishop was also shown; and the New Testament was produced with the authorities to that effect. Then rose the man of arms and the burgess, and said that all that was produced by the poor man and Experience was reasonable, of verity and of great effect, and very expedient to be reformed, with the consent of parliament. The bishop said he would not consent thereunto. The man of arms and the burgess said they were two and he but one, therefore their voice should have more effect. Thereafter the King in the play ratified, approved and confirmed all that was rehearsed.

Before asking how far this summary of the 1540 interlude agrees with the matter in the 1554 text,[1] we must bear in mind that *Ane Satyre* is a play for the times and contains a number of topical allusions. Consequently, successive productions would vary according to time and place. Political, social and religious conditions in 1552 and 1554 were far from the same as those in 1540. A performance, also, in the open air before the men of Cupar-Fife and its neighbourhood, or before the citizens

[1] It is fuller than the 1552 text. See below, p. 43 note 1.

of Edinburgh, would naturally differ from an indoor performance before the Royal Court at Linlithgow.

If we now examine the 1554 text, it is evident that this "note" is not an exact summary of that text. There are several omissions; but we must remember that the "note" was drawn up for a specific purpose, viz. to show Cromwell the feeling in Scotland in favour of church reform. This would explain why the merry parts are shelved, but not why the pardoner is left unmentioned—unless he did not appear in the 1540 play. As to differences, the "note" makes Solace enter first and tell the audience that the play was "a general thing, meaning nothing in special to displease any one". In the 1554 text this is the duty of Diligence, while Solace has a different rôle. The King of 1540 is described as silent till the very end of the play: the King of 1554 is quite different. The bragging guardsmen are absent from the 1554 text. Experience of 1540 is not found in 1554: by 1554 the name had been employed in *The Monarche*. But the "note" shows clearly that the theme of the play as presented in 1540 is the same as in the 1554 play; the intention is the same, the insistence on the grievances of the poor is the same, the attack on the immorality of the clergy is the same. We may, therefore, confidently believe that the 1540 play, whatever its title, was Sir David Lyndsay's *Ane Satyre* in its earliest form.

B. The 1552 performance, at Cupar, was preceded by an interlude—*The Auld Man and his Wife*[1]—with a proclamation. This preliminary matter does not appear in the 1602 edition of *Ane Satyre* by Robert Charteris, but

[1] See below, p. 72.

forms the first interlude in the Bannatyne Manuscript,[1] with the heading:

Heir begynnis the proclamatioun of the play maid be dauid lynsayis of the Month knicht in the Playfeild in the moneth of   the ʒeir of god 155 ʒeiris.

Proclamatioun maid in cowpar of ffyffe.

The sixth line also speaks of "Cowpar toun". Month and day are mentioned in the proclamation (11 sqq.):

> Our purpose is on the sevint day of June
>   Gif weddir serve and we haif rest and pece
>   We sall be sene in till our playing place
> In gude array abowt the hour of sevin.
>   Off thriftiness[2] that day I pray you ceiss
> Bot ordane ws gude drink aganis allevin.

Lines 270 sqq. supply data for discovering the year:

> As for this day, I haif na mair to say yow:
> On witsone tysday cum see our play I prey yow:
> That samyne day is the sevint day of Iune,
> Thairfoir get vp richt airly and disiune.

Since Tuesday of Whitsun week was the seventh of June, Easter had been the seventeenth of April, and consequently the year was 1552.

[1] Folio 164ᵃ (Scottish Text Society, III 87). Bannatyne did not transcribe a complete text of *Ane Satyre*. After the Cupar proclamation and *The Auld Man* interlude, he gives seven extracts, which he introduces thus (folio 168ᵃ, Scottish Text Society, III 101):
> "Heir begynnis ser dauid lyndsay play maid
>   In the grenesyd besyd Edinburgh."
Then Bannatyne explains that he has omitted the "grave matter" because the "abuse" is now reformed and has written only "certain merry interludes". See Laing, II 288, 297 sqq.; and Hamer, II, where Bannatyne's interludes face the corresponding parts of the 1554 text.

[2] For *thriftiness* editors read or suggest *thristiness*. But why not keep the MS. reading? Then the sense is "Don't be frugal that day, but have a supply of good drink ready for us by eleven." Eleven would begin the interval for refreshments; unless the Cupar performance was shortened, so as to finish then. The Edinburgh performance lasted nine hours, not four.

C. The most complete text of *Ane Satyre*, over 4600
lines, is the text of the 1554 performance, at Edinburgh,
printed by Robert Charteris in 1602. In the 1568
edition of Lyndsay's works (which, however, does not
include *Ane Satyre*) Henrie Charteris, after telling Lyndsay's joke[1] played upon the clergy in the King's presence,
continues:

No less earnest and vehement was he against them in his
farces and public plays, wherein he was very skilful and
excellent. Such a spring he gave them in the Play, played
beside Edinburgh,[2] in presence of the Queen Regent and a
great part of the Nobility, with an exceeding great number of
people, lasting from 9 hours before noon till 6 hours at even.[3]

OUTLINE OF 1554 TEXT OF *ANE SATYRE*

PART I

[1] See below, p. 94.
[2] In the Greenside, on the lower slopes of Calton Hill. Bannatyne
mentions Greenside: see above, p. 43, quotation from Bannatyne MS.
[3] Laing, III 231, where the whole of the interesting preface will be
found.
[4] Numbering as in Laing's Edition. The bracketed numbers are those
of the Scottish Text Society Edition.

PART II

SUMMARY OF 1554 TEXT OF *ANE SATYRE*

PART I

Diligence announces the coming of Rex Humanitas to make reformation. Though in youth deceived and wild, the King will meet with Correction, Verity and Discretion.[1] The Three Estates (Lords Spiritual, Lords Temporal and Burgesses) are summoned to compear with dutiful diligence. The spectators are given some idea of the subject of the play and are requested to listen with patience:

> Prudent Peopill, I pray yow all,
> Tak na man greif in speciall;
> For wee sall speik in generall,
> For pastyme and for play:

[1] The only Discretion that appears is Deceit masquerading under that name. If *Discretion* is not here a misprint, the personage might have been intended to act the part taken by Good Counsel.

> Thairfoir till all our rymis be rung,
> And our mistoinit sangis be sung,
> Let everie man keip weill ane toung,
>   And everie woman tway.

Rex Humanitas enters and, acknowledging God as his superior, prays that he may rule well. Wantonness chides him for his gloomy looks:

> Be blyth sa lang as ye ar heir,
>   And pas tyme with pleasure:
> For als lang leifis the mirrie man
> As the sorie, for ocht he can.

He and Placebo will keep the King merry, especially if Solace comes.

Solace enters, singing the praises of the beautiful Lady Sensuality, whom he urges the King to prize above all others. The King rejects this as odious advice:

> Because I haif bene, to this day,
> *Tanquam tabula rasa:*
> That is als mekill as to say,
>   Redie for gude and ill.

"Nay," replies Placebo, "we are not seeking to deceive you, but to help you."

> So that ye be nocht ane young sanct,
>   And syne ane auld devill.

"Lechery is no sin", says Wantonness. "Cardinals and bishops have banished Chastity from Rome." "Till your marriage", advises Solace, "you should have a concubine. Some prelates have three"; and he slyly adds what was a proverbial gibe:

> Speir at the Monks of Bamirrinoch,
>   Gif lecherie be sin.

"Or", suggests Placebo, "ask my Lady Prioress. The Bible says *Omnia probate*."

Lady Sensuality and her attendants are heard singing. Then the Lady is announced:

> Ane perle of pulchritude:
> Soft as the silk is hir quhite lyre,
> Hir hair is like the goldin wyre.

The King has only to see her to love her: what is kingdom or wealth without a merry life? The King bids the lady be summoned, and, overcome by her glowing charms, salutes her:

> Welcum to me, peirles in pulchritude,
> Welcum to me, thou sweeter nor the lamber.[1]

The next scene, though no formal division into scenes is made, opens with the entrance of Good Counsel, who declares that his presence helps kings, his absence ruins them. While welcomed in England, France and Italy, he has been ill-treated in Scotland. Rex Humanitas is overcome by Sensuality and evil counsellors; but there is still hope, and Good Counsel will stay.

Flattery enters, and then his old friend Falsehood, who says,

> Quhen freindis meitis hartis warmis.

Another comrade joins them, Deceit, who has been scared by meeting Good Counsel. He is delighted that his two friends are in quest of Rex Humanitas, for, as he says,

> That samin hors is my awin mair.

Flattery suggests that they should put on religious dress and wear a grave countenance,

> As wee war new cum out of France.

Flattery will be a friar; for, if he cannot preach, he can

---

[1] L'ambre, prized for its ornamental ("lammer beads"), medicinal, cosmetic and magical properties.

wheedle very cleverly; and he may become the King's confessor. Deceit is rebaptized as Discretion, Falsehood as Sapience, Flattery as Devotion. Under these names the Vices, as a stage-direction calls them, are appointed King's Secretary, King's Treasurer, and King's Confessor. When Good Counsel appears, they hurry to drive him away, reporting to the King that he is a shopbreaker.

Verity enters, admonishing kings, judges and prelates to deal justly, walk uprightly, and show a good example. The Vices are afraid of Verity, but Falsehood finds an easy way to get rid of her: they accuse her to the Spirituality of speaking manifest heresy. The Parson would destroy all Lutherans, especially Verity. He demands by what authority she preaches or teaches, threatening her with utter destruction unless she renounces her new opinions. She refuses, and declares that the Spirituality have good reason to fear her coming. Flattery then cries:

> Quhat buik is that, harlot, into thy hand?
> Out, walloway! this is the New Test'ment,
> In Englisch toung, and printit in England:
> Herisie, herisie! fire, fire! incontinent.

"No heresy," she replies, "but Christ's word, a wellspring of truth." She is, however, led away to the stocks.

Next comes Chastity, lamenting that she can find no resting-place. "Try that renowned Prioress", suggests Diligence. "No," replies the Prioress to Chastity, "you are contrary to my temperament." Appealing to the Lords of Spirituality, Chastity is told: "Madam, we know you not"; while the Abbot declares his resolve to live and die with his love, Sensuality. "Go to the nuns", advises the Parson; but Chastity explains that they drove her out of their dormitory and would not let her stay long enough to say her Pater Noster. When she approaches the Lord Temporality and the grave Merchant, Temporality says that they would gladly shelter her, but there is an obstacle:

> For quhy, we twa are maryit.
> Bot wist our wyfis that ye war heir,
> Thay wald mak all this town on steir;
> Thairfoir, we reid yow rin areir,
>   In dreid ye be miscaryit.

Chastity now seeks refuge with two craftsmen, a Tailor and a Shoemaker,[1] who bid her sit down and drink with them, the Shoemaker trolling:

> Fill in and play cap out,
>   For I am wonder dry:
> The Devill snyp aff thair snout
>   That haits this company.

But Jennie, the Tailor's daughter, tells what is going on,

[1] The craftsmen episode, 1288-1395 (1280-1387), has been called an interlude, but it has not the independence of the Poor Man—Pardoner interlude between Part I and Part II. This episode is a later addition, inserted to amuse with its fun, boisterous and in parts coarse. It is not neatly fitted in. For after it finishes, Diligence does not ask Chastity how she fared with the craftsmen, but says,

> "Madame, quhat gars yow gang sa lait?
> Tell me how ye have done debait
> With the Temporall and Spirituall stait.
> Quha did yow maist kyndnes?"

That is to say, line 1396 (1388) is linked in sense, not to 1395 (1387), but to 1287 (1279). When the addition was made, it was forgotten that line 1398 (1390) refers only to clergy, barons and burgesses, not to craftsmen. Another ill-fitted addition occurs later: see below, p. 65 note.

A similar forgetfulness explains a passage in Shakespeare: *Merchant of Venice*, I ii. Nerissa names *six* suitors, who, less than thirty lines later, are spoken of as *four*. Editors hold that there had originally been only four suitors, and that two were afterwards added.

David Laing (II 307 sq. note) says that the craftsmen episode contains local allusions to Cupar-Fife; and some have suggested that it was written for the 1552 performance.

M L   4

and the two wives hurrying up drive away Chastity. They knock their husbands about, first while scolding them, then in silence. The husbands condole with each other, and congratulate priests on not being wedded to such wicked wives. Meanwhile the wives are planning a feast to celebrate their victory. The Shoemaker's wife, getting rid of stockings and shoes, kilts up her clothes and wades through the river to fetch a quart of wine.

Diligence, finding Chastity wandering alone, asks how she has fared with the Spiritual Estate and the Temporal. "Badly", replies Chastity. Diligence recommends her to go to the King for help; and Solace announces her as a fair Lady in white, most like an angel. Sensuality, however, declares that she and Chastity cannot stay in one place. Chastity is then dragged away to the stocks and put beside Verity, who comforts her with the news that Divine Correction is coming.

Correction's Page now proclaims the arrival of his master, who will reform even the Three Estates. Lyndsay again makes apology through the mouth of the Page:

> Sirs, thocht wee speik in generall,
> Lat na man, into speciall,
>   Tak our wordis at the warst:
> Quhat ever wee do, quhat ever wee say,
> I pray yow tak it al in play,
>   And judge ay to the best.

Afraid of reformation, the Vices consider where to find refuge. Flattery will go to the Spirituality, Deceit to the Merchants, Falsehood to the Craftsmen. First, however, Deceit and Falsehood plan to steal the King's moneybox, and Falsehood does so. They quarrel over the division of the money, and fight. Deceit is the victor and runs away with the box.

Divine Correction enters, declaring that he comes to destroy wrongdoers, but without a parliament he will do nothing. No realm prospers without him. A king is simply an official to cause his liege men to live in equity, and, under God, to punish those who transgress against His Majesty.

Good Counsel welcomes Divine Correction, by whose command Verity and Chastity are set free. These four proceed to drive away Sensuality from Rex Humanitas. At first she resents their interference; but Divine Correction shows his power and declares that reformation must begin with the King. Sensuality requests permission to return to Rome. She is quite ready to leave Rex Humanitas; for "as good love comes as goes". She then begs shelter from Spirituality, whose answer is:

> Welcum, our dayis darling,
> Welcum, with all our hart:
> Wee all but feinzeing
> Sall plainly tak your part.

Rex Humanitas now receives Good Counsel, Verity and Chastity, and promises to obey Divine Correction. Divine Correction advises the summoning of Parliament, which the King commissions Diligence to do.

Wantonness, Placebo and Solace promise amendment and are pardoned. Solace pleads:

> Bot, give us leave to sing,
> To dance, to play at chesse and tabills,
> To reid stories and mirrie fabils,
> For pleasure of our King.

These diversions are allowed. Hawking and hunting, also, and learning to couch a lance are honourable pastimes for a king.

Rex Humanitas is informed that Flattery, Falsehood and Deceit have misled him. Good Counsel advises him to do justice, and yet to season justice with mercy. He should read history:

> Thair sall ye finde baith gude and evill report:
> For everie Prince, efter his qualitie,
> Thocht he be deid, his deidis sall never die.

Diligence, with the cry of "Oyez, Oyez", summons the Three Estates to come to Court. He announces that the first part of the play is over, and bids the spectators take refreshments.

A stage-direction says:

Now shall the people make collation; then begins the interlude, the Kings, Bishops and principal players being out of their seats.

INTERLUDE *of the* POOR MAN *and the* PARDONER

The Poor Man enters, entreating the audience to give him alms, for he has "motherles bairns either sax or seavin", or at least show him the way to St Andrews. Diligence bids him begone; but he climbs into the King's chair and refuses to budge till his own time. When the ladder is knocked away, he leaps down. Diligence again bids him begone: his impudence will spoil the play. "Much I care for your play," replies the Poor Man, "for there is very little play at my hungry heart." He lives near Tranent and has been in Edinburgh to seek for law. Finding none either at Court of Session or at Consistory Court, he is on his way to St Andrews. The "black verity" of his progress to poverty is this. He maintained his father, over eighty years old, and his mother, ninety-five:

Wee had ane meir that caryit salt and coill,
And everie ilk yeir scho brocht us hame ane foill.
Wee had thrie ky that was baith fat and fair,
Nane tydier into the toun of Air.
My Father was sa waik of blude and bane
That he deit, quhairfoir my Mother maid great maine.
Then scho deit, within ane day or two;
And thair began my povertie and wo.
Our gude gray meir was baittand on the feild,
And our Lands laird tuik hir for his hyreild.
The Vickar tuik the best cow be the heid,
Incontinent, quhen my father was deid.
And quhen the Vickar hard tel how that my mother
Was deid, fra hand he tuk to him ane uther.
Then Meg, my wife, did murne baith evin and morow,
Till at the last scho deit for verie sorow.
And quhen the Vickar hard tell my wyfe was dead
The thrid cow he cleikit be the heid.
Thair umest clayis,[1] that was of rapploch gray,
The Vickar gart his Clark bear them away.

The Poor Man had also the Parson against him.

The Devil stick him! he curst me for my teind:
And halds me yit under that same proces,
That gart me want the Sacrament at Pasche.

All the wealth the Poor Man has left is an English groat,
which he is keeping to fee a lawyer. Amazed at his
simplicity, Diligence exclaims:

Thow art the daftest fuill that ever I saw;
Trows thow, man, be the law to get remeid
Of men of Kirk! Na, nocht till thow be deid.

For these exactions, the only law, adds Diligence, is con-
suetude. But, says the Poor Man, a custom against the
commonweal should be no law. Diligence explains:

It is thair law, all that thay have in use,
Thocht it be cow, sow, ganer, gryse, or guse.

[1] See below, p. 88.

"Then", says the Poor Man, "it is, I suppose, by custom that prelates violate ladies, maidens, and other men's wives. Is that law evil or good?" Diligence bids him hold his tongue, else he will be hanged. But the Poor Man is past caring; and, as there is no help, he lies down to rest.

The Pardoner enters and at once begins:

> *Bona dies! Bona dies!*
> Devoit pepill, gude day I say yow.
> Now tarie ane lytill quhyll, I pray yow,
> 　Till I be with yow knawin.
> Wat ye weill how I am namit?
> Ane nobill man and undefamit,
> 　Gif that all the suith war schawin.
> 　I am Sir Robert Rome-raker,[1]
> Ane perfyte publike Pardoner
> 　Admittit be the Paip.
> Sirs, I sall schaw yow, for my wage,
> My pardons and my pilgramage,
> 　Quhilk ye sall se, and graip.

He curses the New Testament, for its truth has spoiled his calling; he curses its writers, translators and inbringers. He prays that Luther, Bullinger and Melanchthon had been smothered in the cradle. He wishes that St Paul had never been born and that his books were never read in church, but among friars, in the dark, or riven among rooks. Then, setting out his relics on a board, he continues:

> My patent Pardouns, ye may se,
> Cum fra the Cane of Tartarie,
> 　Weill seald with oster-schellis.
> Thocht ye have na contritioun
> Ye sall have full remissioun
> 　With help of buiks and bellis.

---

[1] One who went to Rome for relics and pardons, or pretended that he went.

Heir is ane relict, lang and braid,
Of Fin Macoull the richt chaft blaid,
   With teith and al togidder.
Of Collings cow heir is ane horne,
For eating of Makconnals corne
   Was slaine into Baquhidder.
Heir is ane coird, baith great and lang,
Quhilk hangit Johne the Armistrang,
   Of gude hemp, soft and sound.
Gude halie peopill, I stand for'd,
Quha ever beis hangit with this cord
   Neids never to be dround.
The culum of Sanct Brydis kow;
The gruntill of Sanct Antonis sow,
   Quhilk buir his haly bell.
Quha ever he be heiris this bell clinck
Gif me ane ducat for till drink;
   He sall never gang to hell,
Without he be of Baliell borne.

Claiming to have power to separate a husband from a shrewish wife, the Pardoner, with indecent formalities, grants "dispensation" to the Shoemaker and his wife—for a consideration: from the Shoemaker five shillings and his shaping-knife and from his wife two shirts. At that moment the Pardoner's boy Wilkin shouts that he has found on "Dame Fleschers midding", a horse's big bone, which women can easily be made to take for a bone of St Bride's cow, good for curing quartan fever. The towns-people, says Wilkin, are calling the Pardoner arrant rogue, *Legatus Natus*, false Saracen, *Diabolus Incarnatus*. The shouting has wakened the Poor Man, who has been dreaming about his lost cows. He prays to St Bride to send them back, and entreats the Pardoner's help. The Pardoner takes the Poor Man's last coin, the groat, and promises him remission of a thousand years of Purgatory

pains. But it is his cows the Poor Man wants, or else the
return of his groat. He gets neither. They fight, and the
Poor Man knocks down the board, tumbling the relics
into the water. Diligence stops this "daffing", and the
stage is cleared for Part II.

PART II

Diligence announces the coming of the Three Estates,
and entreats the audience to listen patiently. The story
is all true, whatever wicked people may say.

The Estates, led by their Vices, appear in the distance,
walking backwards, to the astonishment of Wantonness
and Solace. The King, concerned lest in walking backwards the Estates go wrong, would send them guides; but
Good Counsel advises to leave the matter to Divine
Correction. The Estates turn their faces to the King and
salute. To the question why they go backwards, Spirituality replies:

> Soveraine, we have gaine sa, this mony a year.
> Howbeit ye think we go undecently,
> Wee think wee gang richt wonder pleasantly.

The Court being fenced in due form, Rex Humanitas
as President declares that he will reform abuses and
punish evil-doers, with the help of King Correction.
Spirituality advises delay in reform and moderation in
punishment. But all the oppressed are summoned to
appear and make their complaints. John the Commonweal, accordingly, pushes forward, naked because he
has been among foes, crooked because he has been
overlooked,[1] sad because the Estates go backwards. He

---

[1] Bewitched with the evil eye. So Shakespeare, *Merchant of Venice*,
III ii 15; *Merry Wives*, v v 87.

denounces Covetousness and Sensuality, the Vices of
the Clergy; Public Oppression, the Vice of the Barons;
Deceit and Falsehood, the Vices of the Merchants and
Craftsmen; and Flattery, to whom he says,

> Quhen ye was guyder of the Court we gat litill grace.

Flattery, Deceit and Falsehood are put in the stocks; and,
in spite of Spirituality's threat to complain to the Pope,
Covetousness and Sensuality are chased away.

Good Counsel then gives advice on necessary reforms:

> My worthy Lords, sen ye have taine on hand
> Sum reformatioun to mak into this land:
> And als ye knaw, it is the Kingis mynd,
> Quha to the Commonweil hes ay bene kynd:
> Thocht reif and thift wer stanchit weill aneuch,
> Yit sumthing mair belangis to the pleuch.
> Now, into peace, ye sould provyde for weirs,
> And be sure of how mony thowsand speirs
> The King may be quhen he hes ocht ado.

The old feudal array of husbandmen and commons is no
longer of use. The commons are daily growing very poor.
Some have their dues increased so that they cannot pro-
cure "water kail". Teinds are heightened and consequently husbandmen cannot hold their own. Another
plague is that gentlemen take their steadings in feu, and
husbandmen must either pay higher rents or give up
their farms:

> And sum ar plainlie harlit out be the heid,
> And ar destroyit, without God on thame rew.

This is corroborated by the Poor Man. He has lost horses
and cattle; and now all he possesses is on his back.

John asks Correction to begin his reformation at the
Borders. How can the Scots defend themselves against
the English when they cannot quell the Border thieves

who injure faithful labourers? If John were king, he
would hang all, whether knights or lords or lairds, who
maintain these thieves. He complains also of sturdy
beggars, fiddlers, pipers, pardoners, jugglers, jesters,
gamblers, alchemists, tale-bearers, bards, sluggards,
great fat friars, and all others who wear cowls. Poor
people have other grievances. Justice Eyres are misused: the poor are punished, the rich bribe the judges.
The common people also suffer from the Consistorial
Laws.

Recognizing the truth of John's complaints, Correction
commands the Lords Temporal to expel Oppression, and
the Merchants to keep no company with Deceit. The
Lords Spiritual must feu their temporal lands to men
who labour with their hands,

> Bot nocht to ane gearking gentill man,
> That neither will he wirk nor can.

The Lords Spiritual demand time for deliberation; and,
when ordered to make agreement with John the Commonweal, or be punished, they as well as the Friar claim
papal exemption from secular punishment. The Lords
Temporal and the Merchants take John by the hand and
enter into perpetual agreement with him.

John hesitates to bring his other charges against the
clergy, for it is no joke to complain about priests; but
Correction encourages him to speak his whole mind, if it
is truth. John complains of death dues harshly exacted,
which Poor Man corroborates from his own experience.[1]
John adds that the Parson does not preach: his only concern is to receive his teinds, and spend them. Our white-
surpliced Bishops, says the Poor Man, are rolling in

---

[1] See above, p. 53.

wealth and wallowing in pleasure. Their palaces are like
paradises, full of fair faces. Prelates can always separate
from their wives and take others, while Poor Man himself
is tied to one. The Parson calls Poor Man a liar. Next he
warns John that priests burn men for reckless words, and
John's words, he says, are heresy. "But", John replies,
"they are true." The Bishop, furious that such detraction
of the clergy is permitted, vows to make Poor Man repent
that he spoke of the cow. Good Counsel stops the dispute.
The Merchant proposes that all temporal lands be feued
to such as labour with their hands, who shall be bound to
do war-service for the King. Nothing is to be decided
about corpse-present and cow unless the clergy agree,
but the Bishop says,

> Wee will want nathing that wee have in use,
> Kirtil nor kow, teind lambe, teind gryse, nor guse.

The Lords Temporal suggest writing for the Pope's permission to forbid corpse-present and cow by royal proclamation; and they brush aside Spirituality's formal
dissent. "You are only one Estate and we are two, *et
ubi major pars, ibi tota.*"

John tells how Scotland is drained of gold and silver,
sent daily to Rome in bribes. Were he king, never a penny
should go. The Merchants confirm this: many a hundred
thousand pounds have they advanced to priests for payments to Rome.[1] It is agreed to stop the trafficking for
benefices at Rome, and the holding of pluralities, except
by prelates of the blood royal. Bishops and priests, declares Good Counsel, should be preachers and teachers:

---

[1] The Scottish Parliament had tried, but often in vain, to stop this
flow of money to Rome: in 1471, for example; in 1483, in 1493, in 1496
and in 1540.

that is why they receive teinds. The Bishop demands
where preaching is laid down as their duty, and he is
bidden:

> Luik quhat Sanct Paul wryts unto Timothie:
> Tak thair the Buik, let se, gif ye can spell.

The Bishop answers:

> I never red that, thairfor reid it yoursell.

Good Counsel reads, from the Vulgate, the opening
words of I Timothy iii, describing a bishop's qualifi-
cations. The Bishop protests that laymen are too pre-
sumptuous in meddling with such matters; and, when
reminded that the words are St Paul's words, he adds
that some say it had been good if Paul had never been
born.[1] He swears by Judas[2] that he has never read
either the New Testament or the Old, and never thinks
to do so; for friars say that reading does no good. He is
quite ignorant why the Testaments were bound on his
back at his consecration. "Why then", cries the Merchant, "should the clergy have all these temporal lands
and all these teinds? Not surely for mumbling matins
and keeping vestments clean? Teinds should furnish
teachers." "Yes," agrees Good Counsel, "or sustain
prudent preachers." "Our parson", shouts Poor Man,
"never preached in his life." "What have you to do
with preaching?" asks the Parson; and Poor Man retorts, "Do you think you should have the teinds for
nothing? Had I power, I'd make reformation." John
the Commonweal intervenes, declaring that David I,
"ane sair Sanct to the croun", would repent of founding
so many abbeys were he to see the vicious lives of the

---

[1] The Pardoner, for one, says so. See above p. 54.
[2] One traitor swears by another.

monks. For this the Abbot curses him and accuses him
of heresy in speaking against the law and liberty of the
clergy. John refuses to show his creed to the Friar,
Flattery, but he repeats to Divine Correction what is
essentially the Apostles' Creed. He ends, however, with

> I trow *Sanctam Ecclesiam*,
> Bot nocht in thir Bishops nor thir Freirs,

all of whom he consigns to the "mekill Devill". Correction pronounces John a good Christian.

The Barons and Merchants conclude that only
preachers should receive benefices, whether bishops or
parsons.

Poor Man entreats the Estates to reform the Consistory
Court, unfolding a humorous account of the law's delay.

> Marie! I lent my gossop my mear, to fetch hame coills,
> And he hir drounit into the Querrell hollis:
> And I ran to the Consistorie, for to pleinze,
> And thair I happinit amang ane greidie meinze.
> They gave me first ane thing thay call *Citandum*,
> Within aucht dayis I gat bot *Lybellandum*,
> Within ane moneth I gat *ad Opponendum*,
> In half ane yeir I gat *Interloquendum*,
> And syne I gat, how call ye it? *ad Replicandum*:
> Bot I could never ane word yit understand him.
> And than thay gart me cast out many plackis,
> And gart me pay for four-and-twentie actis.
> Bot or thay came half gait to *Concludendum*
> The Feind ane plack was left for to defend him.
> Thus thay postponit me twa yeir with thair traine
> Syne, *Hodie ad octo*, bad me cum againe;
> And than, thir ruiks, thay roupit wonder fast,
> For sentence silver thay cryit at the last.
> Of *Pronunciandum* thay maid me wonder faine;
> Bot I got never my gude gray meir againe.

Then Temporality says that the Consistory Laws must
be reformed, and also that, following the French way,

Spirituality shall judge spiritual matters, Temporality temporal. That displeases Spirituality; for it would be contrary to the clergy's "profeit singulair". Temporality replies that the clergy's "profeit" is contrary to the Commonweal.

Verity and Chastity state their complaints: Verity has been kept in subjection; Chastity has been banished by the clergy. Verity advises the appointment of learned clerks instead of the present inefficient pastors. An examination of a tailor and a shoemaker proves that they are far more expert in their craft than prelates in their vocation. Diligence is accordingly dispatched to bring devout and learned clerks, whether monk or canon or priest or friar.

The Lords Temporal mention another abuse. Daughters of prelates, on marrying noblemen, receive such large dowries, sometimes as much as two thousand pounds, that the Barons must alienate part of their lands to provide similar amounts; otherwise, their daughters can only curse the proud prelates because they must remain at home unmarried. Correction promises reform of this.

A comic episode is here introduced. Common Theft, a Border reiver from Ewesdale,[1] has heard of the arrival of a king who will head or hang all thieves. He wishes he had the Earl of Rothes' best hackney or Lord Lyndsay's brown jennet to carry him safe home. Suddenly he espies his master, Oppression, in the stocks. Oppression persuades Common Theft to take his place, for half an hour. Common Theft goes into the stocks, where Oppression leaves him for good and all.

---

[1] Border thieves had come plundering as far as the Lothians and Fife. See Introduction, p. xxxv, to *The Complaynt of Scotlande* (E.E.T.S.).

Diligence now returns with three famous clerks, a Doctor of Divinity and two Licentiates, able to preach to the common people and to teach in the Latin tongue. Rex Humanitas welcomes them. Divine Correction advises that investigation be made to discover which of the beneficed clergy are unworthy to hold office. They are to be replaced by worthy men. The Bishop, when asked how he uses his office, asserts that prelates are not accustomed to render an account to any king; but if his questioners will know, he has always done well. He sees to it that his teinds are paid in full, even to the last boll of bere; and he makes sure of all his dues and perquisites. Unable to marry legally, he has four or five concubines. He has given his sons good incomes, and married his daughters to lairds. He is no fool, he rides on an ambling mule. No baron keeps a better table. He has, in his pay, several barons to take his part in any quarrel, right or wrong. He maintains a friar to do his preaching. The Abbot says that he and his monks live a very easy life:

> Thare is na monks, from Carrick to Carraill,
> That fairs better and drinks mair helsum aill.
> My Prior is ane man of great devotioun:
> Thairfor, daylie, he gets ane double portioun.

The Abbot kept his vows very strictly, till he received the papal bulls confirming his appointment. Since then he has lived like his predecessors: he has two fair paramours; he sends his sons to the University of Paris; he dowers his daughters amply. The Parson admits that he cannot preach; but he can play tennis, while he surpasses everyone at football, cards, backgammon and dice. His round bonnet is now square and made of fine stuff. The Prioress declares that she could not entertain Chastity because that did not agree with her temperament, and she follows old use and wont.

The Doctor of Divinity is called upon to preach in English to edify country people. His sermon, formal in style and somewhat latinized, is on Christ's redemption and the two steps to Heaven—love to God and love to one's neighbour. The conclusion admonishes the hearers to shun the seven deadly sins—pride, envy, anger, lechery, covetousness, sloth and gluttony—and to do the deeds of mercy, as feeding the hungry, clothing the naked. The Parson, with his Heaven thousands of miles away, wonders how the blind and the short-legged will reach it in two steps. The Abbot, being himself very stout, fears that he must be drawn up in a tether, or made lighter, or furnished with woodcock's wings, if he is to reach Heaven at all. Nor can the Parson think pride, envy and so on to be sins. "God", says the Doctor, "and the Church have forbidden them." "But", argues the Parson, "were they sins, we churchmen would not indulge in them."

Diligence, observing the Friar whispering to the Bishop, says that, by advice of the Friar, the clergy mean to put the town in uproar. They see the Pope warring on the King of France, and think they should defend their patrimony by force. One of the Licentiates, accordingly, shows that, unlike the churchmen of the day, Christ possessed no land and never intermeddled in temporal things. The Bachelor (the second Licentiate) declares friars to be the chief enemies of truth: they should be banished, if the peace is not to be broken. The Prioress also is useless in Christ's Kingdom.

The Sergeants, seizing the Friar, tell him that the King must be obeyed, but he claims exemption from

kings and queens and from all human laws. This claim
is ignored by the Sergeants, one of whom, with fine sarcasm, chants:

> On Dumisday, quhen Christ sall say,
>   *Venite, Benedicti*:
> The Freirs will say, without delay,
>   *Nos sumus exempti.*

The Friar, when stripped of hood and gown, is discovered,
to the astonishment of Good Counsel, to be Flattery, who
has masqueraded as Devotion.

Then the First Sergeant, turning from the Friar, calls
to the Prioress:

> Cum on, my ladie Priores,
>   We sall leir yow to dance:
> And that, within ane lytill space
>   Ane new pavin of France.

When the Prioress is divested of her habit, she is seen to
be wearing a kirtle of silk, which makes the First Sergeant exclaim that the holy Prioress has turned into a
"cowclink". She curses her kinsfolk who forced her to
become a nun and would not allow her to marry. Nuns
may sing night and day, but their heart does not know
what the mouth says. Nuns are not necessary to Christ's
Church.

> Bot I sall do the best I can,
> And marie sum gude honest man,
>   And brew gude aill and tun:
> Mariage be my opinioun,
> It is better religioun,
>   As to be freir or nun.[1]

[1] Mr Douglas Hamer (*The Library*, x) points out that the Prioress
episode interrupts the Friar business, and is clearly an addition im-
properly joined. Instead of the four lines "Cum on, my ladie Priores",

The Friar Flattery now cries out:

> My Lords, for Gods saik, let not hang me,
> Howbeit, that widdiefows wald wrang me.

He cannot, he continues, struggle to gain a living at plough or harrow, but he would help to hang Falsehood and Deceit. His life is spared on that understanding; and he hurries to the stocks to inform his old friends.

Sentence of deposition is passed on the churchmen. The Bishop threatens to excommunicate whoever touches them, and intimates an appeal to the Pope. The Merchant wonders how such painted sepulchres ever accepted office in the Church: they are very fools. "Greater fools", retorts the Bishop, "were the kings who appointed us." Rebuffed by Sensuality and Covetousness, the churchmen see nothing before them but starvation or hard work. The Bishop blames the friars, who persuaded him that all would be well if they preached for him. The Abbot laments that he is left with two daughters and has now no dowry for them. The young Parson, however, will go to France to become a mercenary soldier.

Divine Correction orders John the Commonweal to be clad in a gorgeous robe and to receive a seat in Parliament. He then announces that, with trumpet sound, the

the Bannatyne MS. has (folio 205ᵃ, Scottish Text Society Edition, III 223):

> "Cum on, ser fflattry, be the mess
> We sall leir zow to dance,
> Within ane bony littill spaice,
> Ane new paven of france."

This threat to hang the Friar Flattery is immediately followed by his appeal for mercy in the Bannatyne MS., with no interrupting Prioress episode. In the 1554 text the Friar's appeal not to be hanged has nothing to lead up to it. The addition, Mr Hamer suggests, was made by Lyndsay himself for the Edinburgh representation.

Acts passed by the Estates are to be proclaimed. These Acts are:

I. Christ's Kirk and Religion to be defended.
II. The Acts of our Prince's last Parliament to be observed.
III. Temporal lands to be feued under military tenure.
IV. Lords to be answerable for thieves on their estates.
V. A Court of Justice to be established at Elgin or Inverness.
VI. By permission of his Holiness, rents of nunneries to be employed to maintain the Court of Justice in Edinburgh and the Court in the North.
VII. Spiritual matters to be judged in spiritual courts, temporal in temporal.
VIII. Benefices to be bestowed only on good and learned men, qualified to preach and teach.
IX. Bishops not to license those unqualified for the priesthood.
X. No benefices to be purchased. Pluralities to be held only by prelates of the blood royal.
XI. Vicar's death dues to be abolished, and also the baron's heriot.
XII. Bishops and parsons to teach the people to refrain from vice.
XIII. No money to go to Rome for benefices, except for archbishoprics.
XIV. Priests to be allowed to marry.
XV. Nobles not to marry bastards of churchmen.

Poor Man blesses Divine Correction for these Acts of Reform, and prays God and St Giles that they be kept. Better to have slept than to make laws and not keep them. He entreats that Deceit, Theft and Falsehood be executed, and Flattery banished.

Common Theft, his head in the halter, directs his dying speech, full of warnings, to Grosars, Nicksons, Bells, Robsons, Hansles, Peels, Littles, Turnbulls, Armstrongs,

Taylors, Earwings, Elwands, Scotts of Ewesdale and
Graemes. Then he, or his figure, is drawn up. Deceit
next addresses the merchants, who know well how

> To sell richt deir and by gude-chaip.

He exposes their wiles: mixing new wine and old, adulter-
ating soap with rye meal and saffron with olive oil, using
an ell wand too short and a pound weight three ounces
too light. He names several famous merchants and
singles out, as deceitful above them all, Tom Williamson,
who in Edinburgh beguiled the bishop and his clerks and
for whose death young merchants will curse the King.
Deceit is then drawn up, or his figure. Falsehood is now
summoned to the gallows. He speaks to the craftsmen,
who without his help will die of hunger. He tells of the
frauds of websters, walkers, millers, fleshers, tailors, brewsters, baxters, wrights, masons, blacksmiths, lorimers,
cordiners, goldsmiths and shepherds. It is a wonder to
find ten true craftsmen in a hundred. Falsehood details
many of their wiles, and in particular curses the "brousters of Cowper toun", who, besides brewing thin ale,
make a horrible compound, called "Harns-out" because it upsets the drinker's brains. Looking up, Falsehood catches sight of his dead comrades and bewails their
loss. When the rope is round his neck, he calls on covetous
kings and unjust conquerors to follow him, shedders of
innocent blood, prelates holding more benefices than
three, wicked clerics, Consistory lawyers, bribed judges,
scolding wives. Would that his own wife, a cursed scold,
were before him in Hell! Her tongue would drive out the
Devil. Falsehood, and not his figure, is drawn up: and
(according to the stage-direction) a crow or a jackdaw
shall be thrown up as if it were his soul.

Flattery congratulates himself on his escape; for he really deserved to be hanged high above the others. He was a greater sinner: he beguiled the Three Estates. Garbed in his friar's habit, he passed for holy, but no holiness could exist in

> Ane wolfe cled in ane wedders skin.

He quits the stage to go (as he says) to serve the Hermit[1] of Loretto and teach him how to flatter.

Here begins The Sermon of Folly, which differs from the other interludes in having Rex Humanitas as one of its characters.

Folly relates his adventures with a sow as he came along the Shoegate.[2] As he ran away, he fell into a midden. He curses the town officials for allowing such obstructions, and appeals to Humanitas and Correction to do justice between him and the sow. Next he describes, with disgusting detail, his wife's drunken sickness. Folly has a "creill" of Folly Hats to sell, but he must first feed his children: his son Stult, and Glaiks,[3] his daughter, who is to marry a friar of Tillilum.

On his way to the King he notices the pulpit and learns, to his great astonishment, that the new bishops have been preaching. He pities the poor friars, who will have no occupation and will die of hunger. If bishops preach, why should not he himself? Then he will sell his hats to his friends in the Three Estates. His text is: *Stultorum numerus infinitus*;[4] and he declares he holds it no

---

[1] See below, p. 107 note 1.

[2] Perhaps the Shoegate in Cupar. The Bannatyne MS. has "the bony gait".

[3] The Bannatyne MS. has "Gukkis". Both words imply silliness, giddiness.

[4] From the Vulgate reading in Ecclesiastes i 15: stultorum infinitus est numerus.

shame to be a fool among fools. Fools are everywhere: kings, nobles, conquerors, seeking worldly dignities, following sensual vanities. Of what avail are their empty honours amid the uncertainty of life? One fool hoards up money, only to have his strong box burgled by another fool. Some act as though they should never die. Folly has hats for all fools, some on horses, some on mules; and especially for his many co-mates of the Three Estates, whose foolishness made them go backwards. Here is a hat for merchants who, not content with a competence, sail the sea in winter, contrary to Act of Parliament.[1] Some lose their property and some their lives. There is a special hat, intended for the feeble dotard of eighty years, with one foot in the grave, the father of six or seven children, who takes to wife a young girl of less than fourteen. Another hat is for prelates who are unable to rule themselves, but undertake, for greed of worldly pelf, to rule dioceses; and who would save the souls of others, while selling their own souls to the devil. "Do you know any such now in the Church?" inquires Diligence. "How can I recognize them?" "Hush", replies Folly.

> *Ex operibus eorum cognoscetis eos:*
> And Fuillis speik of the Prelacie,
> It wil be hauldin for herisie.

Rex Humanitas, however, grants him liberty to speak boldly, even of kings; and Folly cries, "Ye are all fools", bringing out still another hat for princely and imperial fools, who should have ears as long as mules. The pride of princes turns the whole world upside down. They care

[1] In 1535 it was enacted that "na schip saill with staple gudes, fra Simons day and Judes quhill Candlemes", i.e. from 28 October to 2 February.

not though they shed innocent blood. Look at our wars
with England. The Emperor is moving against France;
the Princes of Germany, Flanders and Italy are in a
panic; the Pope has an army in the field. St Peter never
raised such a force, nor St Paul, nor St Andrew. Is this
brotherly love, or mad folly? This was never learned in
Christ's school. These rulers are very fools: let the hat be
parted among them.

Folly concludes his sermon with what he calls a prophecy of Merlin's:

> Flan, fran, resurgent,
> Simul Hispan viribus urgent:
> Dani vastabunt,
> Vallones vasta parabunt:
> Sic tibi nomen in a,
> Mulier cacavit in olla:
> Hoc epulum comedes.[1]

Folly interprets the prophecy as foretelling war among
the friars. They shall not know to whom to say their
Pater Nosters.[2] He commends his audience to Gilly-
Mowband,[3] and entreats their prayers for the soul of
good Cacaphatie, who lately drowned himself in Loch-
leven. So ends the interlude.

Diligence asks the spectators to be indulgent to any
shortcomings in the play, which he promises to make
good by next year. He then dismisses them to drink or
dance; and concludes with

> Rex sapiens, aeterne Deus, genitorque benigne,
> Sit Tibi perpetuo gloria, laus et honor.

---

[1] Lines 1–4 belong to the old prophecy. The others are a sordid
addition. For other versions of the prophecy, see Hamer, IV 238 sq.

[2] See below, p. 117.

[3] One of James V's Court Fools.

THE AULD MAN *and* HIS WIFE

The Proclamatioun maid in cowpar of ffyffe[1]

This interlude, in which the characters are all new, is a
medley consisting of:

    A. Proclamation by Nuntius.
    B. A Cotter and his Wife.
    C. Fyndlaw's bragging.
    D. The Auld Man's Wife and her Wooers.
    E. Fyndlaw and the Clerk.
    F. The Auld Man deceived.
    G. Fyndlaw's discomfiture.
    H. Concluding stanzas by Nuntius.

A. Nuntius proclaims the coming of the King to hold
a meeting of the Three Estates at Cupar-Fife. "On the
seventh of June, weather permitting, the play will begin
at seven hours of the day. Come to the Castlehill, with
plenty of good strong wine; and be not displeased whatever the actors sing or say. Jests, however, are mingled
with grave matters."

B. A Cotter declares that he will be present—if his
wife lets him. She is a devil to scold. He wishes he had
the priests' prerogative and could change his wife as
often as he liked without the Consistory Law. Were his
wife dead, he would never marry again, but live chaste—
like abbots, monks and friars. At that moment his wife
appears and vigorously scolds him for his delay. *She* will
come to the play and *he* shall look after the cows at home.
Meanwhile she orders him away to "milk the ky and muk
the byre", refusing him a penny or two for a drink and

[1] See above, p. 42.

adding blows to quicken his steps. "God's mercy!" he cries,

> Now wander and wa be to thame all thair lyvis,
> The quhilk ar maryit with sic unhappy wyvis.

C. Next enters Fyndlaw of the Foot-band,[1] a braggart captain, boasting of his skill in arms. Had he been at Pinkie, his flashing sword alone would have torn the English to rags. As nobody accepts his challenge to fight, he lies down to rest, praying God to send wars and never peace, that he may fight his fill. The Fool comes and, recognizing in Fyndlaw the first to flee from Pinkie Cleugh, undertakes to frighten the boaster with a sheep's head.

D. The Auld Man leads in his wife, and then lies down to sleep. Wooed by a Courtier, a Merchant, a Clerk and the Fool, she yields to the Fool.

E. Fyndlaw starts up and begins to boast, and is admonished by the Clerk:

> Thay ar not sonsy that so dois ruse thame sell.

Fyndlaw, he says, won no credit at Pinkie. Such braggarts as he have ruined the Commonweal. "May God send us peace, and may you and your fellows be hanged." After more wrangling, the Clerk leaves, and Fyndlaw declares he would have cut off the Clerk's head if he had said another word.

F. The Auld Man, wakening, cries for Bessy, who returns and ludicrously hoodwinks him. He regrets that he ever suspected her—the best wife in Fife.

G. Fyndlaw laments that he has no one to fight with:

[1] Foot Guards. James V had a guard of infantry. See Pinkerton, *History of Scotland under the House of Stewart*, II 428.

he who slew Graysteel and Sir Bevis, he who in hardihood
excels Hector of Troy, Gawain and Goliath. But the
Fool enters, with a sheep's head on a staff. Fyndlaw in
terror imagines that he sees the spirit of Guy, or Merlin,
or some she-ghost, or Gyre Carlin, or Gow-mak-morne.
He offers to surrender his weapons, his purse, and himself. The monster comes still nearer, and Fyndlaw runs
away.

H. "That finishes", says Nuntius, "for to-day. Come
back on Tuesday of Whitsun week, the seventh of June.
Take an early breakfast and be ready to sit out the play."

Ane Satyre has a variety of metres—rhyming couplets
and several types of stanza.

The couplets consist of lines of four feet and five feet,
with a varying number of syllables: 311 sqq., 1882 sqq.,
1952 sqq.

In the stanzas the lines are of two, three, four and
five feet. We find, for example, the ballad metre, *a b a b*,
259 sqq., 1085 sqq.; and the sextain, *a b a b c c*, 3798 sqq.
The Chaucerian heptastich is used, 3784 sqq.; sometimes
with a change in the rhymes of lines six and seven, as
a b a b b c b, 1121 sqq. and *a b a b b a a*, 2356 sqq. Lines
295–310 rhyme *a b a b b c b c c d c d d e d e*.

For serious speeches the metre of Chaucer's *Monk's
Tale* is also employed, *a b a b b c b c*, 14 sqq., 1580 sqq.,
4629 sqq. This type with a bob-wheel, *a b a b b c b c d e e e d*,
occurs 1 sqq. and 214 sqq. In less serious parts and in
comic speeches *rime couée* is frequent—lines of four, three
and two feet, rhyming *a a b a b*, 602 sqq.; *a a b c c b*, 1452
sqq.; *a a a b c c c b*, 70 sqq., 4645 sqq.; *a a a b a b*, 683 sqq.
The last is the form which Burns used with great fre-
quency; see *The Centenary Burns*, 1 336 sqq.

CHAPTER III

LYNDSAY AS POET

Poets sometimes disclaim the title of poet; as Burns in his first *Epistle to John Lapraik*:

> I am nae poet, in a sense;
> But just a rhymer like by chance.

Such disclaimer, critics have declared, merely exhibits a pleasing modesty on the poet's part. In "The Prolog" to *The Monarche* Lyndsay explains why he does not invoke the Muses as do the "pleasand Poetis". He is not one of them,

> For I did never sleip on Pernasso,[1]
> As did the Poetis of lang tyme ago,
> And, speciallie, the ornate Ennius;
> Nor drank I never, with Hysiodus,
> Of Grece the perfyte poet soverane,
>   Of Hylicon, the sors of eloquence,
> Of that melifluous, famous, fresche fontaine.

In other places Lyndsay calls his writing "rurall ryme", "raggit rurall vers", "barbour rusticall indyte"; and speaks of it as deficient in rhetoric and in ornate terms. Again, he bids his book with its rude unrhetorical style flee to rural folk and not keep company with poets. Yet, while yielding to this conventional modesty, he tacitly claims a place among the Scottish poets, living and dead.

---

[1] To excuse rude verse and ignorance of rhetoric, the Franklin in the *Canterbury Tales* is made to say "I sleep never on the mount of Pernasso". Persius (*Prologue to Satires*) may be the ultimate origin:

> "Nec fonte labra prolui caballino,
> Nec in bicipiti somniasse Parnasso
> Memini, ut repente sic poeta prodirem."

Lyndsay's verse, mostly satiric, didactic and chronicle, amounts to about 18,000 lines, wellnigh all of it written in the midst of his busy public life. He had not time, he may not have had inclination, to revise and polish his verses. Consequently, fault might be found with his limited variety of rhymes, and with his readiness to manipulate forms to suit his rhyme. We must, however, be cautious in judging his rhymes, and his language as a whole, for we cannot be sure that we have the forms he wrote. *The Monarche* may have been printed under his supervision. The works printed in his lifetime out of Scotland were not revised by him, and these show variants from the editions printed in Scotland; while Charteris' edition of *Ane Satyre* (1602) has many differences in forms from the Bannatyne MSS. text (1568).

Lyndsay has also been charged with weakness, or forgetfulness, because of his fondness for repeating lines and phrases (in battle scenes he has "ruschit rycht rudelie" four times); while other passages are transferred, almost word for word, from one poem to another. In three poems Lyndsay describes the grief of David I of Scotland had he known how religious life would degenerate in the abbeys which he founded. That Constantine ruined the Church by enriching it is stated in *The Dreme* and *The Papyngo*, two of the earliest works; is repeated in *Ane Satyre*; and appears yet again in his latest work, *The Monarche*. Such repetition, whatever its stylistic defect, has the advantage of making certain what Lyndsay's opinions were, especially when he utters, as his own, in *The Complaynt* or *The Monarche*, the views given to characters in *Ane Satyre*. His contemporaries would not notice the repetition. Those present at a performance of *Ane*

Satyre had not necessarily read *The Dreme*: readers of *The Monarche* were not necessarily auditors of *Ane Satyre*.

Lyndsay has still marks of mediaevalism: love of astronomical lore, and the conventions of dreams, restless tossing in bed, wandering forth on May mornings, allegories and allegorical personages. He sometimes loads his poetry with pedantic erudition, as catalogues of names. For example, he puts the names of the countries of the world into verse, a few lines of which will satisfy:

> Nether Scithia, Trace and Carmanie,
>   Thusia, Histria and Pannonia,
> Denmark, Gotland, Grunland and Almanie,
>   Pole, Hungarie, Boeme, Norica, Rethia,
> Teutonia, and mony divers ma.

Though not a poet of the highest type, Lyndsay was a ready versifier with a command of clear and fitting language. He was a quick observer, a man of shrewd sense, a great humorist, a clever painter of life.[1] *The Monarche* contains long stretches of dreary chronicling of world-history, but also weighty reflections, well expressed, on life and on affairs in Church and State. *Squire Meldrum* has much sprightly narrative and graphic description. Notable for imaginative power is *The Dreme*, perhaps because written when exile from Court afforded Lyndsay leisure. As a rule, his subjects do not lend themselves to the pathetic; but *The Deploratioun*, though it could not be an expression of personal grief, does show pathos.

---

[1] His pictures of low life might at times be termed vulgar, or even obscene. But we must blame the age, not the man; and of the age we might say what A. W. Ward remarks in another connexion: "The grossness...points to the slow progress of aesthetic culture rather than the absence of moral sentiment." *A History of English Dramatic Literature*, I 62. See above, p. 18.

But Lyndsay's strength lies in his dramatic skill. Remember the dates of his dramatic work, roughly 1540 to 1554; and what stage plays there were in England during that period. A. W. Ward says that *Ane Satyre* "in vigour and variety far outstrips any contemporary or analogous English effort"; and, "Altogether, this dramatic satire is ...by far the most elaborate as well as in its way the most powerful of all our mediaeval moralities."[1]

Yet one of Lyndsay's fellow-countrymen calls *Ane Satyre* "a series of interludes loosely combined into a play".[2] A careful study of *Ane Satyre* leaves a totally different impression. The plot is quite good and is well carried out; the varied characters are interesting, even those with abstract names are full of life; there is plenty of lively incidents; the dialogue is grave and gay, its reforming seriousness tempered and enlivened with waggish wit and piercing satire. If some portions of the dialogue are dull to us, we must not forget that the serious matters touched the audiences of Lyndsay's time very intimately. They had suffered from exactions of tithes and other dues; when ecclesiastical immorality was denounced, or ignorance, or neglect of duties, or flaunting of wealth, they could silently think of a culprit, or shout his name aloud. They knew to what friar or pardoner any piece of satire applied, they appreciated topical allusions to marauding Borderers, to·Edinburgh merchants and "the brousters of Cowper toun". To understand the full effect and popular appeal of *Ane Satyre* we must put our-

[1] *A History of English Dramatic Literature*, I 131, 133. While *Ane Satyre* is a morality, it includes comedy—comedy dealing with the manners of the day—and it has also been influenced by the French *sotie*: e.g. Folly's Sermon.

[2] *The Poems of William Dunbar*, I lxxxiii (Scottish Text Society).

selves into the position of the men and women of the time.[1]

[1] John Nichol, Part V of *Sir David Lindesay's Works* (Early English Text Society), and Ward's *Poets*, 1 192 sqq.; E. K. Chambers, *The Mediaeval Stage*, 11 157; T. F. Henderson, *Cambridge History of English Literature*, 111 129; A. J. Mill, *Mediaeval Stage in Scotland*, St Andrews Publications, xxiv, and "Influence of the Continental Drama on Lyndsay's *Satyre*", in *Modern Language Review*, vol. xxv; Janet M. Smith, *The French Background of Middle Scots Literature*. Miss Smith finds French influence, suggestion and imitation, in *The Dreme, Papyngo, Squire Meldrum, Kitteis Confessioun*. She seems too ready to take resemblances as proof; for surely Lyndsay could find material in Scotland without running to French works. It is well to remember that similarity, or even sameness, does not always mean imitation or borrowing. Similar causes produce similar results quite independently.

CHAPTER IV

LYNDSAY AND THE CLERGY

In *The Dreme*, 173 sqq., when Lyndsay visits Hell, he sees churchmen lying in heaps—cardinals, archbishops, bishops, abbots, priors, friars, canons, monks, priests and many more. He inquires of Remembrance the reason of this.

> Scho said, The cause of thair unhappy chance
>   Wes covatyce, luste and ambitioun:
>
> .   .   .   .
>
> Als they did nocht instruct the ignorant
>   Provocand thame to penitence, be preicheing;
> Bot servit warldlie Prencis insolent,
>   And war promovit be thair fenyeit fleicheing,
>   Nocht for thair science, wysedome, nor teicheing;
> Be symonie, was thair promotioun,
> More for deneiris, nor for devotioun.

Another cause of their punishment was their misuse of the patrimony and revenue of the Church.

> Quhilkis suld have bene trypartit in to three;
>   First, to uphauld the Kirk in honestie;
> The secund part, to sustene thair estaitis;
>   The third part, to be gevin to the puris
> Bot thay dispone that geir all uther gaittis,
>   On cartis, and dyce, on harllotrie, and huris;
>   Thir catyvis tuke no compt of thair awin curis:
> Thair kirkis reuin, thair ladyis clenelie cled
> And rychelie rewlit, boith at burde and bed.
>
> Thair bastarde bairnis proudely thay provydit;
>   The Kirk geir larglie thay did on thame spende;
> In thair defaltis, thair subditis wer misgydit,
>   And comptit nocht thair God for tyll offend,
>   Quhilk gart thame want grace, at thair latter end.

Here, in his earliest poem, Lyndsay brings forward his principal charges against the clergy, charges repeated again and again till his latest work, *The Monarche*. What offends him as an honest man is the discrepancy between the profession and the practice of most of the clergy. In *Ane Satyre*, 1069 sqq., Verity, quoting *Sic luceat lux vestra coram hominibus, ut videant opera vestra bona*, tells the prelates:

> In verteous lyfe, gif that ye do indure,
> The pepill wil tak mair tent to your deids,
> > Then to your words, and als baith rich and puir
> Will follow yow baith in your warks and words.

The value of example is emphasized in *The Monarche*, 5431 sqq., where Experience adds:

> Quhat dois availl religious weidis,
> Quhen thay ar contrar in thare deidis?
> Quhat holynes is thare within
> Ane wolf cled in ane wedderis skin?

But the clergy remained obdurate in their evil ways. The Parson in *Ane Satyre*, 3545 sqq., glosses over five of the seven deadly sins. In his eyes pride is no deadly sin but simply honour, dignity, nobility; greed of worldly gain is merely wisdom; anger is boldness; gluttony is nothing other than life's sustenance; the natural sin of lechery is only true love: all these are good.

In nothing was the contrast between profession and practice so glaring as in the attitude of many clerics, high and low, to the obligation of celibacy and the vow of chastity. Though since the days of Hildebrand celibacy had been made obligatory, the obligation had, in many countries, been more or less "a pious fiction".[1] Some

---

[1] See articles in *Encyclopaedia of Religion and Ethics, Encyclopaedia Britannica* and *Chambers's Encyclopaedia*.

priests had married: others, without going through the
marriage ceremony, had taken consorts, with whom they
lived in all faithfulness, their consciences void of offence.
But this course was dangerous; for, if a priest might
break one church law and go unpunished, why should
a layman who broke another law suffer punishment?
Many clerics, however, finding celibacy an impossibility,
neither married nor took consorts, but, forgetting their
vow of chastity, indulged in fornication, adultery and
promiscuous sensuality. These were hated by those whom
they injured and laughed at by others. They became fit
subjects for lewd and ludicrous anecdotes and stories,
songs and poems.

Tracing the degeneracy of the Church from its primitive purity, Lyndsay lays the blame on the possession of
property, which made priests thralls of sensuality. Un-
bound by marriage, they were free to indulge their
appetites as they chose.[1]

Chastity, says Lyndsay, exiled from Italy and France,
and rejected in England, sought refuge in Scotland. Prelates and priests would not harbour a rebel from Rome,
and sent her to the nuns. They welcomed her at first, but,
influenced by property, riches and sensuality, they ex-
pelled her. The friars would have nothing to do with her.
She is now with the "Systeris of the Schenis", whose piety
and poverty keep them unthrall to sensuality.[2]

The example of the Church is cited by Wantonness
(*Ane Satyre*, 235 sqq., 279 sqq.) to prove to Rex Humanitas that lechery is no sin:

---

[1] *Papyngo*, 860 sqq.
[2] *Papyngo*, 871 sqq., 917 sqq.; *Ane Satyre*, 508 sqq.; 1370 sq.; *The
Monarche*, 4690 sq.

> First, at the Romane Kirk will ye begin,
>> Quhilk is the lemand lamp of lechery:
>> Quhair Cardinalis and Bischopis, generally,
> To luif ladies, thay think ane pleasand sport,
>> And out of Rome hes baneist Chastity,
>> Quha with our Prelats can get na resort.

Solace (*Ane Satyre*, 253 sqq.) declares that the Scottish prelates for the most part

>> think na schame to have ane huir,
> And sum hes thrie under thair cuir;

and slyly adds a topical allusion—

>> Speir at the Monks of Bamirrinoch,
>> Gif lecherie be sin.

When the Poor Man (*Ane Satyre*, 2016 sqq.) is told that custom, which to the clergy is good and sufficient law, entitles the vicar to exact death dues, he asks if custom gives them the right to sin with "ladies, maidens and other men's wives". Later in the play (2757 sqq.) he grumbles because, while he himself is bound to one wife, prelates have great prerogatives: without reprimand or punishment, they may put away their wives and take others.[1] They run like rams among the "sillie yows".

The Bishop, questioned how he has discharged his duties, replies (*Ane Satyre*, 3375 sqq.):

>> Howbeit I dar nocht plainlie spouse ane wyfe,
>> Yet concubeins I have had four or fyfe.

In *The Monarche*, 4578 sqq., Experience says:

>> None of his [the Pope's] Preistis dar marye wyfis,
>> Under no less paine nor thair lyfis.
>> Thocht thay haif concubynis fyftene,
>> In to that cace, thay ar ouersene.
>> Quhat chaistytie thay keip in Rome
>> Is weill kend ouer all Christindome.

---

[1] Repeated, with variations, *The Monarche*, 4692 sqq. Compare *The Auld Man*, 40 sqq.

Lyndsay holds that, since the law of celibacy is not observed and the vow of chastity not kept, the obvious course is for the clergy to be free to marry. This view he elaborates in *The Monarche*, 4864 sqq., and he makes permission to marry one of the decisions of Parliament in *Ane Satyre*, 3932 sqq.[1]

John the Commonweal (*Ane Satyre*, 2953 sqq.) declares that if David I could see the great abomination in abbeys and nunneries,

> Thair publick huirdomes and thair harlotries,

he would repent that he had wasted money on these foundations.

The Abbot and the Prioress, says Chastity in *Ane Satyre*, 3397 sqq., "beare ane habite of feinzeit holines", but their actions are far from holy. They solemnly vow to live chaste, but, as soon as they are sure of the papal bulls confirming their appointment, they live in whoredom and in harlotry.[2] The Abbot (*Ane Satyre*, 3418 sqq.) maintains that he kept his three vows strictly till the bulls came:

> Then did I leife, as did my predecessour.
> My paramours is baith als fat and fair,
> As ony wench, intill the toun of Air.

The Prioress (*Ane Satyre*, 3441 sqq.) avows that she would willingly have sheltered Lady Chastity:

> Bot, my complexioun thairto wald not assent:
> I do my office, efter auld use and wount.[3]

What "auld use and wount" meant, we learn from Placebo (*Ane Satyre*, 1834 sqq.):

> Speir at my ladie Priores,
> Gif lechery be sin.

---

[1] Compare *Papyngo*, 1053 sqq.   [2] Compare *Ane Satyre*, 1234 sqq.
[3] Compare *Ane Satyre*, 1216 sqq.

In *The Auld Man*, 49 sqq., the Cotter says that, if his shrewish wife were dead, he would not marry again, and is told that then he must live a chaste life, as is right and proper. "Yes," he replies, "I shall live chaste—like abbots, monks and friars."[1]

While clerical immorality made some people feel indignation or sorrow and in others excited uproarious laughter, bitter ill-will was roused against the clergy, especially among the less well-to-do classes, on account of teinds, corpse-presents, Easter offerings, and also because of the harshness with which these dues were exacted from the poorest by officials of an extremely wealthy church. Covetousness is linked with lust and ambition (*The Dreme*, 186) in bringing churchmen down to Hell; and elsewhere Lyndsay says much about the greed of the clergy, their exactions, their amassing of wealth and their misuse of it.

In *The Dreme*, 976 sqq., John the Commonweal tells that the Spirituality would not listen to his appeal:

> Thair officiaris, thay held me at disdene;
> For Symonie, he rewlis up al that rowte;
> And Covatyce, that carle, gart bar me oute.

In *Ane Satyre*, 2449 sq., the Three Estates enter backwards, Spirituality conducted by Covetousness and Sensuality; and when the two minions are being led to the stocks (*Ane Satyre*, 2499 sqq.), the Bishop threatens to complain to the Pope against such wrong. Covetousness bids the reverend fathers be patient:

> I sall nocht lang remaine from your presence,
> Thocht for ane quhyll, I man from yow depairt,
> I wait my spreit sall remaine in your hart.

[1] See above, p. 72.

The Pie, the Raven and the Kite who gather round the dying Parrot (*The Papyngo*, 647 sqq.) and devour her when dead, quarrelling over their shares of her body, represent, as we saw, a Canon Regular, a Black Monk, and a Friar.[1] The scene is a satire on the eagerness of the clergy to secure for themselves the property of the dying while pretending to give spiritual comfort. Later in the same poem (995 sq.) the unworthy clergy to whom Christ's sheep are entrusted are called "hungrye gormande wolfis"; and in *Ane Satyre*, 3038 sq., the Merchant says:

> The sillie sauls, that bene Christis scheip,
> Sould nocht be givin to gormand wolfis to keip.

One of Folly's hats (*Ane Satyre*, 4542 sqq.) is intended

> For Spiritual Fuillis, that taks in cure,
> The saulis of Great Diosies,
> The regiment of great Abesies,
> For gredines of warldlie pelf.

The Act of Parliament made in *Ane Satyre*, 3080 sqq., to reform the Consistory is opposed by Spirituality, for

> It is againis our profeit singulair:
> Wee will nocht want our profeit, be Sanct Geil.

The clergy are blamed (*Ane Satyre*, 3582 sqq.) because they have no will to be poor; but, unlike their Master Christ, they wish to possess temporal lands. The Bishop (*Ane Satyre*, 3361 sqq.) declares that he has used his office well:

> For I tak in my count twyse in the yeir,
> Wanting nocht of my teind ane boll of beir.
> I gat gude payment of my Temporall lands,
> My buttock-maill, my coattis, and my offrands,
> With all that dois perteine my benefice.

[1] See above, p. 26.

"Tithes were at first contributions made voluntarily as a religious duty, and enforced only by ecclesiastical sanctions. But after the practice of tithe-paying became general in Western Europe the obligation to pay tithe was recognized and enforced as a civil obligation." The paying of tithes has nowhere been generally popular. Chaucer's Plowman, that is, Peasant-farmer, is an exception:

> His tythes payed he ful faire and wel,
> Bothe of his propre swink and his catel.

Exceptional, too, is Chaucer's Parish Priest:

> Ful looth were him to cursen for his tythes,
> But rather wolde he yeven, out of doute,
> Un-to his povre perisshens aboute
> Of his offring, and eek of his substance.

Lyndsay willingly allows that the clergy should have stipends, but he voices the cry of the poor, on whom the exactions fell heavy, and the complaint that very many of the clergy showed more eagerness in exacting teinds, corpse-presents and other dues than in performing their spiritual duties. Cardinal Beaton (*The Tragedie*, 295 sqq.) asks the clergy if they are not ashamed as servants of Christ to take all and give nothing:

> Ye wyll nocht want teind scheif, nor offerandis,
> Teind woll, teind lambe, teind calf, teind gryce and guse;
> To mak servyce ye ar all out of use.

Experience (*The Monarche*, 4682 sqq.) describes how jolly is the proud parson's life, his only toil to take his teind from the parishioners, and spend it:

> Thoucht thay want precheing sevintene yeir,
> He wyll nocht want ane boll of beir.[1]

---

[1] A variant of *Ane Satyre*, 2747 sqq.

The corpse-present, or mortuary, which was considered to be payment of church dues the deceased had failed to pay when alive, was taken from deceased's estate or paid by relatives. This burden, as well as its cruel exaction, was a grievance causing bitter outcry from the poor. In *The Monarche*, 4704 sqq., it is told of the vicar:

> He wyll nocht faill to tak ane kow
> And umaist claith,[1] thoucht babis thame ban,
> Frome ane pure selye housband man;
> Quhen that he lyis for tyll de,
> Haiffeing small bairnis two or thre,
> And hes thre ky, withouttin mo,
> The vicare moste have one of tho,
> With the gray cloke that happis the bed,
> Howbeit that he be purelye cled:
> And gyf the wyfe de on the morne,
> Thocht all the babis suld be forlorne,
> The uther kow he cleikis awaye,
> With hir pure coit of roploch graye.
> And gyf, within tway dayis or thre,
> The eldest child hapnis to de,
> Of the thrid kow he wylbe sure.
> Quhen he hes all than under his cure
> And father and mother boith ar dede,
> Beg mon the babis, without remede:
> Thay hauld the corps at the kirk style,
> And thare it moste remane ane quhyle,
> Tyll thay gett sufficient souertie
> For thare Kirk rycht and dewitie.

Here Lyndsay amplifies and intensifies what John the Commonweal says in *Ane Satyre*, 2725 sqq., about mortuaries. Poor Man corroborates this, giving in brief the story which he has already given in full.[2]

[1] We often hear of "umaist claith", "umest clayis", in this connexion. Sometimes the bed-cover was taken, sometimes an outer garment.

[2] See above, p. 53.

When the abolition of the corpse-present is mooted (*Ane Satyre*, 2818 sqq.), the Bishop shouts:

> Na, na! never, till the day of Judgement:
> Wee will want nathing that wee have in use,
> Kirtil nor kow, teind lambe, teind gryse, nor guse.[1]

But a law is passed (*Ane Satyre*, 3908 sqq.) depriving the vicars

> Baith of corspresent, cow and umest claith,
> To pure commons becaus it hath done skaith.

The Church found another source, a valuable source, of wealth in the belief in Purgatory. Its awful torments were graphically described, and the terror-struck hearers were ready to give or bequeath money and lands for masses and prayers so that they themselves, or their relations or their friends still living or already dead, might find release from such tribulations. In his earliest poem, *The Dreme*, 337 sqq., Lyndsay declares his belief in Purgatory on the authority of great theologians. But by the time he was composing *The Monarche*, 4354 sqq., he was prepared to speak with sarcasm of the Pope, neither God nor man, the mighty "Sanctitude", with power to bind and loose.

> Als he is Prince of Purgatorie,
> Delyvering saulis from paine to glorie:
> Of that dirke dungeoun, but doute,
> Quham evir he plesis he takis thame oute.

Lyndsay, however, talks more boldly (*The Monarche*, 4766 sqq.). Experience, describing the Court of Rome,

---

[1] Not to exact the corpse-present was a serious offence. Thomas Forret, vicar of Dollar, burnt for heresy in 1539, was accused *inter alia* of restoring to his parishioners cow and uppermost cloth and of saying that he had no claim to them. His reply was that he returned them to such as had more need of them than he himself (Pitscottie, I 349; Calderwood, *History of the Kirk of Scotland*, I 126 (Wodrow Society)).

says they claim to be the successors of Peter and Paul, which they are not. The apostles were fishers of men to bring them to the Christian faith. The Court of Rome has many fishers who spread their net over the dry ground as well as over the sea to gather in land, gold and other gear:

> In to thare tramalt nett thay fangit ane fysche,
>   More nor ane quhaill worthye of memorye,
> Of quhome thay have had mony dayntay dysche,
>   Be quhome thay ar exaltit to great glorye;
>   That marvelous monstour callit Purgatorye.
> Howbeit tyll us it is nocht amyable,
> It hes to thame bene veray profytable.
>
> Lat thay that fructfull fysche eschaip thare nett,
>   Be quhome thay haif so gret commoditeis,
> Ane more fatt fysche I traist thay sall nocht gett,
>   Thocht thay wald sers ouerthort the occiane seis,
>   Adew the daylie dolorous Derigeis!
> Selye pure preistis may syng with hart full sorye,
> Want thay that panefull palyce, Purgatorye.
>
> Fairweill, monkrye, with chanoun, nun and freir!
>   Alace! thay wylbe lychtleit in all landis:
> Cowlis wyll no more be kend in kirk nor queir,
>   Lat they that fructfull fysche eschaip thare handis,
>   I counsall thame to bynd hym fast in bandis:
> For Peter, Androw, nor Johne culd never gett
> So profytable ane fysche in to thare nett.

Money was amassed by the clergy in other ways. For, says Lyndsay, it was money-making everywhere. Christ commanded Peter to feed his sheep, and Peter obeyed. To that command, however, the churchmen of to-day pay little heed (*The Monarche*, 4794 sqq.):

> Bot Christis scheip thay spulye petuouslye;
>   And with the woll thay cleith thame curiouslye.
> Lyk gormand wolfis, thay tak of thame thare fude,
> Thai eit thair flesche and drynkis boith mylk and blude.

Another grievance sprang from the method of enforcing payment of church dues. If teinds, for example, were not paid, the clergy used the weapon of excommunication, familiarly called "cursing". When the Poor Man (*Ane Satyre*, 2006 sqq.) has described how the vicar treated him, he is asked: "Was not the parson your good friend?" "No", he replies:

> The Devil stick him! he curst me for my teind:
> And halds me yit under that same proces,
> That gart me want the Sacrament at Pasche.

How then did the clergy use their abundant wealth? Lyndsay's answer is that they misused it. The patrimony and revenue of the Church should (*The Dreme*, 197 sqq.) be divided into three parts: one for the proper and seemly upkeep of the buildings; another for the maintenance of the clergy; the third for the poor. Instead, the poor are neglected, and churches are allowed to become ruinous. The money is squandered on cards and dice, and on mistresses, who are finely dressed and richly adorned.[1]

Churchmen also lavishly spend the wealth of the church on their bastards. The Bishop describes how well he has used his office, making provision for his sons and marrying all his daughters to lairds (*Ane Satyre*, 3377 sq.). Similarly, the Abbot says he has sent his sons to Paris, to the University (he trusts they shall be no fools), while all his married daughters have been well provided for (*Ane Satyre*, 3423 sqq.). But when he is deposed, he laments

[1] Compare what the vicar of Dollar (see above, p. 89) replied to the charge of having said that churchmen were not entitled to teinds, offerings and corpse-presents: "I said not so, but I say it is not lawful for churchmen to spend the teinds and the patrimony of the Church as they do on harlots and whores and elegant clothing, riotous banqueting and wanton playing at cards and dice, and the church ruined and the pulpit down" (Pitscottie, 1 348).

that he has still two unmarried daughters, both con-
tracted, and he knows not how he is now to pay their
dowry (*Ane Satyre*, 3767 sqq.). The huge dowries given
by prelates with their daughters the nobles and gentry
felt to be a special grievance. Lyndsay voices their complaint in *Ane Satyre*, 3182 sqq.:

> Schir, we beseik your soverane celsitude,
>   Of our dochtours to have compassioun;
> Quhom wee may na way marie, be the Rude,
>   Without we mak sum alienatioun
>   Of our land for thair supportatioun;
> For quhy? the markit raisit bene sa hie,
>   That Prelats dochtours of this natioun
> Ar maryit with sic superfluitie:
> Thay will nocht spair to gif twa thowsand pounds,
>   With thair dochtours, to ane nobill man:
> In riches, sa thay do superabound:
>   Bot we may nocht do sa, be Sanct Allane:
>   Thir proud Prelats our dochtours sair may ban;
> That thay remaine at hame sa lang unmaryit.

Again and again Lyndsay assails the appalling ignorance and incompetence shown by the clergy, and not by
the lower ranks only.

In *The Papyngo*, 976 sqq., the Raven, that is, the Black
Monk, while admitting that the clergy have degenerated,
seeks to lay the blame on princes, who have put unsuitable
men in office. If doctors of divinity or of law held high
office, things would be well. Then what pleasure to hear
a bishop preach, to find an abbot who could teach his
convent, to meet a parson full of philosophy! But that is
to wish for the impossible.[1] Experience (*The Monarche*,
5349 sqq.) says that ignorant prelates are of as much use
for their duty as ice would be to kindle a fire. No wonder

[1] Compare *The Complaynt*, 332 sqq.

the people slide when they have blind men for guides. Prelates who cannot preach, or teach God's law, are the dumb dogs of Isaiah. And yet many such ignorant prelates are now in office.[1]

Latin, though the language of the church services, was to some of the clergy practically unknown and by others known only uncertainly. In *Kitteis Confessioun* one of the clerics is styled Sir John Latinless (line 76); and of another Kittie says (lines 43 sq.):

> And mekil Latyne he did mummill,
> I hard na thing bot hummill bummill.

Beaton (*The Tragedie*, 344 sqq.) admonishes princes not to appoint unworthy men as bishops or abbots but to select those fitted to do their duty. Offices should not be given to ribald rascals, stable grooms, street-walkers, publicans, flatterers, tattlers, or boobies[2]—men with no university training, with no instruction in theology. They may be arrayed in ecclesiastical vestments, but all they can do is to

> Mummyll ouer ane pair of maiglet matenis.

Bishops, abbots, parish priests and vicars should all be chosen with the scrupulous care used in selecting a brewer, a cook or a tailor. Lyndsay delights in contrasting ignorant clerics with skilled craftsmen; as tailor and shoemaker in *Ane Satyre*, 3128 sqq. One of the Acts of Parliament (*Ane Satyre*, 3884 sqq.) runs:

---

[1] Compare *The Complaynt*, 321 sqq. and *The Tragedie*, 288 sqq.

[2] The word is "cowhubeis"=calves. We might say "stirks", after Burns, *Epistle to John Lapraik*:

> "A set o' dull, conceited hashes,
> Confuse their brains in college classes,
> They gang in stirks and come out asses."

Als becaus of the great pluralitie
　Of ignorant preists, ma than ane legioun,
Quhairthroch, of teichouris the heich dignitie
　Is vilipendit, in ilk regioun:
　Thairfoir, our Court hes maid ane provisioun.
That na bischops mak teichours, in tyme cumming,
　Except men of gude eruditioun,
And for preistheid qualifeit and cunning.

Siclyke as ye se, in the Borrows toun,
　Ane tailzeour is nocht sufferit to remaine
Without he can mak doublet, coat, and gown,
　He man gang till his prenteischip againe:
　Bischops sould nocht ressave, me think certaine,
Into the Kirk, except ane cunning Clark:
　Ane idiot preist, Esay compaireth, plaine,
Till ane dum dogge, that can nocht byte nor bark.

According to Henrie Charteris, in his 1568 edition, Lyndsay employed the tailor's skill to give point to a joke at the expense of the higher clergy:

He never ceased both in his grave and merry matters, in earnest and in jest, in writing and in speaking, to accuse and censure them. There comes to my memory a clever trick which I once heard reported of him. The King's Grace, James the Fifth, being on one occasion accompanied by a great number of his nobles, and a great crowd of bishops, abbots and other prelates standing about, Lyndsay quickly and cleverly invented a clever trick to annoy them. He comes to the King and after great "God Save you" 's and salutations, he makes as though he would request something important of the King's Grace. The King observing this, demands what he would have. Lyndsay answers: "Sir, I have long served your Grace and look to be rewarded as others are. And now your master tailor is, at God's pleasure, departed this life. Therefore I would desire of your Grace to bestow this little kindness upon me as a part of reward for my long service, to make me your master tailor." The King, believing indeed his master tailor to be deceased, says to him, "Why wouldst thou be my tailor? Thou canst neither shape nor sew." He answers, "Sir, that does not matter, for you have given bishoprics and benefices to many standing here about you, and yet can they neither teach nor preach. And why may I not then as well be your tailor though I can neither shape nor sew? Since teaching and preaching are no less necessary to their vocation than shaping and sewing to a tailor's." The King immediately perceived his smart device, and laughed merrily thereat, but the bishops at such jesting laughed never a bit.

It was notorious in Lyndsay's day that very many of the clergy were ignorant of the contents of the Bible. In *Ane Satyre*, 2910 sqq., the Bishop is offered the Vulgate New Testament:

> Tak thair the Buik, let se gif ye can spell.

He refuses it, and, when asked if he has never read the New Testament, replies:

> Na, Sir, be him that our Lord Jesus sauld,
> I red never the New Testament, nor Auld;
> Nor ever thinks to do, Sir, be the Rude;
> I heir freiris say that reiding dois na gude.

Lyndsay is here alluding to a remark by the Bishop of Dunkeld when finding fault with the good Vicar of Dollar, Thomas Forret, who said he had read the New Testament and the Old. Thereupon the Bishop declared:

> I thank God that I never knew what the Old and the New Testament was. Therefore, Dean Thomas, I will know nothing but my Portuise and my Pontifical.

Hence arose a proverb in Scotland: "Ye are like the Bishop of Dunkeld, that knew neither the New Law nor the Old."[1]

Buchanan (*Historia*, xv, 29) mentions the reading of

---

[1] Calderwood, *History*, I 126 sq.; and Laing's *Knox*, I 97.

the New Testament as being classed among the most serious crimes, and adds:

So great blindness was there that very many of the priests, offended by the name "New", asserted that the book had lately been written by Martin Luther, and asked again for the Old Testament.

Lyndsay gives another instance of ignorance of the Bible in *Ane Satyre*, 3501 sqq. The Doctor of Divinity in his sermon calls love the ladder with only two steps which leads to heaven.

Diliges Dominum Deum tuum ex toto corde tuo, et proximum tuum sicut teipsum: in his duobus mandatis, &c.

> The first step suithlie of this ledder is
>   To luife thy God, as the fontaine and well
> Of luife and grace; and the second, I wis,
>   To luife thy nichtbour as thou luiffes thy sell.

Both Abbot and Parson fail to recognize the passage. Their Heaven is a material Heaven thousands of miles distant from the earth. How could the short-legged, the crooked or the blind reach it by a ladder of two steps? "Or", adds the portly Abbot, "a stout fellow like me?"

Though pride is the chief of the deadly sins and has been regarded as the source of the others, yet the Parson calls it honour, dignity.[1] Pride, says John the Commonweal (*The Dreme*, 981), has chased away humility from the clergy; and Beaton (*The Tragedie*, 62 sqq.) confesses that his prideful heart would not allow him to be satisfied with any position but the highest.

The pride of the clergy was manifest in various ways. One was to ride on mules. The Bishop mentions that to

---

[1] See above, p. 81.

show how well he exercised his office (*Ane Satyre*, 3379 sq.):

> I am na fuill,
> For quhy? I ryde upon an amland muill.

Compare *The Complaynt*, 332 sqq., and *Ane Satyre*, 3734 sqq.

Pride is also seen in the fine clothes of the clergy, in the rich trapping of their mules, in their grand houses. The dying Parrot (*The Papyngo*, 1044 sqq.) says,

> And in thair habitis thay tak sic delyte
> Thay have renuncit russet and raploch quhyte
>
> Cleikand to thame skarlote, and crammosie,
>   With menever, martrik, grice and ryche armyne:
> Thair lawe hartis exaultit ar so hie,
>   To see thair Papale pompe, it is ane pyne.
>   More ryche arraye is now, with frenyeis fyne,
> Upon the bardyng of ane Byscheopis mule,
> Nor ever had Paule, or Peter, agane Yule.

The Parson (*Ane Satyre*, 3433 sq.) declares:

> Our round bonats, we mak thame now four nuickit,
> Of richt fyne stuiff.

In *The Monarche*, 4532 sqq., we read:

> Abbottis, Byschoppis, and Cardinallis
> Hes plesand palyces royallis:
> Lyke Paradyse ar those prelattis places.

A third exhibition of pride appears in the titles claimed by the clergy, as Experience tells in *The Monarche*, 4658 sqq.:

> The seilye Nun wyll thynk gret schame,
> Without scho callit be Madame;
> The pure Preist thynkis he gettis no rycht
> Be he nocht stylit lyke ane knycht,
> And callit Schir, affore his name,
> As Schir Thomas and Schir Wilyame.
> All monkrye, ye may heir and se,
> Ar callit, Denis, for dignitie:

> Quhowbeit his mother mylk the kow,
> He mon be callit Dene Androw,
> Dene Peter, Dene Paull and Dene Robart.[1]

The Pope (*The Monarche*, 4326 sq.) is called *Sanctissimus*, though Saint Peter is styled merely *Sanctus*.

Finally, in their pride, the clergy demand precedence at table and in Parliament (*The Monarche*, 4674 sqq.):

> My lorde Abbote, rycht venerabyll,
> Ay marschellit upmoste at the tabyll;
> My lorde Byschope, moste reverent,
> Sett abufe Erlis in Parliament;
> And Cardinalis, duryng thare ryngis,
> Fallowis to Princis and to Kyngis;
> The Pope exaltit, in honour,
> Abufe the potent Empriour.

Ambition is classed by Lyndsay (*The Dreme*, 186) as one of the causes why prelates are found in Hell. Beaton (*The Tragedie*, 55 sqq.) confesses that his heart had been set on riches, dignity and glory. He would not be anything less than Cardinal and Legate. Even supremacy in the Church was not enough: he must be also Chancellor of Scotland. Beaton was not alone in his ambition. In *The Monarche*, 5346 sq., Lyndsay charges the degenerate clergy with seeking nothing but riches and dignity; and with the ambition of ruling in secular affairs and even of being above the king (*The Dreme*, 190 sqq., *The Complaynt*, 316 sqq., *Ane Satyre*, 3040 sqq., 3363 sq.). His summing up is in *The Dreme*, 984 sqq.:

> Lords of Religioun, thay go lyke Seculeris,
> Taking more compt in telling thair deneris,
>   Nor thay do of thair constitutioun,
>   Thus ar thay blyndit be ambitioun.[2]

---

[1] *Dene, Denis* = Sir, Sirs. So *dan, daun* in Chaucer; e.g. *Canterbury Tales*, B. 3982, "Sir Monk or Dan Piers by your name."

[2] See below, pp. 172, 193.

Lyndsay does not object to innocent amusements (*The Dreme*, 8 sqq., *The Complaynt*, 87 sqq., *Ane Satyre*, 1840 sqq.); but he attacks the clergy for wasting church revenues on cards and dice, and for devotion to sports instead of to religious duties. Beaton (*The Tragedie*, 78 sqq.) describes his princely prodigality, in which he outdid the French prelates, and his lordly liberality in banquets, in card-playing and in dice-playing:

> In to sic wysedome I was haldin wyse.
> And sparit nocht to play, with Kyng nor Knycht,
> Three thousand crownis of gold, upon ane nycht.

And so he warns his brother prelates to amend their lives in time and leave gaming (*The Tragedie*, 302 sqq.). He calls on princes not to make bishops, abbots, parsons or vicars of such as are qualified only in playing cards, dice, chess and backgammon (*The Tragedie*, 365 sqq.). Besides cards and dice and backgammon, tennis and football are what the Parson excels in, though he does not preach (*Ane Satyre*, 3428 sqq.).

The Abbot tells about the easy life he and his monks have. No house from Carrick to Crail enjoys better fare or more wholesome ale. The Prior, being a man of great devotion, is allowed a double portion of food and drink (*Ane Satyre*, 3412 sqq.). Experience ironically says (*The Monarche*, 4669 sqq.) that monks have really a hard time:

> With Christ thay tak ane painfull part,
> With dowbyll clethyng frome the cald,
> Eitand and drynkand quhen thay wald.[1]

Clergy, who were a byword for pride, ambition, covetousness, lust and ignorance, could not be expected

---

[1] Compare the story told in *Satirical Poems of the Reformation*, I 239 (Scottish Text Society).

to pay due attention to religious work; and Lyndsay brings forward many charges of neglect.

In *The Papyngo*, 838 sqq., he points out that in the early Church the clergy became enthralled by the peerless beauty of Riches and Sensuality:

> Soune thay foryet to studye, praye and preche,
>   Thay grew so subject to dame Sensuall,
> And thocht bot paine pure pepyll for to teche.

And the same is true of Scottish churchmen (*The Papyngo*, 1039 sqq.):

> As for thair precheing, quod the Papyngo,
>   I thame excuse, for quhy, thay bene so thrall
> To Propertie and his ding Dochteris two,
>   Dame Ryches and fair lady Sensuall,
>   Thay may nocht use no pastyme spirituall.

Their neglect of preaching and teaching, and their absorption in public affairs have caused their appearance in Hell (*The Dreme*, 190 sqq.). They ought to preach unfeignedly, minister the sacraments faithfully, and leave vain traditions (*Complaynt*, 319 sqq., 411 sqq.). This is their duty by Christ's example and command, and by the injunction of Canon Law (*The Monarche*, 4480 sqq., 4829 sqq., 5367 sqq.).

The Bishop in *Ane Satyre*, 2901 sqq., is frankly astonished when told that he ought to preach himself. Like other bishops, he thought that it was enough to employ a friar to take his place (*Ane Satyre*, 2925 sqq., 3389 sqq., *The Tragedie*, 309 sqq.). With what result we learn from Experience (*The Monarche*, 2597 sqq., 4490 sq.):

> Thay send furth Freris to preche for thame,
> Quhilk garris the peple now abhor thame.

Folly (*Ane Satyre*, 4452 sqq.), when told that a bishop has come to preach, says that it must be a red-letter day:

> Than stryk ane hag into the poast,
> For I hard never in all my lyfe
> Ane bischop cum to preich in Fyfe.

The Parson is too busy with his teinds and his sports to find time for preaching (*Ane Satyre*, 2747 sqq., 3428 sqq.).

Kitteis Confessioun, 95 sqq., tells how the confessor failed in his duty. He should have shown Kittie God's abhorrence of sin and her need of repentance. He should have exhorted her to love God and her neighbour.

It is enacted (*Ane Satyre*, 3716 sqq., 3916 sqq.) that negligent clergy should be deposed; and that in future bishops, priests and other churchmen must faithfully perform their duties.

In *The Monarche*, 4358 sqq., Lyndsay, when describing the marvellous domination of the Papacy over body and soul, denounces confession since it is one of the chief instruments of the power of the clergy:

> Oure secreit synnis, every yeir,
> We mon schaw to sum preist or freir,
> And tak thare absolutioun,
> Or ellis we gett no remissioun;
> So, be this way, thay cleirly ken
> The secretis of all seculare men;
> Thare secretis we knaw nocht at all:
> Thus ar we to thame bound and thrall.
> Quhat evir thare ministeris commandis
> Most be obeyit, without demandis.

We see the process of worming out secrets in *Kitteis Confessioun*.[1] The Curate puts questions to Kittie and discovers that she has stolen a peck of bere, that Will Leno

---

[1] Lines 9 sqq.

and she have misbehaved, that her master reads English
books,[1] and has spoken ill of the King. The Curate does
not consider himself bound by the seal of confession. He
will report about the bere to the owners, who have asked
him to investigate. He will tell Will's wife, with whom he
himself wishes to be intimate. Naturally, he will inform
the bishop about the heretical books and the King about
the treasonable talk.

Kitteis Confessioun[2] discloses another objection to the
confessional as it then was: it often led to immorality.
When Kittie was confessing, the Curate would have
kissed her, though he kept a face grave, devout, modest
and demure. At the close of his examination, he told
Kittie to come in the evening to his chamber to be absolved. Kittie refused and sought another confessor, who
was very inquisitive about Kittie and her lover—when
they embraced, how often, in what way and where. He
wished he had been there. He absolved her for a
"plack", and imposed penance. She was to say an Ave
Maria every day, and eat no fish for five Fridays ("But
butter and eggs are better fare", interjects Kittie). She
must also buy a Mass and go a pilgrimage ("The very
way to wantonness", she remarks).[3] The penance
pleased Kittie; for she knew the price of stealing and
of other sins.

Simony, the exchanging of spirituals for temporals,
had, by canon law, been declared a heinous sin, a kind
of heresy. Yet it was very prevalent in the Middle Ages.
In spite of the efforts of popes like Gregory VIII and

---

[1] The English Bible, or writings by some of the Reformers.
[2] Lines 3 sqq. and 29 sqq.   [3] See below, p. 107.

Innocent III to root it out, it flourished everywhere, especially in Rome, where Nicholas III,[1] Boniface VIII, Clement V and Alexander I were shameless offenders. An epigram on Alexander runs:

> Vendit Alexander claves, altaria, Christum.
> Emerat ille prius: vendere jure potest.

George Buchanan writes:

> *In Pium Pontificem.*
> Vendidit aere polum, terras in morte reliquit:
> Styx superest Papae quam colat una Pio.

At one time spiritual offices were openly sold in Rome. Roman citizens, says Lyndsay (*The Monarche*, 4937 sqq.), have lost their noble name; for they have turned the home of saints into a tabernacle for Simon Magus. The officials of the Roman Curia (*The Monarche*, 4792 sq.) are described as making huge profits by simony, which "they hold little vice". In Scotland, too, simony rules all the clergy (*The Dreme*, 979); by simony "dyke-low-paris" crowd into the Church (*The Papyngo*, 992 sq.); and Beaton (*The Tragedie*, 386 sqq.) tells:

> Nocht qualyfeit to bruke ane benefyse,
>   Bot throuch Schir Symonis solysitatioun,
> I was promovit on the samyn wyse.

The Church authorities in Rome (*The Monarche*, 4787 sqq.) export their merchandise to all countries—stamped lead, wax, parchment, pardons and dispensations—in value exceeding a temporal prince's revenue. In such trafficking they are not negligent. In *Ane Satyre*, 2839 sqq., John the Commonweal points out how Scotland is completely denuded of gold and silver, sent daily to

---

[1] See Dante, *Inferno*, xix 54 sqq., where Nicholas is in Hell because of simony, and Boniface and Clement are mentioned as coming soon.

Rome for bribes. The Merchant corroborates. The merchants of Scotland have furnished priests with the sum of a million pounds, which has gone out of the country to the detriment of the Commonweal:

> For throw thir playis[1] and thir promotioun,
> Mair for denners nor for devotioun,
> Sir Symonie hes maid with them ane band,
> The gould of weicht thay leid out of the land.

Good Counsel says that formerly only great bishoprics were sped at Rome, but now a priest goes there for the sake of a poor vicarage. A worthless lout runs to Rome and takes charge of a bishop's mule, and then comes home, with many a false story, carrying a pile of benefices on his back. The Lords Temporal would have priests forbidden to go to Rome. They are always wasting the wealth of the country for pleas and private profit. In consequence, the realm is bare of money. Parliament, therefore, decrees (*Ane Satyre*, 3924 sqq.) that, as the clergy squander the wealth of the country for bills and processes in seeking benefices, no money shall henceforth go to Rome except for archbishoprics.

The apostles, says Experience (*The Monarche*, 4745 sqq.), were noble fishers, bringing men and women to the Christian faith. But their successors have spread their net on rich revenues, gold and other goods. They have caught indeed a great part of all temporal lands, and, besides, the tenth of all movables—wonderfully profitable fishing. Their hose-net daily draws to Rome the most fine gold in Christendom. Within this half-century Rome has "ressett" out of Scotland, for bulls and bene-

---

[1] Pleas.

fices, as much as might very well have paid a king's ransom.[1]

The authoritative view regarding sacred pictures and statues had been for long that these were in churches not to be worshipped but to teach the ignorant. Educated people learned by reading what was written, the uneducated were instructed by looking at pictures or statues. Unfortunately many regarded the picture or statue as the dwelling-place of the sacred being it represented and as itself full of divine influence. This erroneous belief, or superstition, was, according to Lyndsay, encouraged by the clergy. In *The Complaynt*, 418 sqq., he calls on King James to cause the clergy to give up their vain traditions which deceive their people, such as superstitious pilgrimages and praying to graven images, expressly against God's command. In *The Monarche*, 2087 sqq., 2279 sqq., Experience describes the beginning of image-worship, which continued to flourish because, for one thing, it brought "singulaire proffeit" to priests, painters, goldsmiths,[2] masons, wrights. St Peter with the keys, St Catherine with sword and wheel, St Giles with the hind, St Andrew with his cross, St Anthony with the

[1] See Bishop Dowden's *The Medieval Church in Scotland*, pp. 320 sqq. (1910); and Miss Annie I. Cameron's *The Apostolic Camera and Scottish Benefices*, 1418–1488. From Miss Cameron's materials I calculate that in twenty-five years (1463–88) official dues totalled over 32,400 gold florins, equal (at the exchange fixed in 1431) to £12,960 sterling, and much more in Scots money. Variations in exchange make it difficult to state the exact value of each payment, but clearly large sums were paid officially. Add to this, the necessary bribes and gifts; travelling and other expenses if the cleric visited Rome; if he did not, procurator's fees; or a banker's commission. For banks undertook this business, often as a speculation (*The Apostolic Camera*, pp. xxxi sqq.). Truly "trafficking" in benefices was no inappropriate expression. See below, p. 113.

[2] The Acts of the Apostles, xix 23 sqq.

sow, and many others, stand on the altars. The priests
cry for offerings while we, the laymen, kneel worshipping
the images:

> With offerand and with orisoun,
> To thame aye babland on our beidis,
> That thay wald keip us in our neidis.

That is exactly the same as the idolatry of the Gentiles;
still we have permission to make images, which are the
books of the unlearned. The Cross reminds us of Christ's
Passion; statues of saints remind us of their sufferings for
the faith;

> Or, quhen thou seis ane portrature
> Of blyssit Marie, Virgen pure,
> One bony Babe upone hir kne,

then remember the prophet's words that she should be
both mother and maid.

Lyndsay (*The Monarche*, 2397 sqq.) asks what reason
there is, what law or authority, what authentic scripture,
for adoring stocks and stones or for giving them oblations.
The Bible is full of admonitions against such idolatry,
and of instances of its punishment. The clergy are to
blame for consenting to this superstition and for assisting
in this idolatry.[1]

With the superstitious adoration of images was asso-
ciated the abuse of pilgrimages. It is natural to visit some
holy place; and when the purpose is good, the act is
laudable. But by Lyndsay's time the good custom of
pilgrimages had for generations been corrupting the
world. Some pilgrims indeed still went for religious
reasons; but others were seeking cures for bodily ailments
or hoping to obtain some wish, to have lost property restored, to save a sow or a cow (*The Monarche*, 2359 sqq.).

[1] See below, p. 117.

Naturally the pilgrims gave offerings; and this led the clergy to exploit the supposed powers of the saints at the various shrines. Lyndsay attacks the bishops for countenancing such an abuse (*The Monarche*, 2649 sqq.) merely for the profit of some crafty priest or false hermit, and especially (*The Monarche*, 2685 sqq.)

> that Heremeit of Lawreit.
> He pat the common peple in beleve
> > That blynd gat seycht and crukit gat thare feit,
> The quhilk that palyard no way can appreve.[1]

Pilgrimages became not merely times of merry-making, as we find Chaucer's Pilgrims enjoying, but also occasions of shocking immorality. Lyndsay brings forward instances of this (*The Monarche*, 2653 sqq.) from Loretto, from Fife, from Angus. He pointedly charges the bishops with winking at this abuse (*The Monarche*, 2669 sqq.); and warns laymen (*The Monarche*, 2693 sqq.) not to allow their wives or daughters to make pilgrimages,

> To seik support at ony stock Image:
> For I have wyttin gud wemen passe fra hame,
> > Quhilk hes bene trappit with sic lustis rage,
> Hes done returne boith with gret syn and schame.[2]

In the Middle Ages the Catholic doctrine of indulgences was "complicated and abstruse". Whatever it might be that was remitted by the indulgence, or pardon (as it came to be called), the phrase "a poena et a culpa",

[1] The "Heremeit of Lawreit" was Thomas Douchtie, who returned from abroad with an image of the Virgin. Near Musselburgh he founded he chapel of our Lady of Loretto, which became a popular pilgrim shrine. The Master of Glencairn composed an amusing satire on the Franciscans, which he put in the mouth of the hermit. Laing's *Knox*, I 72 sqq.

[2] Compare *Kitteis Confessioun*, 79 sqq. Walter Mill, the martyr of 1558, declared that no greater whoredom existed anywhere than at pilgrimages—except in common brothels. Laing's *Knox*, I 553. See below, p. 167.

applied to plenary indulgences, led to the popular belief, fostered by unscrupulous pardoners, that the indulgence freed the sinner from guilt as well as from temporal penalty. When Lyndsay was still a young man, Western Europe had been startled by Luther's attack on indulgences, the sale of which had become a regular means of raising money for the Holy See. The immediate cause of Luther's outburst was the glib tongue of Tetzel, one of whose remarks was that as soon as the coin clinked in the chest, the soul would be freed from Purgatory. Luther's views about indulgences (and about other points of doctrine) had influenced the Vicar of Dollar, Thomas Forret, who set forth these views to his parishioners. When the professional seller of indulgences, the pardoner, came to Dollar, Forret warned his people that pardoners were deceivers and that only through the blood of Christ could sinners obtain pardon.[1] Long before Luther's time, however, the pardoner had been strongly denounced and amusingly satirized.[2] The denouncing was not always done on principle: sometimes it came from self-interest. Parish priests were angry at the intrusion of pardoners who by their clever harangues drained the parishes of money to the loss of the priests:

> But with thise relikes, whan that he [the Pardoner] fond
> A povre person dwelling up-on lond,
> Upon a day he gat him more moneye
> Than that the person gat in monthes tweye.
> And thus, with feyned flaterye and Iapes
> He made the person and the peple his apes.
>
> Chaucer, *Prologue*, 701 sqq.

[1] Calderwood, *History*, i 129.
[2] See Chaucer, *Canterbury Tales*, A. 669 sqq., C. 318 sqq., with Skeat's notes, vol. v. Consult also G. G. Coulton's article "Indulgence" in *Encyclopaedia Britannica*, Eleventh Edition.

Lyndsay, accordingly, seizes on this well-known figure and, with great gusto, ridicules all his trickery, cheating and greed.[1]

The Pardoner (*Ane Satyre*, 2042 sqq.) in his address declares his hatred of the New Testament, which has spoiled his trade; boasts of his skill in deceiving women; describes his faked relics; cheats a husband and wife into believing that he can dissolve their marriage; does not wince either when his boy shouts that he has discovered on "dame Fleschers midding"[2] a great horse's bone which can be passed off as a bone of St Bride's cow, or when he hears the opprobrious names given him; and swindles Poor Man out of his last groat.[3]

The Consistory, properly an ecclesiastical court, had come to absorb civil business,[4] and was in bad repute for its long-drawn-out procedure, its expense, its partial

[1] See above, pp. 54 sqq.

[2] A Franciscan treatise of the time of Edward III mentions the use of filthy bones for relics. See the quotation from "Fasciculus Morum" in Carleton Brown's Edition of Chaucer's *Pardoner's Tale*, p. ix (Clarendon Press, 1935).   [3] See below, pp. 142 sq.

[4] Cosmo Innes, *Liber Officialis Sancti Andree*, p. ix, says: "For a long period preceding the Reformation, the officials or Episcopal judges of Scotland had extended their jurisdiction over a great proportion of purely civil questions, in addition to suits which are now considered the only proper subjects of consistorial law." Innes makes the same statement in his *Scotch Legal Antiquities*, pp. 238 sq. Compare Robertson, *Statuta*, II 296; and Dowden, *The Medieval Church in Scotland*, pp. 297 sq.

In *An Introductory Survey of the Sources and Literature of Scots Law* (The Stair Society, 1936), p. 137, Dr F. C. Walton writes: "...in course of time, the ecclesiastical courts throughout Europe had drawn to themselves jurisdiction over many matters not obviously *inter spiritualia*. 'There was', Craig says [*Jus Feudale*, I 3. 19], 'indeed no end to the ingenuity displayed by the Church Courts in discovering means for extending their powers....The result in all realms was that they acquired a jurisdiction at least as extensive as that properly belonging to the lawful sovereign.'"

decisions. The poorer classes suffered most from unjust administration. Their complaint (*The Monarche*, 4733) is that law is oppression's own brother. The Poor Man (*Ane Satyre*, 1970 sqq.) has sought law in Edinburgh

> this monie deir day:
> Bot I culd get nane at Sessioun nor Seinzie;
> Thairfor, the mekill din Devill droun all the meinzie.

Later (*Ane Satyre*, 3054 sqq.) he declares that the Consistory has more need of reformation than Pluto's Court; and he tells his experience.[1] The Lords Temporal say the Consistory laws must be reformed. Their infamy is so great:

> I wist ane man, in persewing ane kow,
> Or he had done, he spendit half ane bow.

Let the Consistory confine itself to ecclesiastical matters. The Lords Spiritual object, for that would be against their "profeit singulair" (*Ane Satyre*, 3080 sqq., 3868 sqq.).

On the Day of Judgment, says Experience (*The Monarche*, 5757 sqq.),

> Officialis with thare Constry clerkis
> Sall mak compt of thare wrangous werkis,
> Thay and thare perverst Procuratouris,
> Oppressiouris boith of ryche and puris,
> Throw delatouris full of dissait,
> Quhilk mony one gart beg thare meit.
> Gret dule that day to Jugis bene,
> That cumis nocht with thare conscience clene:
> That day sall pas be Peremptouris,
> Without cawteill or dillatoris;
> No Duplicandum nor Triplicandum,
> Bot schortlye pas to Sentenciandum,
> Without continuatiounis,
> Or ony appellatiounis:
> That sentence sall nocht be retraitit,
> Nor with no man of Law debaitit.[2]

---

[1] See above, p. 61.   [2] See below, pp. 143 sq.

Contrary to the age-long custom of the Church and to the views of the clergy, Lyndsay strongly advocated the use of the vernacular in church services. In *Ane Satyre*, 3453 sqq., after the deposing of the old clerics, the Doctor of Divinity, who is qualified to teach in Latin in theological schools, is called upon to preach in English to edify country-people.

Before beginning to tell of the Creation (*The Monarche*, 538 sqq.), Lyndsay defends the vernacular. Why should the Bible story be known only to the learned? The unlearned cannot understand Latin more than they do the cawing of crows. The Law on Mount Sinai was in the mother tongue of the Israelites, while Plato and Aristotle wrote in Greek, Cicero and Virgil in Latin. Lyndsay laughs at nuns chanting and praying in Latin without understanding, like parrots or starlings. Why should children and ladies of honour repeat Pater Noster, Ave and Creed in Latin? Surely it would be as pleasant to their spirit to say "God have mercy upon me" as "Miserere mei Deus". Jerome translated the Bible into Latin. Had he been born in Argyll, he would have turned it into Gaelic. St Paul writes that five words understood are better than a thousand in an unknown tongue. Of praying in an unknown tongue Lyndsay says:

> I thynk sic pattryng is not worth twa prenis.

What is necessary for salvation—the Bible, preaching, Pater Noster, Ave and Creed—should be in the vernacular.[1]

---

[1] Compare what Pitscottie (I 349 sq.) tells in narrating the trial of the vicar of Dollar (see above, p. 89). Accused of teaching the Ten Commandments, Creed, and Lord's Prayer in English contrary to the decree of the Pope and the Church, the vicar put forward Christ's command and St Paul's declaration that he would rather speak five words to the under-

Lyndsay satirizes the clergy because they would prohibit the reading of the English New Testament.[1] The
Pardoner (*Ane Satyre*, 2054 sqq.) says that it has ruined
his trade:

> I give to the Devill, with gude intent,
> This unsell wickit New Testament,
>   With thame that it translaitit.
> Sen layik men knew the veritie,
> Pardoners get no charitie
>   Without that thay debait it.

To the Reformers the New Testament meant the truth,
but to the supporters of the old regime it meant heresy.
In *Ane Satyre*, 1097 sqq., when Verity arrives, New Testament in hand, she is at once denounced as a heretic and
put in the stocks:

> Quhat buik is that, harlot, into thy hand?
>   Out, walloway! this is the New Test'ment
> In Englisch toung, and printit in England:
>   Herisie, herisie! fire, fire! incontinent.[2]

standing than 10,000 in a language not understood. "Where find you
that?" cried the accuser. "Here," replied the vicar, "in my book which
is here in my sleeve." The accuser snatched the book from his hand and
showed it to the people as the book causing all the contention and trouble
in holy Church and among the prelates. "No book of heresy," said the
vicar, "but the true scripture of God." As the New Testament in English,
however, was contrary to the acts of the Church and forbidden by the
Pope, the vicar was condemned to death. Calderwood (*History*, 1 128)
makes the "book" incident occur at the vicar's execution and says:
"Another taketh the New Testament out of his bosom, holdeth it up
before the people, and crieth 'Heresy! heresy!' Then the people cried,
'Burn him! burn him!'"

[1] The Scottish bishops had issued a decree forbidding the use of the
English New Testament on pain of death. This led to the publication in
1533 of the work entitled *Alexandri Alesii Epistola contra decretum quoddam
episcoporum in Scotia quod prohibet legere Novi Testamenti libros lingua
vernacula*. See A. F. Mitchell, *The Scottish Reformation*, p. 37, where other
evidence is given about this enactment.

[2] See above, pp. 32, 48, 102.

The supreme authority of the Church, the Roman Pontiff or the Roman Curia, had to do with affairs in the various countries—hearing appeals from the clergy, bestowing exemptions from local courts, granting dispensations, taking part in conferring benefices (sometimes called "trafficking in benefices").[1] All these cost money, and huge sums flowed to Rome. Every interference from Rome, every penny going to Rome, meant somebody's grievance.

In *Ane Satyre*, 2499 sqq., when Covetousness and Sensuality are to be arrested, the Bishop intimates an appeal to the Pope. He hesitates to fall in with the reforms proposed (*Ane Satyre*, 2696 sqq.) and, when threatened with punishment, cries,

> Schir, we can schaw exemptioun,
> Fra your temporall punitioun.

Against the proposal to abolish pluralities, the Bishop urges that the Pope has given churchmen dispensations to hold more benefices than one (*Ane Satyre*, 2869 sqq.). When it has been decreed to deprive prelates of their offices and strip them of their vestments, he declares (*Ane Satyre*, 3728 sqq.):

> I mak ane vow to God, and ye us handill,
> Ye sallbe curst and gragit with buik and candill:
> Syne we sall pas unto the Paip, and pleinzie;
> And to the Devill of hell condemne this meinze.

Friars, members of the mendicant orders, had at first dedicated themselves whole-heartedly to poverty and simplicity: they had as few possessions as possible—"no lands, no funded property, no fixed sources of income". But in a comparatively short time the orders grew powerful

---

[1] See above, p. 105.

and wealthy, while many of the members became self-indulgent and often dissolute. The secular clergy did not always love the friars, who were frequently regarded as interlopers. They were responsible only to the head of their order, who in turn was accountable to the Pope alone.

Friars claimed the widest exemption and were naturally the most hated. They claimed exemption from ecclesiastical as well as civil jurisdiction, from bishops as well as magistrates (*The Papyngo*, 719 sqq., *Ane Satyre*, 771 sqq.). When Flattery, the Friar, is stripped of gown and hood by the Sergeants, he claims exemption from kings and queens and from all human law (*Ane Satyre*, 3632 sqq.). To this the First Sergeant adds that the Friars

> ar exempt, I yow assure,
> Baith fra Paip, King and Empreour;

and the Second Sergeant sarcastically prophesies that, at the Day of Judgment, when Christ says, "Come, ye blessed", the Friar will immediately reply, "We are exempted".[1]

In *The Papyngo*, 669 sqq., the greedy Kite introduces himself to the dying Parrot as a holy friar, with power to bring her alive to Heaven. His conscience is clear; and he will pronounce offhand the prayers for the dead if the Parrot will bequeath something to the brethren of his order: God knows they are much in need of food. "Your dress", says the Parrot, "may be religious, but I suspect your conscience is not good. I saw you secretly steal a chicken from its mother." "True," replies the Kite, "it was my teind. We sustain the faith, and the Pope has

[1] See above, p. 65.

decreed that we live on the teind. You are fortunate in having such holy men about you. Confess your sins,[1] and we shall make your funeral, bury your bones,

> Syne trentalls twenty trattyl all at onis."

The Parrot dies: the birds tear her to pieces: nothing is left but her heart, with which the greedy Kite flies away (*The Papyngo*, 1144 sqq.).

In *The Monarche*, 4822 sqq., Lyndsay ridicules the belief that anyone dying in a friar's robe is granted full remission of sins and passes straight to Heaven. He adds, with grave earnestness,

> Be thare sic virtew in ane Freris hude,
> I thynk in vane Christ Jesus sched his blude.

In many dioceses friars had a monopoly of preaching. Bishops could not, or would not, preach (*The Tragedie*, 309 sqq., *Ane Satyre*, 747 sqq., 3762 sqq., 4449 sqq.). The friars' preaching was often far from the truth (*Ane Satyre*, 3602 sqq.), but they were eager to preach because it gave scope for flattery, in which they excelled. Thus they won influence and received many offerings. Friars were special favourites with women, who, however scanty the harvest might be, would not let the friars want (*Ane Satyre*, 753 sqq.),

> For quhy, thay ar thair confessours,
> Thair heavinlie prudent counsalours:
> Thairfor the wyfis plainlie taks thair parts
> And schawis the secreits of thair harts
> To Freirs, with better will, I trow,
> Nor thay do to thair bed-fallow.

Kitteis Confessioun, 95 sq., tells us:

> "Freiris sweiris be thair professioun
> Nane can be saif but this Confessioun."

Since flattery was characteristic of the friar, it was very
appropriate that Flattery (*Ane Satyre*, 740 sqq.) should
declare he would counterfeit a friar. He is reminded that
he cannot preach, and replies:

> Quhat rak, bot I can richt weill fleich!
> Perchance I'll come to that honour,
> To be the Kings Confessour.
> Pure Freirs ar free at any feist
> And marchellit ay amang the best.

When Flattery leaves the stage (*Ane Satyre*, 4278 sqq.),
he says,

> Adew! I will na langer tarie,
>   To cumber yow with my clatter:
> Bot I will, with ane humbill spreit,
> Gang serve the Hermeit of Lareit:[1]
>   And leir him for to flatter.

Hypocrisy is also attributed to the friars by Lyndsay. The
Pardoner (*Ane Satyre*, 2063 sqq.) was taught all his wiles
by a friar called Hypocrisy. Flattery mentions as one of
his sins how he beguiled the Three Estates by his hypocrisy. In his friar's hood he always passed as a good man.
Put the most arrant knave in a friar's habit and the
women will certainly hold him for a very saint (*Ane
Satyre*, 4253 sqq.). Then he confesses:

> I knaw that cowle and skaplarie
> Genneris mair hait nor charitie,
>   Thocht thay be blak or blew:
> Quhat halines is thair within
> Ane wolfe cled in ane wedders skin,
>   Judge ye gif this be trew.

John the Commonweal (*Ane Satyre*, 2617 sqq.) in-
veighs against "great fat friars"—Augustinians, Car-
melites, Cordeliers and all other wearers of the cowl—

[1] See above, p. 107 note 1.

who labour neither in spiritual things nor with their hands, and yet have plenty to eat. He calls them idle dogs and well-fed hogs. They profess poverty, but flee fast from necessity.

Friars (*Ane Satyre*, 3570 sq., 3614 sqq., *The Monarche*, 2541 sqq.) are also blamed for stirring up strife and leading princes to shed innocent blood. If they would only fight with each other, the devil may care who wins (*Ane Satyre*, 4621 sq.).

In *The Monarche*, 2509 sqq., the friars are fiercely attacked as "fosterers of idolatry", since instead of discouraging the adoration of images, they actually encourage it.

Toward the end of his Sermon (*Ane Satyre*, 4617 sqq.), Folly says,

> Sa, be this Prophesie plainlie appeirs
> That mortal weirs sal be amang Freirs:
> Thay sal nocht knaw weill, in thair closters,
> To quhom thay sall say thair Pater Nosters.

This is certainly a topical allusion. About the middle of the sixteenth century, a dispute, we are told, raged in St Andrews whether the Pater Noster might be said to saints as well as to God the Father.[1] A Prior of the Black Friars from Newcastle had in a sermon at St Andrews taught that the Pater Noster should be said to God alone.

---

[1] This may appear to us an improbable controversy but we hear of it in England, Switzerland and Germany as well as in Scotland. In *The Monarche*, 2311 sqq., Lyndsay mentions statues of saints,

> "To quhome, we Commounis, on our kneis,
> Doith wyrschip all thir imagereis;
> In kirk, in queir, and in the closter,
> Prayand to thame our Pater Noster."

Henry Balnaves (Laing's *Knox*, III 518) says: "We praye commonly the *Pater Noster* (that is *Our Father*) to the image of this or that saint made of tree or stone."

One of the Gray Friars was chosen to answer this doctrine.
His sermon gained him the nickname of Friar Pater-
noster. The dispute grew hotter; and "To whom say
you your Pater Noster?" came to be a common query.
A formal debate at the University failed to settle the
matter; and a Provincial Church Council in Edinburgh
succeeded no better.[1] In St Andrews two pasquils had
appeared, one in Latin, one in English. The Latin speaks
of the University doctors arriving at the same conclusion
as Lucifer:

Quod sancti sunt similes Altissimo.

The English verses name Doctors of Theology and Gray
Friars who would be called Rabbi and Magister Noster,

And wot not to whome to say their Pater Noster.

At last John Wynram, sub-prior of St Andrews, was
appointed to pronounce on the question, and his deliver-
ance was that the Pater Noster should, as a rule, be
addressed to God alone.[2] The late Professor A. F.
Mitchell (Preface to facsimile reprint of Hamilton's
Catechism, pp. xxiii, xxiv) thought that, assuming Wynram to have been the chief author of the Catechism, we
have echoes of his judgment on the controversy in what
the Catechism says on the Lord's Prayer: "And sa this
word, qui es in celis, may nocht be trewly said bot to God
only" (folio clxxvii[a]): "Quhairfor O Christin man and

---

[1] The Concilia have no record of this; unless it was to be in the un-
finished Statutum of 1549 (Robertson, Concilia, II 121, 295; Patrick's
Translation of Concilia, 127). See below, p. 121 note 1.

[2] The authority for the story is Foxe (Cattley's Edition, v 641 sqq.),
who says he records it on evidence brought from Scotland. See Calderwood, History, I 273 sqq.; Spottiswoode, History of the Church of Scotland,
I 180 sqq.; D. Hay Fleming, Reformation, p. 141 sq.; Christie, Influence of
Letters on the Scottish Reformation, p. 186 sq.

weman say thi *Pater Noster* to God oft tymes distinctlie and devoitly" (folio clxxv^a). Lyndsay's attitude is the same. Christ, he says (*The Monarche*, 2621 sqq.), teaches in Matthew vi how and to whom we should pray a short prayer every day, addressed not to any apostle or saint or angel, but only to Our Father, God Himself, the prayer we call Pater Noster.

CHAPTER V

ARE LYNDSAY'S CHARGES WELL GROUNDED?

CAN we accept a friend's praise as absolutely true? Can we admit the truth of an enemy's blame? An enemy's praise or a friend's blame is a different story. As far as is known, David Lyndsay was not a professed Protestant; but, if he can be reckoned a friend of the Roman Church, he must be termed a candid and a critical friend. Sir Thomas Dempster looks upon him as an enemy and speaks of the godless writings of Knox, Lyndsay, Buchanan and others, for which an antidote must be found to protect the unwary.[1] Modern readers of Lyndsay, unacquainted with Scottish Church History, 1530–60, and viewing the Roman Church of to-day, regard his charges as in part untrue, in part exaggerated, and wholly untrustworthy. I propose, from official documents of the Roman Church, from state records, and from the writings of faithful members of the Roman Church, to show that Lyndsay, satirist and humorist though he was, had a solid foundation for his charges, that in fact they are substantially true.[2]

[1] *Scotia Illustrior*, p. 54, Lugduni [Batavorum].
[2] Compare Dowden, *The Medieval Church in Scotland*, p. 314: "Nothing could be more unreasonable than to accept the picture presented by such a humorous satirist as Sir David Lyndesay, if it were unsupported by other evidence. But the evidence for the immorality of the Scottish clergy in the middle of the sixteenth century is, unhappily, so copious and unimpeachable that one hesitates to say that the poet was guilty even of exaggeration in the indictment which he sets forth in *The Thrie Estatis*."

PROVINCIAL COUNCILS

Ecclesiae Scoticanae Statuta, the official records of the Councils of the Scottish Church,[1] contain enactments to prohibit various kinds of wrongdoing and vice among the clergy. Now, the existence in any community of laws against murder, for example, does not necessarily indicate a great prevalence of man-killing in that community. But when, within a short space of time, ordinance after ordinance on some particular evil or shortcoming is enacted, often with a declaration that a previous enactment has proved ineffective, we rightly infer continued prevalence of wrongdoing. We have, however, something stronger than mere inference. The preamble to the proceedings of the Provincial Council which met in Edinburgh, 27 November 1549, contains a significant statement.[2] The prelates and clergy there assembled diagnose the grievous evils in the church. Two causes in particular of dissension and heresy are mentioned: first, the corruption of morals and the wicked lewdness in almost all ranks of ecclesiastics; and then, their gross ignorance of literature and of all arts.[3]

To remove the scandals arising from clerical incontinence it was agreed by this Council to adopt the decree of Basel (1431 and following years) *De Concubinariis*. Any cleric of whatever rank or dignity who is known to keep a concubine must put her away, or suffer severe penalties.

---

[1] *Concilia Scotiae: Ecclesiae Scoticanae Statuta tam Provincialia quam Synodalia quae supersunt*, edited by Joseph Robertson (The Bannatyne Club, 1866): English Translation by David Patrick (Scottish History Society, 1907). These are referred to as R. and P.

[2] R. ii 81 sq.; P. 84.

[3] The record says: "morum corruptela ac vitae profana obscaenitas, cum bonarum literarum artiumque omnium crassa inscitia."

Ordinaries refusing to punish offenders shall themselves
be punished. The decree, *mutatis mutandis*, shall apply
also to nuns.[1] Another scandal must be stopped, arising
from the fact that deans and other visitors have taken
bribes from concubinaries and adulterers to pass over
their offences.[2] Negligent supervision of houses of canons
regular, monks and nuns has weakened discipline.
Abbots, priors, commendators, and administrators of
exempt monasteries must strive to reform the life, morals,
piety and learning in these houses and bring back the
old conditions.[3]

Concubinage was of long standing in the Church and
widespread—a custom not to be speedily altered. Decrees had been enacted against it in the thirteenth
century and the fourteenth. One of the synodal con-
stitutions (to be published annually) of Andrew Forman,
Archbishop of St Andrews, 1516–21, runs:

In spite of repeated warning from himself and his predecessors, the clergy of the diocese are, to the great scandal
and prejudice of the whole Church, still keeping wenches and
concubines. These must be put away and repudiated so that
no suspicion or scandal may appear at all.[4]

Did the members of the 1549 Council believe that
the decree concerning concubines would, or could, be

[1] R. II 86 sqq.; P. 89 sqq.　　[2] R. II 93 sq.; P. 96 sq.
[3] R. II 91 sq.; P. 94 sq. Conscientious visitors sometimes found reform
no easy task. The Abbot of Soulseat, in Galloway, was commissioned by
the Father Abbot and the General Chapter of Premonstratensians to
reform abbots, priors, and religious men, places, kirks and lands, spirit-
ually and temporally, in head and in members. Afraid that abbots,
priors and monks would resist, he entreated the King to support him,
and the King instructed his lieutenants, sheriffs, earls, barons, bailies of
abbeys, and others to give the Abbot of Soulseat "all help, supply,
maintenance and assistance" (*Register of the Privy Seal*, 24 July 1532).
[4] R. I cclxxi sq.; P. 262 sq.

carried out? Among them were men of immoral life. Archbishop Hamilton, who presided, Bishop Gordon of Aberdeen, Bishop Hepburn of Moray, and other prelates as well as many of the inferior clergy had each two or more bastards, in some cases by different mothers.[1] Within little more than six months after this Council met, Bishop William Chisholm of Dunblane had two children legitimated, 8 June 1550: Mr Alexander Erskine, sub-dean and official of Dunkeld, had a son legitimated 27 February 1547–48, when he is styled "venerabilis": Mr Arthur Tailliefere, rector of Creithmond, had four sons (two named John) legitimated, 20 June 1550.[2]

Were these clerics hypocrites? Were they like the Scribes and Pharisees of Matthew xxiii 2 sqq.? They sat in Moses' seat: they said and did not: laying heavy burdens and grievous to be borne on men's shoulders, they themselves would not move them with one of their fingers. Ophelia (*Hamlet*, i iii 47 sqq.) would have addressed them:

> Do not, as some ungracious pastors do,
> Show me the steep and thorny way to heaven;
> Whiles, like a puff'd and reckless libertine,
> Himself the primrose path of dalliance treads,
> And recks not his own rede.

Portia (*Merchant of Venice*, i ii 15 sq.) might have been more tolerant; and might have said,

> It is a good divine that follows his own instructions.

Good divines, however, were rare in Scotland in 1549. Shall we say that the spirit was willing but the flesh was weak? In 1552 and even in 1559, the Council has

[1] R. II 283; Hay Fleming's *Reformation*, pp. 51 sqq.
[2] *Register of the Privy Seal*, under these dates.

to lament that the decrees of 1549 have not been enforced.[1]

Yet these legislators seem alive to the necessity of example as well as precept. Ordinaries are specially entreated to amend their own lives and morals, lest they should be zealous in sternly correcting the morals of others while they themselves are entangled in notorious faults; for that causes the greatest scandal and much of the prevalent heresy.[2]

The Provincial Council of Edinburgh, 11 March 1558–59—10 April 1559, had, as one item of business, to consider Articles sent by the Queen Regent, which she had received from certain of the Lords Temporal and Barons.[3] These were neither Lutherans nor Calvinists, but sincere well-wishers of the Roman Church.[4] The first Article is very important. It shows the general condition of the Spiritual Estate then and in the years preceding, and proves that the 1549 ordinances had never been enforced or had been ineffectual:

First, remembering that our Sovereign Lord of good memory that last deceased, in his late Acts of Parliament[5] for the common weal of this realm, thought necessary to make a public exhortation to my Lords the Prelates and the rest of the Spiritual Estate for reforming of their lives and for avoiding of open slander that is given to the whole Estates through the said Spiritual men's ungodly and dissolute lives; and in the same way remembering in divers of the late Provincial Councils holden within this realm that point has been treated of, and sundry statutes synodal made thereupon, of the which nevertheless there has flowed none or little fruit as yet, but rather the said Estate is deteriorate,

---

[1] R. II 128 sq., 153 sq.; P. 135 sqq., 163.
[2] R. II 118; P. 124.   [3] R. II 146 sqq.; P. 156 sqq.
[4] See the last three Articles: R. II 150 sq.; P. 159 sq.
[5] James V in Parliament 1540–41: Act. Parl. Scot. II 370.

nor amends by any such persuasion as has been hitherto used; and since the said Estate is mirror and lantern to the rest, it is most expedient therefore that they presently condescend to seek reformation of their lives, and for executing duly of their offices, every one of them according to their own vocation and care committed unto them to do, and namely that open and manifest sins and notorious offences be forborne and abstained from in time to come, etc.

This Council (1559) approves of the statute of 1549 against concubinaries, which is to be strictly enforced on archbishops and bishops as well as on all other clerics. Archbishop Hamilton of St Andrews and Archbishop Beaton of Glasgow willingly submit themselves, to a commission of six, for inquisition and correction, that they may not seem to bind heavy burdens on their suffragans and the lower clergy while they themselves, by virtue of privileges and exemptions, indulge themselves too freely.[1] The lack of good example by bishops and abbots to priests and monks, and of archbishops to bishops and abbots, is manifest from what we find in Joseph Robertson's note to this statute:[2]

Shortly before, the Dean and Chapter of Aberdeen had appealed to their Ordinary, Bishop Gordon, to cause his clergy to reform their shameful way of life and to remove their open concubines, great as well as small. They promised to reform themselves and their subordinates; and they prayed their Ordinary that, for God's honour, for his conscience' sake, and for the good of his diocese, and because opponents of Christianity promised obedience to prelates if they reformed themselves and their subordinates, he would show a good example and put away his concubine.

Archbishop Hamilton's *Catechism*,[3] printed in 1552 by his command and at his expense, has a passage recalling

[1] R. II 153 sq.; P. 163 sq.   [2] R. II 301 sq.
[3] See below, p. 152.

that Saint Paul sets fornicators and lecherous men and women in the first place of all them that shall be excluded from the kingdom of Heaven.[1] At the time when the *Catechism* was printing, the Archbishop was treated for asthma by Cardan, the Italian physician, who gave him the following advice on another matter:

De Venere, certe non est bona neque vtilis; vbi tamen contingat necessitas, debet vti ea inter duos somnos, scilicet post mediam noctem, et melius est exercere eam ter in sex diebus, pro exemplo ita vt singulis duobus diebus semel quam bis in vna die, etiam quod staret per decem dies.

The preamble of the 1549 statutes mentions as the second occasion of heresy the gross ignorance of the clergy in literature and the liberal arts.[2] Add to this a great lack of religious knowledge and of theology. This deficiency was one reason[3] why there was hardly any preaching and hardly any teaching of scripture truths to the people. The Councils cry out for men qualified to teach and preach as well as to be ensamples of good living. There were, of course, and had been in the Scottish Church men of learning, of upright life, attentive to their duties, as Bishop Elphinstone of Aberdeen, Bishop Reid of Orkney, Archibald Hay, and others; but most of the lower clergy, and not the lower clergy alone, were grossly ignorant and extremely incompetent. From time to time efforts were made to remedy this. Archbishop Forman orders absentee clerics to reside at their churches and chapels, or to study at St Andrews; and he enjoins on abbots, priors and commendators to send a quota of religious to the University.[4] The Council of 1549 decrees

---

[1] Folio lv[b], Law's Edition, p. 94.   [2] See above, p. 121.
[3] Another reason was negligence.
[4] R. 1 cclxxii, cclxxxiv; P. 263, 276 sq.

that lecturers in theology and canonists be appointed in cathedral churches, and theologians in monasteries; and that monasteries send suitable men to the Universities for a four years' course in theology and the Holy Scriptures.[1] The Councils of 1552 and 1559 lament that these decrees have not been carried out.[2]

The Council of 1549 attempted also to stop the neglect of preaching. Bishops and ordinaries are enjoined to preach, either themselves or by qualified substitutes, at least four times a year. Ordinaries who are less able to preach than they ought to be, are to equip themselves as soon as possible. Rectors, if competent, are also to preach at least four times a year. Of those who cannot preach, the young who have abilities are to study in Colleges, while such as are through age unable to study must appoint substitutes, whose preaching they are to countenance by their presence.[3] Some of the clergy had, in their ignorance, to ask what and how they should preach, and the Council lays down rules. The discourse is to begin with an explanation of the epistle or the gospel, and to proceed to give instruction in the rudiments of the faith or an exposition of the Creed, the Ten Commandments, the seven deadly sins, the seven sacraments, the Lord's Prayer, the Ave Maria, and the works of mercy.[4]

The Council of 1552 re-affirms the injunctions about preaching, and, as they had not been carried out, adds penalties.[5] Even the 1559 Council has to re-affirm the order to preach; with the addition that preaching is to be oftener than four times a year, if convenient. A bishop

---

[1] R. II 95 sqq., 100 sqq., 104 sqq.; P. 98 sqq., 104 sqq., 108 sq.

[2] R. II 128 sq., 161, 165; P. 135 sq., 171 sq., 176.

[3] R. II 95, 97 sq., 99 sq.; P. 98, 101, 103 sq.

[4] R. II 104; P. 108.   [5] R. II 129; P. 136.

must also visit the whole of his diocese at least every two years and preach in the places visited.[1]

This increase fell short of the demand of the Temporal Lords and Barons in the Articles which the Council of 1559 had before it.[2] Their demand is for sermons in every parish church on all Sundays and other Holy Days; at least on Yule, Pasch, Whitsunday, and every third or fourth Sunday. Where people are most ungodly and ignorant of their duty to God and man, preaching should be most frequent and most earnest. Preachers are to be sound in doctrine, of good manners and of competent knowledge and condition.[3]

A statute of the 1549 Council had required in ordinands learning, morals and title (that is, nomination to a benefice sufficient to support them). It is significantly added that very many of those in charge of parish churches are utterly lacking in learning, morals and discretion as well as in other essential qualities. They must all be examined by their ordinaries. Those found qualified will be continued in office: the unqualified will be advised to resign: non-compearance will involve dismissal.[4] This proved another futile decree, and the 1552 Council has to order its enforcement.[5] But all in vain; for in 1559 clerics are still lacking in clerical qualities. The Lords Temporal and Barons ask that in future no curates or vicars be appointed unless sufficiently qualified to administer the sacraments in proper form. They are to be able to read, distinctly and plainly,

[1] R. II 161 sq.; P. 171 sq. This Council also gives orders what to preach on various points of doctrine and ritual which the Reformers attacked: R. II 163 sqq.; P. 173 sqq.

[2] See above, p. 124.   [3] R. II 147; P. 156 sq.
[4] R. II 106 sqq.; P. 109 sqq.   [5] R. II 129 sqq.; P. 136 sq.

the *Catechism* and other directions given by the ordinaries so that every man and woman may turn from their disorderly ways and in word and in deed live according to what they have seen and heard.[1] The Council consents to pass a decree to that effect, but manages to divert to lay patrons[2] and to the Crown part of the blame for admitting unsuitable persons to benefices. To avoid, in the future, the scandal of unfit clergy, no presentee would be admitted unless qualified in age, morals and learning. The Queen is to be petitioned not to present unqualified persons to bishoprics and other Crown preferments. The Pope is prayed not to grant or allow such promotions. The presenting to priories of infants had for many years caused great infamy and great injury to the Church.[3]

The Council of 1549 denounces any who desire the admission of unqualified persons. Those who do so through guile, goodwill, partiality or negligence, are liable to punishment at God's hands as well as amenable to canonical penalties.[4]

[1] R. II 147; P. 157.
[2] The Lords and Barons would themselves be patrons.
[3] R. II 166; P. 176 sq. Five illegitimate sons of James V, while still infants, obtained *in commendam* some of the richest religious houses in Scotland—James (the elder), Kelso and later also Melrose; James (the younger, afterwards the Regent Moray), St Andrews and Pittenweem; Robert, Holyrood; John, Coldingham; and Adam, Charter House, Perth. For James's negotiations with Rome for these appointments, see A. Theiner's *Vetera Monumenta*, pp. 599, 611. Even archbishoprics were bestowed on princes of uncanonical age. The Duke of Ross, son of James III, was appointed to St Andrews in 1497, but being only eighteen could not be consecrated. He died at twenty-four, still unconsecrated. His successor was Alexander, an illegitimate son of James IV. He also was a youth and was killed at Flodden before he reached canonical age. See Dowden, *The Bishops of Scotland*, pp. 35 sqq.
[4] R. II 107 sq.; P. 111 sq.

Another scandal was the giving of church preferment to sons of clergy. In the Council of 1549 this preferment, whether direct or indirect, was prohibited.[1] The Council of 1559 re-enacted the statute, and declared that any such collation or provision would *ipso facto* be null and void. In addition, the Queen was to be earnestly implored to send supplicatory letters to His Holiness, the Pope, beseeching him not to grant any more dispensations from this statute. Any dispensation fraudulently obtained by making no mention of the statute would *ipso jure* be null and void.[2]

It was not merely preaching that the clergy neglected: they were also slack in regard to the Mass and the rest of their religious duties. In the Council of 1559 prelates and other clerics are entreated and exhorted to celebrate Mass, in the sight of the people, oftener than they are wont to do, in order that their flocks may be more readily moved to piety and religion. Ordinaries are to inquire if priests and beneficed clergymen recite the canonical hours daily and are present at the sacrifice of the Mass, at least on the Lord's day or other festivals.[3]

The record of this Council concludes with an exhortation, in the vernacular, to the congregation before communion. The celebrants are admonished to minister the blessed sacrament in a more godly and proper manner than they have been wont to do, and with greater reverence. The parishioners are not to be allowed to come forward irregularly. They are to be put in order before the altar, to listen to the exhortation without noise or din, and to sit still in devout meditation and emotion,

[1] R. II 89; P. 92.   [2] R. II 155; P. 165.
[3] R. II 157; P. 167.

till in an orderly way they are served with the blessed sacrament.[1]

Impressed by the general lack of religious knowledge, the Council of 1552 resolved to compile a *Catechism*, which is not a series of questions and answers, but a manual of instruction in the Catholic faith and religion.[2] It contains an explanation of the Ten Commandments, instruction in the articles of faith and the seven sacraments, and an exposition of the Lord's Prayer and the Ave Maria. Laymen were not allowed to have the book unless they were discreet, of good faith and approved by the ordinaries. After public reading, the clergyman is not to answer questions unless the ordinary is satisfied of his competence to do so. The necessity for the *Catechism* is itself proof of the unsatisfactory condition of the clergy of that time. The contents indeed do not furnish direct evidence of this; we find, however, hints, more or less direct, about the state of the Church. But the injunctions issued by the Council to those in charge of congregations regarding the use of the *Catechism* show conclusively how ignorant and incompetent the average clergyman was.

The gist of the Council's injunctions is:

Jesus Christ, that great Shepherd of the sheep, laid on all pastors the duty of preaching, that their flocks might be well instructed in the rudiments at least of the Catholic faith. The inferior clergy, however, and the prelates have not advanced far enough in knowledge of sacred learning to be able by their own efforts to instruct the people rightly in the Catholic faith and in other matters necessary to salvation, or to convert wanderers. Therefore, to assist their pious endeavours and further their diligence, and in order also that the true, Catholic and Apostolic faith, all errors

[1] R. ii 177 sqq.; P. 188 sqq.
[2] R. ii 135 sqq.; P. 143 sqq. See also below, pp. 152 sqq.

excluded, may be preserved uninjured and impregnable, the decree of the Council is that a book compiled in the Scots vernacular, and, after the most exact revision, approved by the decisions and votes of the wisest prelates of the kingdom, the most learned theologians, and other ecclesiastics, members of this convention, is to be put into the hands of rectors, vicars and curates as much for their own instruction as for that of the Christian people under their care.

The *Catechism* is to be read in sequence, a portion every Sunday and Holy Day when the people are bound to hear Mass. The clergyman, in surplice and stole, shall, with the utmost reverence, read from the pulpit for half an hour before Mass, in a loud voice so as to be understood, distinctly, clearly, articulately, and according to the punctuation; he is to read from the book in full and with no stammering, nothing added, altered, suppressed or omitted, but just as the words stand, so that the people may hear with profit, may derive edification and may drink in knowledge of salvation.

To accomplish this better and more easily, and with greater reverence and profit on the part of the people, the clergy must take care not to go into the pulpit without being duly prepared, but they must with all zeal and application equip themselves for the reading by frequent, constant and long-continued[1] rehearsing of the lesson, lest they expose themselves to the derision of the hearers, when being unprepared they have stammered and stumbled in the middle of the lesson. They are also to endeavour to read, not languidly and listlessly, but with the greatest possible spirit, voice and look and gesture in full accord with the utterance, so that what is read may be imprinted on the minds of the hearers by the force of the living voice.

The *Statuta* contain many details, often rather complicated, regarding the amounts of the various teinds. The details need not detain us, interesting though many of them are. What we notice is that, however burden-

---

[1] Patrick has "daily", evidently translating *diurna*, but Robertson reads *diuturna*.

some teinds and other customary dues were felt to be by the payers, the clergy clung to them and refused, till the very last, to make any relaxations. They even employed scandalous means to enforce payment. In the thirteenth century we find a statute headed: "The Sacrament of the Eucharist should not be denied to parishioners for the non-payment of tithes or offerings."[1] Certain priests shamelessly refuse (we are told) to administer the Eucharist on Easter day unless Christ's people first bring their offerings to the altar; and on that day the priests make exactions from the laity, holding the body of Christ in their hands as if they were saying, "What are you willing to give and I shall hand Him to you?" This the statute forbids altogether under adjuration of divine judgment. Priests are, however, allowed by means of church censures to compel parishioners at a fitting time to pay tithes and other dues.

This scandal was still in existence in 1559. One of the Articles sent to the Queen Regent by the Lords and Barons complains of it. The Article[2] declares that "the corpse-presents, cow and uppermost cloth"[3] and the silver commonly called "Kirk richts", and Easter offerings usually taken at Easter from men and women for the distribution of the Sacrament of the blessed Body and Blood of Jesus Christ, were at the beginning simply offerings and gifts at the discretion and goodwill of the giver alone. Now, however, the clergy are accustomed to compel payment by authority and jurisdiction, so that they will not only fulminate their sentence of "cursing", but also debar men and women from the

---

[1] A synodal statute of the See of Aberdeen, R. I clxxxix, II 40; P. 42.
[2] R. II 148 sq.; P. 158 sq.   [3] P. 178 note.

Sacraments of Holy Church, till they receive full and
exact satisfaction. This proceeding is not grounded on
the law of God or of Holy Church, and gives occasion
for the poor to murmur very much against the State
Ecclesiastic. It is, therefore, thought expedient that no
man shall in future be compelled to make these payments
by authority of Holy Church, but that it shall be in the
free will of the giver to give as alms and for maintenance
of priests and ministers of the Holy Church.

To remove the outcry and grumbling against the
mortuary dues, the 1559 Council resolves, for the relief
and aid of the poor, that certain relaxations and modi-
fications should be made; and, to benefit poor husbandmen or tillers of the soil, it is agreed to make alterations
in regard to teinds.[1] Joseph Robertson notes that, twenty-
three years earlier, James V is said to have urged that
corpse-presents, church cow and uppermost cloth should
be given up, and that every husbandman should be
granted a lease of his tithes for a certain fixed payment.[2]

Another statute[3] of the 1559 Council says that Christ
instituted sacraments free and that they should be administered free. But, especially at Easter, during the
Sacrament of the Body and Blood of Christ, the ministers
are so much concerned in exacting smaller teinds and
certain other offerings that, to the great scandal of
Christians, they seem, to the common people and to all
who have been in church, to put up for sale that most
sublime Sacrament in consideration for the giving of a
garment. Vicars of parishes, therefore, are shortly before
Lent to make a bargain for the smaller teinds, personal

---

[1] R. ɪɪ 167 sqq., 170 sq.; P. 178 sq., 181 sq.
[2] R. ɪ cxxxvi sq., ɪɪ 305.   [3] R. ɪɪ 174; P. 185 sq.

or mixed, and for other offerings due to the Church. Thus, at the solemn service of Easter, the people may more freely have leisure for prayer and may receive the Sacrament with warmer piety and with divine fervour. After the service, free-will offerings may be accepted from those willing to give.

The clergy, whether from greed or necessity, sought to make money in other ways. A statute of the 1549 Council enjoins the clergy not to engage in secular pursuits, especially trading to make profits, or leasing farms. This had been prevalent for many years and was a cause of the neglect of spiritual work.[1] The Council of 1559 orders the previous decree to be strictly observed. Prelates and other clerics who themselves, or by others, trade in victuals, fish, salt, butter, wool or any other merchandise, shall be fined and the goods shall be confiscated.[2]

It had come to be a custom for the clergy to provide dowries for their illegitimate daughters out of the patrimony of the Church. Here are two examples from Joseph Robertson:[3]

When the Bishop Chisholm of Dunblane—perhaps the poorest of all the Scottish sees—married his daughter to Sir James Stirling of Keir, A.D. 1542, he gave her a dowry of £1000 and a lease of tithes, and became bound to keep her and her husband for five years.

When Cardinal Beaton married his daughter to the Master of Crawford, A.D. 1546, he gave her a dowry of 4000 merks, the same sum which the Regent Arran, the first subject of the realm, gave in marriage with one daughter to the Earl of Eglinton, A.D. 1545, and with another to Lord Fleming, A.D. 1555.

No wonder the less wealthy temporal lords found it

[1] R. II 89; P. 92.　　　　[2] R. II 156 sq.; P. 166.
[3] R. II 303.

difficult to get husbands for their daughters.[1] The Council of 1549 declared against this giving of dowries from the patrimony of Christ to marry daughters of ecclesiastics to barons.[2] The custom continued, and the 1559 Council re-enacted the prohibition, with the modification that it did not apply if the baron's or landowner's yearly rental was less than one hundred pounds.[3]

The 1549 Council had also forbidden churchmen to use the patrimony of Christ to make their sons barons.[4] This prohibition was repeated in 1559, modified, however, just as in the case of dowries: the sons must not be made barons or landed gentry with a yearly rental of more than a hundred pounds.[5] The statute also decrees that clerics shall not in any way, directly or indirectly, make over or let church lands or other lands pertaining to benefices to their foresaid offspring, or to their concubines.

Many holders of benefices misused their rights over church lands to secure for themselves greater revenue. An ordinance was passed in the 1549 Council that glebes must not be granted in feu-farm.[6] The statute of the 1552 Council is more explicit.[7] Glebes and teinds had been let on long tacks, alienated, squandered and dissipated merely to glut the greed of the present holder or through affection to increase the wealth of relations and friends, to the irreparable loss of the parish and the impoverishment of successors in the benefice. This abuse was forbidden; but it continued to the detriment of the Church, the impoverishment of the lieges of the realm and the

[1] See above, pp. 62, 92.
[2] R. II 89; P. 92.
[3] R. II 155 sq.; P. 165.
[4] R. II 89; P. 92.
[5] R. II 156; P. 165.
[6] R. II 94; P. 97.
[7] R. II 134; P. 141 sq.

great damage arising through lack of able men to defend the country. It was accordingly decreed in 1559 that church lands are not to be let in feu-farm, emphyteusis or other forms of leasing and renting, except to the old native tenants, occupiers and tillers of the lands.[1]

Several statutes deal with unclerical dress. In the Council of 1549 it is laid down that beneficed clergy and clerks in holy orders are to wear round bonnets. Doublets and top boots are forbidden. So too are such clothes as yellow, green and parti-coloured. In churches, cities, towns and larger villages the cassock must go to the ankles. For journeys short cassocks are allowed. White shirts with white seams are the proper wear. The penalties for non-observance are suspension and excommunication, till caution is found for future obedience; with fines, increasing in amount for future transgressions.[2] Prelates and all other ecclesiastics, to show their gravity, are to wear graver garments than hitherto customary, garments of sober colour, of wool rather than of silk. They are also reminded of St Bernard's strictures on bridles with gold ornaments.[3] The Council of 1559 declares that the dress law is to be strictly enforced, even against abbots, priors and commendators. Archbishops and bishops, in public and in church, are always to wear linen vestments, in particular their rochets at proper times.[4]

A statute of the 1549 Council forbids beards: all clerics must be shaved: first, to distinguish the clergy from the laity, and secondly, to avoid disparaging jokes at the beards. All churchmen, at least those in holy

[1] R. II 168 sqq.; P. 179 sqq.   [2] R. II 89 sq.; P. 92 sq.
[3] R. II 91; P. 94.   [4] R. II 157; P. 166 sq.

orders, to have the tonsure. The tonsure command was repeated in 1559.[1]

Andrew Forman, Archbishop of St Andrews, 1516–21, in his ordinance for annual synods, is very explicit on dress. At the synod meeting, deans, rectors, vicars, curates and chaplains are to wear clean surplices and to have their hair becomingly shortened.[2] Another ordinance denounces clerics who do not dress according to their order and status. Provosts, deans, rectors, vicars, chaplains are expressly warned to discard unsuitable gowns and garments, fashioned at the back like organ-pipes, having long, wide and ample sleeves, and in the upper part loose and open with lacings. When they appear in public, with locks which hang over their shoulders and flowing beards, their birettas bound with cords, after the style of laymen, contrary to the life and dignity of clergymen and to good manners, they are a public disgrace to the Church. For the future they are to wear garments befitting their status as clerics—neither too short nor too long. Birettas are to be round, and the hair is to be shortened as is becoming.[3]

Excessive eating and drinking had also to be checked. In the Council of 1549, prelates and other clerics are enjoined to keep in future a more frugal and more moderate table, abstaining, according to status and rank, from a choice superfluity of foods and drinks, that they may the more liberally and bountifully help the needs of the poor. They are also themselves and their households to avoid the public violation of fasts prescribed by the Church, lest evil example cause the laity to stumble.[4]

[1] R. II 90, 157; P. 93, 167.   [2] R. I cclxx; P. 261.
[3] R. I cclxxvii; P. 269.   [4] R. II 90; P. 93.

"The household's misbehaviour means the householder's dishonour." This sentence of Bonaventura's concludes a statute of the 1549 Council admonishing prelates to have well-behaved households. Attendants and servants should not be such as are by repute gamblers, fornicators, drunkards, brawlers, night-prowlers, blasphemers of God's name, addicted to swearing horrible oaths; but they should be those who are regarded as Catholics of upright life, good morals, seemly behaviour, an example to the good and a terror to the evil.[1]

The Council of 1549 orders a visitation of religious houses, including nunneries, which are to be amended where necessary. Visitors are instructed to find if there are rumours about exempt monks as regards decorum of monastic life, proper repair of buildings, and administration of revenue.[2] In 1552 the visitation has not yet taken place;[3] nor even in 1559. For in that year's Council ordinaries are enjoined, as they shall answer to the Supreme Judge, to carry out the statute of visitation strictly. They, or their commissioners, are to inspect all houses of monks, even exempt monks, and of nuns. Three points are specially to be investigated: Do the houses maintain a sufficient number of religious according to resources and revenues? Are the monks and nuns liberally provided with food, raiment and other necessaries? Are ruinous and dilapidated buildings put into a state of repair?[4]

In the 1549 Council ordinaries are enjoined to see that hospital and other endowments are duly administered; that buildings, walls as well as roofs, are in proper repair;

[1] R. II 91; P. 94.
[2] R. II 93 sq.; P. 96 sq.
[3] R. II 130; P. 137.
[4] R. II 158; P. 167 sq.

and that distribution is made to the poor as in former days. The members of the Council say that they are moved by pity towards Christ's poor, for whose support hospitals were first founded.[1]

The Council of 1559 passes a general ordinance that all ruinous and dilapidated churches be repaired in walls, roofs, ornaments and other necessaries, according to use and wont, that is, the chancel by the rector, the nave and churchyard walls by the parishioners.[2]

While very many of the clergy were negligent in their sacred duties and were themselves irregular in attendance at the services, which indeed were often carelessly performed, they sought to compel their flocks to attend regularly and to behave with decorum in and near the church. One statute[3] of the 1552 Council says that during recent years very great contempt for divine mysteries has prevailed in Scotland so that very few in the most populous parishes condescend to be present at Mass on Sundays and other double, i.e. solemn, festivals, or at preachings of the Sacred Word. The decision of the Council was threefold. First, those wilfully absent should be noted and punished. Next, ecclesi-

---

[1] R. II 113 sq., 132; P. 119, 139 sq. The views of "Christ's poor" on hospital foundations were made manifest in the famous Beggars' Summons, fixed on friary gates on 1 January 1559. In the name of the blind, crooked, bedridden, widows, orphans and all other poor unable to work, the Summons called upon the sturdy friars unjustly holding these hospitals to remove out of them before the Feast of Whitsunday, so that the lawful proprietors may enter. Otherwise, the rightful owners will, with God's help and the assistance of His saints on the Earth, take possession and summarily eject the friars. "Let him, therefore, that before has stolen steal no more; but rather let him work with his hands, that he may be helpful to the poor." Laing's *Knox*, 1 320 sq.; Calderwood, *History*, 1 423 sq.

[2] R. II 158 sq.; P. 168.   [3] R. II 131 sq.; P. 138 sq.

astical censure and such penalties as the ordinary pleases should fall upon those who make a habit of hearing Mass without reverence and without devotion; or who, in church at time of sermon, jest or behave like buffoons; or who, in church porches or in churchyards, presume to indulge in mockeries or to busy themselves with profane bargainings. Lastly, in order to remove opportunities for these abuses, vicars and curates are to forbid in church porches and churchyards all trading in time of divine service on Sundays and holy days, and are to order that no wares be for sale or on show near church precincts. All parishioners must give earnest attention to holy prayers and rosaries or to preaching of the Divine Word. For contravention, there is a fine of two hundred shillings.

The 1559 Council ordered "monitorial letters" to be sent to rectors that all parishioners shall devoutly attend Divine Service, especially the sacrifice of the Mass. Diligent inquisition is to be made about those who will not obey.[1]

Archbishop Forman found it necessary to instruct his clergy of every rank—abbots and priors as well as parish priests and chaplains—how to behave at meetings of synod. The clergy compearing in the holy synod are commanded, in this church and in other places, to refrain altogether from unlawful acts, indecorous words, unseemly gestures; and, fitly, holily and devoutly according to good manners, to behave with reverence, with decorum and without noise. They are to take their places according to their degrees; to remain within the church silent and attentive during the service and the sermon,

[1] R. II 173; P. 184 sq.

bending towards the ground during invocations; and
not to retire till the synod is ended and till permission is
granted, under penalty of major excommunication.[1]

The Provincial Councils of our period are all but silent
on the extravagances of pardoners. The Council of 1549
adopts a decree, passed by the Council of Trent in 1546,
that pardoners begging for alms[2] shall not, either themselves, or by deputy, presume to preach. If they dis-
obey, bishops and ordinaries are to restrain them by
appropriate remedies.[3] In 1562 the Council of Trent
went further and, persuaded of the scandal of pardoners,
abolished both "nomen" and "usus".

As early, however, as the thirteenth century attempts
were made to curb the pardoner's activities. A Scottish
statute decrees that, since certain pardoners by various
deceits lead astray the souls of the simple, when any
pardoner comes into a church the ministrant shall rever-
ently explain to the parishioners the pardoner's business
in terms of his letter from Pope or ordinary, so that the
pardoner may not go beyond what the letter says.
Neither is the pardoner to enter the same church on the
same business on any day within a year. The reason for
this prohibition lies perhaps in the wish not to injure a
special collection. For the statute goes on to ordain that,
from the beginning of Lent to the Octave of Easter, on
all Sundays and feast days, the scheme for the building
of the Glasgow church be faithfully and earnestly brought
to the notice of the people by intimation and exhibited

[1] R. I cclxx; P. 260 sq.
[2] Licensed by Pope or bishop to grant an indulgence in return for
money given for a specified church purpose. They have been called
"itinerant hawkers of indulgences and relics".
[3] R. II 99; P. 103.

writing. An indulgence is to be granted to such as contribute to the scheme. Within the period mentioned no collection is to be taken for any other purpose.[1]

Towards the close of the fourteenth century, when an indulgence was granted for building the nave of the Cathedral of Aberdeen, pardoners were forbidden to sell the indulgence. If this should be done, the indulgence would be invalid.[2]

In the Council of 1549 a discussion took place on various wrongdoings of procurators in the Consistory Court: e.g. offering to delay actions or suits for one year, two years, or even more. It was decreed that processes should be shortened to avoid complaints about the law's delay; that obstructive arguments must not be interposed; that witnesses must not be suborned; that while a procurator is speaking (using the vernacular as little as possible) the others are to listen in silence.[3] The decree was futile.

The Lords and Barons, in one of their Articles, 1559, asked that Consistory proceedings should be shortened and expenses lessened. They declare that a poor man's just action has often to be given up because of the long-drawn-out process and the exorbitant expense as well in the first instance as by appeals from place to place, from judge to judge, and finally to Rome, even on small

[1] R. II 25; P. 24 sq.

[2] *Registrum Episcopatus Aberdonensis*, I 131 sq. (Spalding Club). A century earlier the Synod of Exeter (Robertson, II 288, quotation from Wilkins's *Concilia*) described the pardoner as commonly an ignoramus, of shameful life also, feigning to be skilled, showing a pretence of holiness. This he does to allure the minds of the simple to lavish ampler alms, which afterwards he does not blush, in the sight of all, to squander prodigally in carousals and lewd excesses.

[3] R. II 121 sqq.; P. 128 sqq.

matters. "Albeit men obtain sentences never so many by the ordinary judges of this realm", an appeal to Rome holds up execution. The Council's decree is that previous statutes be enforced for shortening processes and checking protracted suits. Mention is specially made of fine and suspension of procurator or advocate if he has brought forward "frivolam exceptionem replicandam, duplicandam, triplicandam, quadruplicandam".[1]

The Lords and Barons also petitioned that in every parish church on Sundays and other holy days the Common Prayer with Litanies should be said in "our vulgar tongue" after the Divine Service of the Mass, and that Evening Prayers should also be in the vernacular.[2] The petitioners were in favour of the *status quo* as regards the Mass and other Sacraments, ceremonies and rites, while they were against the destruction of church buildings and ornaments. But all the reply given was that the Council had no power to authorize prayers in the vernacular.[3]

Excommunication, or "cursing" as it was appropriately called, had been for centuries employed by the Church; and to enforce penalties the help of the civil power was at times invoked. Under a statute of 1552 the treatment of excommunicated persons, if obstinate, was made more severe and the penalties were increased. Names are to be read out every Sunday and placarded on chancel rails and in other places in public. The excommunicated are liable to the punishment decreed by Act of Parliament.[4] The statute says that excommunica-

---

[1] R. II 171; P. 182 sq. Compare Scott's *Abbot*, chap. I: "Answers, replies, duplies, triplies, quadruplies, followed thick upon each other."
[2] R. II 148; P. 158.
[3] R. II 300. See Leslie, *History*, II 398 (Scottish Text Society).
[4] R. II 132 sq.; P. 140 sq.

tion, the severest of all ecclesiastical censures, has everywhere become completely futile, owing to men's corrupt
and dissolute morals. But the statute omits another
reason, perhaps the weightiest reason, for the contempt
in which excommunication was held and for the irrita-
tion against it and its authors. Cursing had for a long
time been a weapon to enforce payment of Church dues;[1]
and even of small debts.[2] Despising the censures of the
Church was declared heresy by the Council of 1549.[3]

Before 1549 complaints were common about the dis-
honesty of clerical executors, and enactments had been
passed against this. The Council of 1549 ordered every
executor to render an account of the execution of testaments.[4] A statute of the thirteenth century enacts
that Cistercians and members of other exempt orders
(exempt from the jurisdiction of the bishop of the diocese)
should not be appointed executors or allowed to take any

[1] R. II 148 sq.; P. 158. When bishops failed to pay any charges owing
to the Roman camera, they incurred the penalties of suspension, excommunication and interdict (Dowden, *The Medieval Church in Scotland*,
pp. 325, 330). Miss Cameron, in *The Apostolic Camera and Scottish Benefices*,
pp. 331 sq., records the excommunication of the Prior of Pluscarden,
November 1482, for non-payment of annates.

[2] Hay Fleming (*The Reformation in Scotland*, pp. 160 sq. and Appendix J)
gives from official sources a case where monastic tenants were sentenced
to pay a debt of fifty shillings, within fifteen days, under pain of excommunication. Another use of cursing was to secure the return of lost or
stolen property. Friar William Arth told how excommunication was
vilipended. The priest would stand up and cry: "Ane hes tynt a spurtill.
Thair is ane flaill stollin from thame beyound the burne. The goodwyiff
of the other syd of the gait hes tynt a horne spune. Goddis maleson and
myne I geve to thame that knowis of this geyre and restoris it not."
Arth added an anecdote of a husbandman's joke that a letter of cursing,
which cost only a plack, kept their corn better than the sleeping boy,
who would have a year's fee of three shillings besides a shirt and a pair
of shoes (Laing's *Knox*, I 38; Calderwood, *History*, I 83 sq.).

[3] R. II 119 sq.; P. 126.   [4] R. II 110 sq.; P. 115.

part in administering the effects of deceased persons.
This exclusion lends point to the satire on Canon Regular,
Monk and Friar in *The Papyngo*.[1]

Pluralities were of long standing and, though sanc-
tioned under papal dispensations, occasioned much
scandal. The Council of 1549 ordains that the holding
of several metropolitan or cathedral churches should be
forbidden. Churchmen who already have several benefices are to choose one and surrender the rest within a
specified time. Inferior benefices are similarly dealt with.[2]
Pluralities, however, continued; and in the Council of
1559 all that is said is that pluralists must show ordinaries
their dispensations before the month of August.[3]

The Preamble of the proceedings of the Council of
1559 gives a gloomy picture of the times. Wolves are
devouring the scattered sheep, subverting the right use
of sacraments, contemning the ceremonies of the Church,
seeking to overthrow the temple of God and the saints.
The Council must devise means to guard the Church;
to keep the flock in the Christian faith, to feed it with
wholesome food, to bring back the strayed sheep, and to
govern the Church in peace, till a General Council pro-
vides fitter means to redress these great evils. All the
clergy are called upon to put in practice the statutes
passed in the present Council, and "be sure that by God's
grace and the Queen Regent's help we will see them enforced". The clergy are to care for their flocks; to train
them in the traditions of the Church; and to reject
novelties and doubtful opinions.[4]

---

[1] R. II 18; P. 17. Compare Dowden, *The Medieval Church in Scotland*,
p. 302; and see above, p. 86.
[2] R. II 108 sq., 113; P. 113, 118.   [3] R. II 159; P. 169.
[4] R. II 151 sq.; P. 161 sq.

These were excellent sentiments, well intended; but they came too late, and where were the men to translate them into reality? Reform of the Church must come from outside, if religion was not to perish in Scotland.

RECORDS OF LEGITIMATION

The evidence of clerical immorality in the *Concilia* is quite general: no churchman is charged by name. Popular talk, however, unhesitatingly singled out offenders and did so with truth; while ludicrous nicknames arose and merry anecdotes circulated to the discredit of this, that and the other ecclesiastic. Andrew Durie, Abbot of Melrose (afterwards Bishop of Whithorn), was "sometimes called for his filthiness Abbot Stottikin".[1] Friar Arth was credited with telling a scandalous story of Patrick Hepburn, Prior of St Andrews (afterwards Bishop of Moray).[2] In 1542 Kirkcaldy of Grange considered the Prior of Pittenweem "a vile whore-master", and bluntly described him to James V as "a manifest forcer of women and the greatest defouler of wives and maidens in Scotland".[3] Abbeys, too, as Balmerinoch and Scone, were notorious for profligacy.[4] Popular talk, however, tends to exaggerate; and its details must not be too readily accepted. Still "there's aye some water whaur the stirkie drouns". But we possess the strongest evidence to convict many churchmen of breaking their vows of

[1] Laing's *Knox*, 1 261.

[2] Laing's *Knox*, 1 40; Calderwood, *History*, 1 85; A. F. Mitchell, *Scottish Reformation*, pp. 244 sq.

[3] Sir James Melville of Halhill, *Memoirs*, p. 66 (Bannatyne Club).

[4] See above, p. 46; and Laing's *Knox*, 1 361 sq.; Calderwood, *History*, 1 473. When Scone was destroyed, an old woman who lived near said it had been a den of whoremongers.

chastity—evidence from the legitimations entered in the *Register of the Privy Seal* and the *Register of the Great Seal*.[1] Legitimations recorded in the father's lifetime may rightly be considered a voluntary confession of his breach of the vow of chastity. One purpose of legitimating bastards was to secure that succession should not fall to the Crown as *ultimus haeres*. In the record of legitimation of Abrahe Waus (*Register of the Privy Seal*, 18 February 1506–7) hereditary succession is expressly granted as if he were legitimate, and the King renounces "totum jus, clameum, juris titulum et escheatam" to lands, revenues, possessions and "bona mobilia et immobilia". In another record (*ibid.* 30 January 1541–42) Alexander McIlwyane receives as a gift of escheat all the goods whatsoever, debts, jewels, money, etc., of his predecessor as vicar, William Vaus, escheated to the King, by the law of the realm, because the said William Vaus was born bastard and died bastard without lawful heirs of his body gotten and without lawful disposition made by him of the said goods in his lifetime.

A scrutiny of the *Registers*, 1510–60, discloses an enormous increase,[2] beginning about 1530, in the legitimation entries of "natural" sons and daughters of churchmen. Anyone who has not access to the printed

---

[1] *Registrum Secreti Sigilli Regum Scotorum*, and *Registrum Magni Sigilli Regum Scotorum*. Add Bishop Dowden's remark (*The Medieval Church in Scotland*, p. 315) about breaches of the vow of celibacy in the sixteenth century: "...the publication of the *Calendar of Papal Registers* supplies in the long lists of dispensations for the ordination of the sons of priests evidence of an unimpeachable kind."

[2] I suggest that the reason for this increase was the desire to prevent reversion to the Crown of the huge alienations of Church lands and other "immobilia" which Cardinal Sermoneta declares to have taken place during the forty years before the Reformation (see below, p. 159).

or manuscript Registers must be grateful to Dr Hay Fleming[1] for assembling entries of legitimations of children of the clergy from 1529 to 1559. Adding these up, I find that during those years over four hundred and fifty sons and daughters of some three hundred churchmen were legitimated.[2] In the Preface to the first volume of the printed *Register of the Privy Seal*, Matthew Livingstone says that there is "evidence of a great deal of looseness on the part of the recording officers". To legitimations "the attachment of the Great Seal was required"; yet we find some legitimations entered in the *Privy Seal Register* and not in the *Great Seal*, others in the *Great Seal Register* and not in the *Privy Seal*. Further "some of the acknowledged sons of the clergy were not legitimated or their legitimations unregistered", and "most of the daughters were not recorded".[3] As a matter of fact, the recorded legitimations of sons are about eight times those of daughters. Either many of the daughters were not legitimated or their legitimations were left unrecorded. For we cannot believe the birthrate of sons to have exceeded the birthrate of daughters to such a degree; unless many of the mothers of the clergy's natural children obeyed Macbeth's injunction to Lady Macbeth: "Bring forth men-children only."

[1] *The Reformation in Scotland*, pp. 540 sqq.

[2] About one-sixth of these are not designated clergymen in the *Registers*, but have simply "Dominus" *before* the Christian name. That indicates a cleric, as Dominus John Gordon, contrasted with "Dominus" *after* the Christian name, which indicates a lord, as John Dominus Gordon. (See second volume of printed *Register of the Privy Seal*, p. xxix.) Besides, several names with "Dominus" only in the *Privy Seal Register* have in the *Great Seal* "capellanus" added. Even if we omit those with "Dominus" only, the number is more than enough to prove the unashamed disregard of the vow of chastity.

[3] Hay Fleming's *Reformation*, p. 544.

The three hundred, or two hundred and fifty, churchmen involved belong to various grades: the Cardinal-
Archbishop of St Andrews and his successor, Archbishop
Hamilton, bishops and abbots in abundance, besides
priors, archdeacons, chancellors, deans, rectors, vicars,
chaplains and others. The chaplains are the most
numerous, about one-fourth of the whole: vicars come
next, about one-half of the chaplains. Chaplains were
arrant concubinaries. Deeds founding chaplainries
regularly contained a clause declaring that a known
concubinary who kept his concubine openly and after
warnings could not hold the post.[1]

In the list of offenders appear the names of prelates
who took part in enacting statutes, in the Council of
1549, against concubinage. Among them is the name
of Archbishop Hamilton, whose *Catechism*[2] contains a
scathing denunciation of the breakers of the commandment against adultery and fornication. Hardly a corner
of Scotland but supplies instances, from Caithness to
Wigtown, from Stronsay to Holyrood.

Let us now select a few examples of these entries. We
begin with three from the *Privy Seal Register* recording the
legitimation of children of the Cardinal-Archbishop:

5 March 1530–31—George Betoun, Elizabeth Betoun
and Mar^te Betoun, bastards, natural son and daughters of
David, Abbot of Arbroath.

4 November 1539—James Betoun, Alexander Betoun and
John Betoun, natural sons of David, Archbishop of St
Andrews.

2 August 1545—David Betoun, James Betoun, Alexander
Betoun and John Betoun, natural sons of David, Cardinal, etc.

[1] Hay Fleming's *Reformation*, pp. 69 sqq. John Major mentions another
characteristic of chaplains: see below, p. 164.
[2] See Law's Edition, pp. 90 sqq.

Archbishop Hamilton, while Bishop of Dunkeld, had one son legitimated, 22 January 1546–47, and another, 24 September 1548 (*Privy Seal Register*). Bishop Gordon of Aberdeen legitimated three sons, 26 February 1553–54 (*ibid.*); the reverend father in Christ, John, by divine compassion, Bishop of Brechin, legitimated four sons, 1 February 1542–43 (*ibid.*). On 4 October 1545 (*Great Seal Register*) legitimation was granted to Adam, Patrick, George, John and Patrick junior, natural sons of Patrick Hepburn, Bishop of Moray, two of whose daughters were legitimated 14 May 1550 (*Privy Seal Register*).

The following are also from the *Privy Seal Register*:

Robert Forester, Abbot of Balmerino: 28 August 1536, one son, 26 August 1547, one son and one daughter;

John Rowle, Prior of Pittenweem: 24 February 1540–41, two sons, 18 May 1546, two sons;

George Dury, Archdeacon of St Andrews and Commendator of Dunfermline: 30 September 1543, two sons;

Dominus Michael Disart, Chancellor of the Chapel Royal, Stirling: 16 October 1551, four sons and one daughter;

Mr Arthur Hamilton, Provost (of the Collegiate Church), Hamilton: 27 April 1543, four sons;

Dominus Paul Fresall, Dean of Ross: 28 March 1544, four sons;

Dominus Richard Hay, Chaplain: 16 May 1552, four sons;

Mr Adam Stewart, Rector of Stronsay: 22 October 1541, two sons and one daughter; and

Mr Robert Skeyn, Vicar of Logymar: 27 February 1553–54, five sons.

The *Register of the Privy Seal* from 1488 onwards also shows the legitimations of many bastard children of laymen; naturally, for, as Chaucer says (*Prologue*, 500 sqq.),

> if gold ruste, what shal iren do?
> For if a preest be foul, on whom we truste,
> No wonder is a lewed man to ruste.

Nicol Burne speaks of John Knox as having, on account of his marriage, incurred "eternal damnation by breaking of his vow and promise of chastity".[1] Then, will a severer punishment be meted out to the Roman clerics who broke their vows without marrying? "No, a less severe punishment", would be the reply. For centuries the Roman Church had held that for a priest to go through the marriage ceremony was more heinous than to commit fornication or adultery.[2]

ARCHBISHOP HAMILTON'S *CATECHISM*

The efficient cause of the compiling and publishing of the *Catechism* lay in the prevalent ignorance and incompetence of the Scottish clergy.[3] The book, however, proves that there were good men in the Church: men of ability, of learning, of high ideals, who produced a fine work, a praiseworthy, if belated, attempt to instruct priest and people. Though the *Catechism* was intended to instruct, still it discloses, directly and indirectly, certain of the faults of the church officials of the day.

---

[1] *The Disputation concerning the Controversit Headdis of Religion*, p. 161 (Scottish Text Society Edition of *Catholic Tractates*).

[2] Pitscottie (*Historie*, I 351) puts it bluntly: "For they would thole no priests to marry but they would punish and burn them to the death, but if he [Norman Galloway] had used ten thousand whores he would not have been burned."

[3] See above, p. 131. The *Catechism* is traditionally held to have been, for the most part, the work of John Wynram, sub-prior of the Augustinian Monastery, St Andrews. Printed in 1552 at St Andrews by Archbishop Hamilton's command and at his expense. Edited by T. G. Law (Oxford, 1884).

In "The Preface", the Archbishop admonishes all parsons, vicars and curates to use the *Catechism* for their own instruction and spiritual edification; and not to be negligent in their duty. If negligence is to be censured in all men and women, it is certainly most to be censured in those who have the care of Christian people. He reminds them of St Augustine's words: "Nothing in this life is in the eyes of men easier, lighter and more acceptable than the office of bishop, priest or deacon. But if that duty is done in a perfunctory, that is a negligent, manner, nothing in the sight of God is sadder, more unhappy, and more to be condemned." Therefore, it is expedient for them to use this *Catechism*, first, for their own instruction, remembering what is written: "Ignorance, mother of all errors, should most of all be eschewed in priests, who have received the office of teaching among the Christian people." Secondly, in accordance with the decree of the Provincial Council,[1] his will is that they read the *Catechism* diligently, distinctly and plainly, each to his own parishioners, for their common instruction and edification.[2]

The Archbishop tells all his spiritual curates that his whole intention is to help the Christian people, their parishioners, out of blind and dangerous ignorance into knowledge of what belongs to their salvation. The *Catechism* is, therefore, to be read on Sundays and principal holy days till God provide a sufficient number of able preachers, which will, he trusts, be within a few years.[3]

The following extracts from the *Catechism* corroborate

[1] See above, p. 132.
[2] Law's Edition, p. 5.
[3] Law's Edition, pp. 6 sq.

some of Lyndsay's charges or throw light on some of his statements.

After giving the commandment[1] which forbids the making and worshipping of graven images as gods, the *Catechism* declares that images may be made and possessed, provided they are well and lawfully used. The wrong use is to make images for the purpose of worship. Bede's saying is quoted:

No holy writ forbids the making of images, for the sight of them, especially of the crucifix, gives great compunction to those who behold it with faith in Christ; and to those who are unlettered, it gives a lively remembrance of Christ's Passion.[2]

Images of apostles and martyrs remind us of their true and constant faith and inspire us to follow their example:[3]

The image also of our Lady, the glorious Virgin Mary, bearing in her arm the bonnie image of her Son, commonly called the Baby Jesus, represents to us the blessed Incarnation and holy Birth of our Saviour...therefore the image by representation teaches us to honour and love the glorious Virgin as the Mother of God.[4]

The second commandment (our third) is broken by all negligent and ignorant prelates and parsons who neglect or refuse to set forth the word of God and instruct the people.[5]

Strict observance of Sunday is required. Parishioners are to attend service, hear Mass, and the preaching of the Word. Fathers should teach their children, masters their servants, the articles of the faith, the Pater Noster,

[1] Folios vii[b], xii[a]. Law's Edition, pp. 31, 37.
[2] Folio xxiii[b]. Law's Edition, p. 52.
[3] Folio xxiv[a]. Law's Edition, p. 52.
[4] Folio xxiv[a]. Law's Edition, p. 53.
[5] Folio xxxii[b]. Law's Edition, p. 64.

the commandments, and should instruct them to avoid the deadly sins. Christian people should abstain especially from money-making; forbear vice and sin; eschew idleness, vain talking, backbiting, slandering, blaspheming, and contention; shun every occasion of sin, such as dancing, unnecessary drinking, wantonness, lecherous songs and touching, whoredom, cards and dice; and in particular refrain from carolling and wanton singing in the church.

All the deeds of mercy and charity to the poor should be done on Sunday more than on any other day.

Sunday-breakers are those who do not attend church services; those who do not allow their servants to attend, but keep them at work; those who go to church but do not worship in spirit and in truth; and those who in the church during the time of God's word or service, occupy themselves in vain, evil or any worldly talking, laughing, scorning or any such doings.[1]

When we come to the exposition of the sixth commandment[2] (our seventh) we wonder what Archbishop Hamilton and other prelates felt as they read the denunciation of "incorrigible whoremasters, inveterate fornicators, detestable adulterers, and other violators of chastity, which they should keep by the command of God and their own special vocation".

In this connexion the authors of the *Catechism* cite

[1] Folios xxxv^b—xxxvi^b. Law's Edition, pp. 68 sq. The late Professor A. F. Mitchell (Facsimile, 1882, edition of *Catechism*, pp. xx, xxi) points out the resemblance of "the long accepted Scottish view as to the sanctity of the Lord's day" to the principles and practice laid down here. Except for the injunctions about the Mass, this declaration would serve as "a directory for the public and private sanctification of the day which would go far to satisfy the straitest sect among us".

[2] Folios li^a—lvi^b. Law's Edition, pp. 88–95.

the fate of Hophni and Phinehas (I Samuel ii 22 and iv 11)
as "a special example to be noted of all kirkmen".[1] The
fate of Hophni and Phinehas was the consequence of
their sin: they were "given to great wantonness and
whoredom, abusing the women who came to make
sacrifice". Scottish churchmen have this fate specially
pointed out to them, because the same scandal had arisen
in Scotland. Bishops and priests had been guilty, sometimes within the sanctuary itself, of defiling women who
had come for confession and absolution. Statutes denounced this sin and prescribed penalties—fifteen years
of penance for a bishop, twelve years for a priest, with
deposition if the matter should become known to the
people. Those statutes, however, belong to periods before
1500.[2] But David Patrick holds that the citing of the
punishment which deservedly overtook Hophni and
Phinehas, indicates that the compilers of the *Catechism*
and the members of the Provincial Council sanctioning
it seem to admit "that this abominable vice was still rife
amongst clergymen in the sixteenth century".[3]

Among breakers of the seventh (our eighth) commandment the *Catechism* reckons all patrons of benefices

when they present or promote any unworthy and unqualified man to any dignity or benefice in the Church, for

[1] The Hophni and Phinehas incident is employed as a warning in
"The Bishop Hely", *The Gude and Godlie Ballatis*, pp. 180 sqq. (Scottish
Text Society).

[2] R. II 29, 48 sq., 55; P. 29, 51, 60.

[3] *Statutes of the Scottish Church*, lxxxix sq. See also Bishop Dowden, *The
Medieval Church in Scotland*, p. 316: "The confessional was a source of
danger then, as, indeed, it has always proved to be. And it is impossible
that such rigorous condemnation of the sins of priests with their female
penitents should find a place in the ecclesiastical statute-books without
a cause."

love of temporal gear to their own advantage, or to that of any other, friend or stranger. Why should not that be called theft that is given for love of gear, which should be given freely for the love of God and in respect of learning and virtue?[1]

This commandment is broken by beneficed clergy[2] who receive the patrimony of Christ, that is, teinds and offerings, sometimes in greater measure than they should, and yet will not in return minister either the Word of God to the people for the food of their souls, or the Holy Sacraments for their spiritual consolation. Neither will they give any part of their benefice for the sustentation of poor people within their parish. For undoubtedly they are merely dispensers or stewards of the patrimony, to be dealt out to themselves as far as they require for their proper maintenance, and also to the poor people of their own parish in particular, and the repairing the choir of their church when necessary.[3]

Simony is declared to be an express transgression of this commandment. Whoever buys any of the Seven Sacraments also commits manifest simony. Nevertheless a poor priest saying Mass or dispensing any other Sacrament may take money, not as a price for the Sacrament but as a suitable fee for his necessary maintenance; for then he has no intention to sell the Sacrament. Moreover, those who give any benefice, especially if it has the care of souls, for money or money's worth, commit open simony. Again, if a patron gives a benefice to his near kinsman or any other friend, even though qualified, still if he gives it on condition that the receiver of the benefice

---

[1] Folio lviii[b]. Law's Edition, p. 97.
[2] A finger points to this as specially important.
[3] Folio lix[a]. Law's Edition, p. 98.

shall provide a living for the friends of the giver, in so doing he commits manifest simony. It is a far more serious transgression of this commandment if any one gives or takes a benefice *in commendam*; and if any one gives a benefice with the condition that the holder shall have only a trifling stipend so that the giver may receive the rest for himself and his maintenance.[1]

In discussing orders, the *Catechism* lays down that, besides administering the Sacraments, priests are bound to preach or teach God's word as far as necessary for the general instruction of the people, and also to pray to God daily for the people.[2]

One of the admonitions which conclude the book is addressed to all parsons:

Be diligent to do your duty, that is to say, to teach and preach the gospel sincerely to your parishioners according as you are bound to do by the law of God and Holy Church. Do not believe that in the sight of God you will be freed from performing that duty by this *Catechism*; for in truth the *Catechism* is not set out with the intention of giving you any presumption or opportunity for negligence and idleness. Therefore, for the tender mercy of God and for the love you have or should have to the bitter Passion of Christ Jesus our Saviour, whose spiritual flock bought with his own precious blood you have taken to keep and feed, do not fail to do your duty, every one to your own parishioners, seeing that they pay to you their duty sufficiently. Consider well and doubt not that ye are as much bound to them as they are bound to you.[3]

[1] Folio lix^b, lx^a. Law's Edition, p. 99.
[2] Folio clxiii^b. Law's Edition, p. 233.
[3] Folio ccv^b. Law's Edition, p. 289.

PAPAL NEGOTIATIONS

The volume of Papal Negotiations[1] contains very important statements regarding the condition of the Church. Father Pollen in his introduction (p. xviii) says that, in the decades just before 1560, the superintendence of morals in the Scottish Church, of doctrine, and of the election of prelates had been almost altogether neglected, though supervision of religious discipline was particularly necessary.

In a letter of 1556, Cardinal Sermoneta, who acted at Rome as representative for the Kingdom of Scotland, tells Pope Paul IV, on the authority of the Queen Regent, Mary of Lorraine, that almost one-half of the revenues of the whole kingdom comes into the Church. A letter from Blois signed by Mary Queen of Scots, 27 December 1555, declares that the greatest and least injured part of the wealth of Scotland is held by the Church.[2]

The unbridled licence of the monks is attributed by the Cardinal to over-great revenues.[3] He also says that, in spite of great wealth, many clerics, even prelates, use their riches to rent farms and estates; and to traffic in cattle, fish, hides and other goods, to the dishonour of the clerical order and the indignation of the laity.[4] From the same letter we learn that for about forty years prelates and other churchmen have alienated as much as possible of the most valuable part of the immovable property

[1] *Papal Negotiations with Mary Queen of Scots*. Edited from original documents in the Vatican Archives and elsewhere by John Hungerford Pollen, S.J. (Scottish History Society, 1901).

[2] Pp. 524 sq. See also pp. 1 sqq. Of course, the Queen's letter was inspired by the Queen Regent.

[3] Pp. 526, 529.   [4] Pp. 527, 530.

(real estate, i.e. lands, houses) pertaining to churches, monasteries and other benefices.[1]

Sermoneta also reports that in all the nunneries (and especially among the Cistercians) abbesses, prioresses, and sisters have become so brazen that they utterly despise the safeguards of chastity. Not only do they wander shamelessly outside the bounds of their convents, through the houses of seculars; but they also allow all sorts of worthless and wicked men within their convents and have immoral intercourse with them. The nuns defile the sacred precincts with the birth of children; bring up their progeny about them; go forth accompanied by their many sons; and marry their daughters with ample dowries from the revenues of the Church. The only possible remedy for this scandal is from the Pope, for the nuns claim exemption and will not submit to any admonition or visitation from the ordinaries.[2]

The Cardinal recommends that an account should be taken of the revenues of the monks. Then, after a suitable portion for their maintenance has been set aside, the surplus should be employed to restore churches and other buildings that are decaying, as well as for the enclosure of such religious houses. Very many stately churches and monasteries have, within the last ten years or so, been reduced to ruins by enemy inroads, or are crumbling to decay through the avarice and neglect of those in charge. The Pope is entreated to compel ecclesiastical authorities to restore the buildings and to spend one-fourth of the income from the benefices they hold on the restoration of churches, monasteries and benefices.[3]

---

[1] Pp. 526 sq., 529. Compare p. 8. See above, p. 148.
[2] Pp. 526, 528 sq.   [3] Pp. 527, 529 sq.

A letter of Pope Paul IV to Cardinal Trivulzio (27 October 1557) refers to a communication from the Queen Regent, stating:

(1) That for certain years back ecclesiastical discipline has been very much relaxed in Scotland.

(2) That ecclesiastics of all grades alienate Church property.

(3) That they neglect the fabric of the churches, allowing them to fall into ruin and decay from age, and omitting repair and restoration.

(4) That nuns and other dedicated women go out of bounds, and wander through houses of laymen, admit suspects into their convents, and make bold to indulge in pleasures and carnal lusts.

(5) That men and women, ecclesiastics of various ranks, seculars and regulars, commit crimes, iniquities and scandalous enormities, offending God, shaming Christianity, causing loss of souls, bringing scandal to Christ's faithful.[1]

The Pope at the same time commissioned Cardinal Trivulzio to visit Scotland by deputy, who *inter alia* was to see that the fabrics of all churches of every kind should be repaired and restored. In the middle of 1559 this was still to be done; for in June Henry II of France wrote to Paul IV asking that some one should be delegated to reform the Scottish Church, and to correct the corrupt customs and the depraved and dissolute lives of the ecclesiastics.[2]

When Nicolas de Gouda, the papal legate, was in Scotland in 1562, some good Catholics gave the following as causes of the fall of the old Church:[3]

(1) Benefices bestowed on children and on absolutely unworthy persons, who cared for nothing so little as for God's honour and the service of the Church. One and the same cleric would hold several benefices, sometimes even in

[1] Pp. 4 sqq.   [2] Pp. 13 sqq.   [3] Pp. 127, 138.

the same church. An example was cited of a prelate's son holding the archdeaconry and two canonries in his father's church.

(2) The extremely licentious and scandalous lives of priests and clerks.

(3) The supine negligence of the bishops.

The lives of the bishops, says de Gouda, he will not describe, nor the example they set. They are indeed such that it is no wonder that wolves assail the Lord's flock and destroy everything.

JOHN MAJOR

John Mair, or Major, "the last of the schoolmen", was renowned in both French and Scottish Universities as a profound thinker, an able lecturer, and a learned writer. It is mainly with his *History of Greater Britain*[1] that we are concerned, and only to a small extent with his *Commentary on the Sentences of Peter Lombard* (1509 and following years) and his *Commentaries on the Gospels* (1529). In his writings Major did not deliberately set out to describe the state of the Scottish Church; but here and there something crops up to induce him to remark on ecclesiastical matters. What he says is uttered not in fierce anger or biting satire but gravely, in the tone of a logician. He was a loyal son of the Roman Church, holding its doctrines with sincerity. At the same time he was not blind to the faults of the clergy, which he wished to be reformed by the Church itself. In dedicating the *Commentaries on the Gospels* to James Beaton, Archbishop of St Andrews, Major praises his defence of the Church against Lutheranism, and commends the recent execu-

[1] *Historia Majoris Britanniae tam Angliae quam Scotiae* (Paris, 1521). Translated by Archibald Constable (Scottish History Society, 1892).

tion of Patrick Hamilton. The *Commentaries* throw light on some of Major's views.[1] He condemns heretics who deny the doctrine of transubstantiation:[2] he defends the monastic life, while admitting the need of reform in certain monasteries and nunneries:[3] he approves of images in churches,[4] and of the worship of saints, though abuses may arise in connexion with this:[5] his belief in the miracles of saints is buttressed by the narrative of three villages in East Lothian,[6] each possessing St Baldred's body.[7]

What, then, are the faults which Major saw in the churchmen of his day and in Church affairs? He considers the Scottish ecclesiastical polity as generally inferior to the English; and he mentions two instances of the inferiority.[8] First, the Scottish bishops admit to the priesthood men altogether unskilled in music:[9] priests should at least understand the Gregorian chant. We must remember Major's fondness for music: witness the oft-quoted passage telling how, when he was at Christ's College, Cambridge, he would lie awake many a night to listen to the melody of the bells.[10] Second, in some districts of Scotland there is only one parish church for thirty villages, lying far apart: the villages may be four, five, even ten miles from the church. The wide parishes

---

[1] See Archibald Constable's introduction to translation of *Historia*, to which I am indebted for references to the *Commentaries*.

[2] *In Ioann.* folio cclxxxviii.　　　　[3] *In Matth.* folio lxxii.

[4] *In Ioann.* folio cccxiii.　　　　[5] *In Ioann.* folio cccxxii.

[6] Near Haddington, his birthplace.

[7] *Historia*, II vii, with Constable's note.　　[8] *Historia*, I vi, III vi.

[9] Elsewhere (*In Matth.* folio lxxx) Major condemns the granting of benefices to unworthy priests, and the preferring of a less suitable candidate to one who is more suitable.

[10] *Historia*, III i.

result in cures, large and wealthy; and the wealth makes the holders disinclined to serve their charges in person. Major would have an increase in the number of cures, with a decrease in the amount of each stipend.

He explains that villagers living far from their parish church may attend services by their landlord's chaplain. Every small laird has one chaplain, and the great lords may each have five or six. These chaplains are no despicable soldiers; they are ever ready to gird on sword and shield, and follow their lord to battle. Major calculates that Britain has 40,000 priests fit to be matched as fighting men with a like number from any nation.[1] This custom he condemns; for priests should pray, not fight. He allows, however, that clerics may take up arms to defend their country or themselves.[2]

Major dislikes pluralities,[3] *in commendam* appointments, and all absenteeism. When speaking of the poor endowments and the few scholars at the University of Glasgow, he adds: "And yet the Church possesses many fat prebends; but in Scotland such revenues are enjoyed *in absentia* just as well as they would be *in praesentia*, a practice which is lacking both in justice and in common sense."[4] In his *Commentary on the Sentences* he describes a prelate who is invested with a benefice *in commendam* as a reeve rather than a prelate.[5] While highly praising James Kennedy, Bishop of St Andrews, Major disapproves of two points in his conduct: that with so rich a see he held the priory of Pittenweem *in commendam*, poor though it was; and that he spent a huge sum of money

---

[1] Men like the Clerk of Copmanhurst in *Ivanhoe*.
[2] *Historia*, I vi, VI iii.   [3] *In Matth.* folio lxxx.
[4] *Historia*, I vi.
[5] *In Quartum*, 21st question of 24th distinction.

on his costly tomb. The wealth possessed by bishops is not intended for their own use: like abbots, they should employ it for pious purposes.[1]

Major agrees with James I in censuring David I's lavish expenditure on monasteries and nunneries, which impoverished the Crown. If David, he adds, had foreseen what manner of life the religious would come to lead, he would not have wasted the royal revenues on religious houses. "That wealth was indeed the offspring of a truly pious sentiment, but the wanton daughter ended by suffocating her mother." The early abbots made a pious use of their riches; and princes imagined that it would be so for ever. But now we have for many years seen shepherds whose only concern is to find pasture for themselves, and who neglect their sacred duties. See what the possession of great wealth may do to religion. By means of flattery undisguised, worthless sons of noblemen obtain the control of monasteries *in commendam*. It is the ample revenues they covet, not for the benefits they might bestow on the brethren, but simply for the lofty position, that they may be in command and may have the opportunity of filling their own pockets. Under a wicked head all the members are wicked; for "when the head is sick, the other members suffer". A wealthy abbot must maintain an unruly retinue, showing a bad example to the religious. Often he bids farewell to the cloister and speeds to the king's court, never heeding the wise saying: "Sicut piscis sine aqua caret vita, ita sine monasterio monachus."[2] Even if his body happens to be

---

[1] *Historia*, VI xix.
[2] Chaucer (*Prologue*, 179 sq.) applies this proverbial saying to his Monk.

in the cloister, yet in spirit and in conduct he himself is as one outside. He may have ruined the tenant-farmers of the monastery by raising their rents for the benefit of his private purse and may still think—but in this he is much mistaken—that he has acted rightly. The religious should dwell in the cloister, away from the society of secular persons: they should not hanker after the flesh-pots of Egypt nor remember the gifts of fortune. An abbot who is his own land-steward has assumed a function very much alien to the practice of true religion: Judas kept the purse and was exposed to greater danger than the other apostles. The true end and aim of religion is better promoted by a moderate competence than by superfluity. An abbot's wealth should not permit him to keep more than two or three servants.[1]

In his *Commentary on the Sentences* Major advocates the curtailing of the huge retinues of bishops.[2] He blames the beneficed clergyman who cares for his own flesh and blood more than for Christ's orphans and poor. They can barely get anything as relish for their bran loaf, while he himself is plump and sleek and in good case, a pig of Epicurus' herd.[3] Major disapproves of the praise heaped on prelates who fare sumptuously and give their house-holds not only barn-door fowls to eat but also partridges and pheasants.[4]

---

[1] *Historia,* III xi, with Constable's note.

[2] Attempts were made to limit retinues to thirty horsemen or fewer. They had all to be hospitably entertained when a bishop made a visitation to a parish or a religious house. In 1470 the Abbot of Arbroath—a wealthy foundation—appealed to the Pope against the Archbishop of St Andrews, who would come sometimes with one hundred horses, sometimes with two hundred. See Dowden, *The Medieval Church in Scotland,* pp. 118 sq.   [3] Horace, *Epistles,* I iv 15 sq.

[4] *In Quartum,* 18th, 20th and 22nd questions of 24th distinction.

The indiscriminate employment of ecclesiastical censures, especially for frivolous offences, is abhorrent to
Major. In certain cases, he says, sentence of excommunication may be so unjust as to be null and void, and
not to be dreaded. Such excommunication is no more
excommunication than a corpse is a living man. It is
only for mortal sin that one can be liable to be excommunicated; and only for contumacy can this sentence be
inflicted by man.[1]

Major utters a warning against pilgrimages, because
of the danger to morals. Confessors should not, as many
are wont to do, enjoin pilgrimages, least of all on women.
It is harmful for married women to go on pilgrimage
without their husbands; perchance, even with them.
Neither is it becoming for maidens to roam afield: they
can see saints at home.[2]

The misuse of the wealth of the Church is denounced
by Major. Writing about the levy to pay the ransom of
James I, he says that the collectors, the Bishop of Dunblane and the Abbot of St Columba, exacted money
from the commons only. The levy should have been
imposed, in due proportion, on nobles and gentry, on
ecclesiastics, and on the common people. In this way,
the whole and more could have been raised without
difficulty. Then he continues: "What shall I say about
the ecclesiastics? Their conscience does not prick them
when they recklessly lavish Church property on kinsfolk
and connexions; but if in their King's hour of need, in
his captivity, they are called upon to give help out of the

[1] *Historia*, iv vii.
[2] *Historia*, v xxiii. Friar Arth gave a similar warning to the men of
St Andrews (Laing's *Knox*, i 39; Calderwood, *History*, i 84).

funds of the Church, they straightway make it a matter of conscience. They strain out a gnat and swallow a camel. For the funds of the Church, beyond supplying the necessities of churchmen, should be devoted to relieving the poor and to ransoming such captives as may not otherwise be readily ransomed. Ecclesiastics should be glad to do this, since taxation must then press less heavily on the poorest people."[1]

JOHN BELLENDEN

John Bellenden, Archdeacon of Moray and Canon of Ross, translated Boece's *Scotorum Historiae*, to which he made additions.[2] Two of the additions may be noticed.

In a poetic address to his book, he writes:

> Schaw how of kirkis the superflew rent
>   Is ennimie to gud religion,
> And makis preistis more sleuthfull than fervent
>   In pietuus werkis and devotion;
>   And not allanerly perdition
>   Of common weill, be bullis sumptuus,
>   Bot to evill prelatis gret occasion
>   To rage in lust and life maist vicuus.[3]

The evil effects of wealth on the commonweal and on churchmen are enlarged upon in the account of the reign of David I. Bellenden approves of James I's description of David as "ane soir sanct for the crown", who left the Church too rich and the Crown too poor. He also quotes from "Master John Mair" the statement that David gave the Church "LX.M pundis Scottis". This the

---

[1] *Historia*, vi xi.
[2] *The Hystory and Croniklis*. Printed by Thomas Davidson (*c.* 1536). *The History and Chronicles of Scotland*: written by Hector Boece...and translated by John Bellenden (Edinburgh, 1821).
[3] Edition of 1821, i cx.

Church still possesses to no less damage of commonweal than "perditioun of gud religion". For if David had considered the manners and fostering of devout religion, he would not have endowed the churches with so great riches nor built them with such magnificence. For "the superflew rentis of kirkis, as now used, are not only occasion to evil prelatis to rage in maist insolent and corruppit life", but a "sicker" net to draw all manner of gold and silver out of Scotland. The drain on the wealth of the country would be less if abbots were appointed by the ordinaries, with no dispensation from habit or religious manners; ordinaries by their primate, without any exemption; and the primate by the Provincial Council. Till seventy years ago[1] no kind of benefice, except only bishoprics, went to Rome; and since then we see what infinite amount of silver and gold is taken out of the realm by their continual promotion. The realm must, through this never-ceasing promotion of prelates, be brought to such incurable poverty that it shall be an easy prey to our enemies. It cannot sustain a great charge in time of war as was done formerly by our forefathers. But because neither spiritual nor temporal estate of this realm has any love for the commonweal thereof, but each man is set only for "his awin singular way, I will (says Bellenden) deplore no more the calamities daily befalling through their imprudence".[2]

[1] This would roughly be 1460; but money for benefices other than bishoprics was flowing to Rome before that date. Consult Miss Cameron's *Apostolic Camera and Scottish Benefices*. See above, p. 105.

[2] Edition of 1821, II 300.

JOHN LESLIE

John Leslie, Canonist of University and King's College, Aberdeen, and Bishop of Ross, was the most distinguished champion of Mary Queen of Scots and an ardent defender of the Roman Church. His great history is *De Origine, Moribus et Rebus Gestis Scotorum*, Rome 1578, translated, 1596, into Scots by Father James Dalrymple,[1] of the Benedictine Monastery of St James, Regensburg, Bavaria.

Leslie declares that when James III, with the Pope's concurrence, appointed abbots to Paisley and Dunfermline in 1472, he originated the intruding of seculars into religious houses by royal command. The result was that monasteries became scenes of idleness, luxury and all bodily pleasures, while God's service began to be neglected, hospitality to be despised and wealth to be prized most of all. What was intended to help the poor was misused to satisfy the voluptuousness of the rich. No longer did the monks elect godly and devout abbots; but kings nominated their chief favourites. Churchmen came to be hated and envied, especially by the commons.[2]

The scrambling for bishoprics and abbeys, as in the years after Flodden, and the bestowal of these posts on men not distinguished for learning, or for goodness of life, or for capacity to rule a diocese or a community, are blamed by Leslie and declared to have probably allowed heresy to come into Scotland.[3]

He refers to decrees of the 1552 Provincial Council

[1] This translation was edited for the Scottish Text Society by E. G. Cody and W. Murison, 1888–95.

[2] Book VIII; Dalrymple's Translation, II 90 sq. The practice was known much earlier.

[3] Book IX; Dalrymple's Translation, II 163 sq.

as very necessary for the cleansing of the morals of the clergy.[1]

In answer to any who ask why the welter in religion came about, Leslie admits as "almost the fountain of all mischief" the fact that the people saw that when they were children they had not been taught the catechism. The clergy neglected to give sound instruction on what they should believe as certain. Their empty minds, accordingly, readily drank in false doctrines. In addition, many ecclesiastics were stained with avarice and licentiousness. The reformers asked how the light of the gospel could dwell in the black darkness of vice.[2]

THE COMPLAYNT OF SCOTLANDE

The Complaynt of Scotlande was compiled soon after the Scots had been defeated at Pinkie, 1547, and was printed in Paris, *circa* 1549.[3] The anonymous author was an ardent patriot, a determined opponent of England, and a staunch adherent of the old Church.

Chapter VII tells how he saw a lady, Scotia, with a long mantle that had once been of great beauty but was now torn and defaced. In the middle part there had been "graved in characters, books and figures, divers sciences divine and human with many charitable acts and supernatural miracles". But the fine workmanship was spoiled. No one could extract a profitable meaning or good example from any part of it. This typifies the clergy of Scotland now degenerated from their first excellence. Scotia's three sons appear—Nobility, Spirituality,

---

[1] Book x; Dalrymple's Translation, II 346.

[2] Book x; Dalrymple's Translation, II 465 sq.

[3] Edition by J. A. H. Murray, E.E.T.S. 1872. See *Cambridge History of English Literature*, III 152 sq.

Labourers. The second son is seated in a chair, clad in a long gown, of grave aspect, in his hands a book, "the clasps were fast locked with rust". The rusty clasps graphically depict the clergy's neglect of study. Scotia exhorts her sons, blaming them for the sad condition of the country.

In chapter xv, the third son recounts his troubles. His two brothers, the nobles and clergy, are more cruel than the English. Corn and cattle are taken from him, he is evicted from his leaseholds and farmsteads, the rent of his land is increased so much that he and his wife and children must drink water. His corn teinds are not only heightened out of all proportion to the fertility of the soil, but they are also taken out of his hands by his two tyrant brothers. If he makes money as trader or artisan, he is compelled to lend it to his cruel brothers. If he craves his debts, he is threatened, hurt and sometimes killed. Their wickedness causes all his troubles. For as their ill-gotten gains multiply, so their inordinate pomp increases, and their dainty idleness also, with misunderstanding of God. This makes them ambitious in their state, covetous of goods, and desirous to be governors of the realm—"misgovernors" is the right word.

In chapter xix Scotia reproves her second son, Spirituality. The clergy ought to be degraded from office. Their faults are far less excusable than those of nobles or labourers. The clergy cannot plead ignorance. They possess knowledge not only of divine learning but also of the humanities, the liberal arts and moral and natural philosophy. They should use their talents to promote unity in the land. Their negligence in duty has caused dissension and discord. In conformity with their profession and learning they should give good example in behaviour. Evil example deserves greater punishment than disobedience. It is very necessary for churchmen to give good example in life and behaviour so that ignorant people may follow in their footsteps. Example is better than doctrine.

The philosophour plutarque rehersis ane exempil of the partan, quhilk repreuit ane of hyr zong partans, be cause the zong partan vald nocht gang euyn furtht, bot rather sche zeid crukit, bakuart, and on syd. than the zong partan ansuert, quod sche, mother, i can nocht gang of my auen natur as thou biddis me, bot nochttheles, vald thou gang furtht rycht befor me, than i sal leyrn to follou thy futsteppis.

The clergy's abuses and maladministration of their office have doubtless been the cause of the schism troubling Christianity. Short of killing all heretics, the schism can be cured only if the clergy reform themselves.

Scotia declares (chapter xx) that the chief vices of the nobles and the clergy are pride, envy and avarice.

COMMENTARY ON THE RULE OF ST AUGUSTINE[1]

Like other orders, the order of Augustinian Canons, or Black Canons, had its ups and downs, its flourishing and fading. In the late fifteenth century and the early sixteenth there were strenuous efforts at reform; and one of the reformed houses was the Abbey of St Victor in Paris, which became renowned as a training school in theology. Among the Augustinian foundations in Scotland was

[1] Edited for the Scottish History Society by G. G. Coulton, 1935. The original was printed in Paris, 1530, with the title "Exegesis in Canonem diui Augustini recens aedita per Fratrem Robertum Richardinum celebris Ecclesiae Cambuskenalis canonicum". On this book Dr Coulton based chapter xx of his *Scottish Abbeys and Social Life* (1933), an expansion of his Rhind Lectures.

Cambuskenneth. Alexander Mylne,[1] a man of fine character, became its head in 1517, and began a series of reforms. As he found that in his monastery men of learning were well nigh extinct, he planned to send promising novices to St Victor. One of the novices sent was this Robertus Richardinus (Richardson or Richards), a brother perfectly loyal to the Church—he has no kind word for Luther[2]—and to his order. He desires above all things that the Augustinians may be restored to their pristine form. His Abbot had frequently asked him to send from Paris an account of the reformed canons there and a commentary on St Augustine's Rule. Hence the "Exegesis". Richardinus, however, does not stick closely to his theme, but portrays how the discipline of the unreformed monasteries was weak and how the monks failed to keep the rules. He does not always indicate where his instances come from; but whether they come from Scotland or not, Scottish monasteries are not held up as free from the faults of religious houses in general.

The Augustinian Canons bound themselves by the usual vows of obedience, chastity and poverty, to oppose the deadly sins of pride, lechery and greed.[3] Yet, says Richardinus, the vows are not kept; the monks break rules, both when inside and when outside the monastery. He bids his brethren remember that their house is neither a palace, nor a tavern, nor a brothel, but a place

[1] In 1532 Mylne was appointed President of the Court of Session.

[2] *Lubricus serpens Luttherus*, p. 20 of Coulton's Edition; *Hic Lutherus antichristi praeco...serpens ille lubricus*, *ibid.* p. 112. *Lubricus* is slimy, with the further notion of lewd.

[3] Page 42. *Contra superbiam uouerunt obedientiam ueram: contra luxuriam, castitatem synceram: contra auaritiam, paupertatem inexcusabilem.*

of holiness, where the inmates bewail their sins, pray for the founders, and in particular honour God and the Blessed Virgin. To-day we show no good example, but, through our bad example, are become a laughing-stock.[1]

One main cause of monastic degradation was "pro-prietas", the illegal possession of private property by monks. This was clean against the principle of the original foundation of monastic orders, and against the vow of poverty, which (as Coulton puts it) was the chief claim of cloisterers to be "Pauperes Christi" *par excel-lence*. Coulton quotes from Abbé C. Fleury: "Monks' places...were sought after as mere worldly establish-ments by men who then led a thoroughly worldly life."[2] Richardinus emphasizes the evils[3] of "proprietas", which should be abolished, and denounces the sorry subterfuges of the monks to gloss over breaches of the vow of poverty in the spirit while they pretend to keep it in the letter. To embezzle for private use what bene-factors have given for religious purposes is simply sacrilege.[4] He ends with the wish that monks would show the same strenuous effort and the same clever shrewdness in learning good and holy literature or in reading the story of the "Biblia Catholica", as they do in cramming their coffers with money destined to perish.[5] He also describes the indecent haste with which, when a rich man falls ill, monks fly to his house, not to give consolation to

[1] Pp. 25 sqq., 43.
[2] Introduction, pp. xxix sq.
[3] Pride, lechery, greed, p. 42.
[4] Pp. 33 sqq., 37, 101, 175 sq.
[5] Page 43. Richardinus (p. 145) quotes Jerome's remark: "Nostrae diuitiae sunt in lege domini meditari die ac nocte."

the dying soul, but, like greedy kites, to see what they can grab.[1]

The statutes of the order regarding dress and food were also ignored. In Scotland and England the Augustinian garb was white surplice, black cassock and black mantle.[2] Religious, says Richardinus, should dress in quiet colours, avoiding red, dark brown and green. Their clothes should be neither too long nor too short, neither too expensive nor too cheap.[3] How utterly incongruous that preachers of grief and sorrow for sin should stand "gleaming in purple and gold".[4] He censures the excessive eating and drinking. Many who had little to eat outside the monastery will have all manner of dainties. They seek foods from everywhere: they invite as guests men and women, people of every sort. Their aim is not to live a holy life, but to be seen to banquet sumptuously.[5] Some monks tipple from morning to night. At vespers they disturb the chant and are a disgraceful spectacle. After supper they start bacchanalian revels—"commessationes" is the term—and consequently next morning

---

[1] Pp. 28 sq. In *The Papyngo*, 647 sqq., as we saw, the birds of prey that swoop down on the dying Parrot, the Pie, the Raven and the Kite, represent a Canon Regular (a Prior of the Augustinians), a Black Monk or Benedictine, and a Friar. Richardinus gleefully relates a story told in public by a famous Paris lecturer. An avaricious churchman, eager to obtain a benefice the holder of which was at the point of death, rode fifty miles in four hours to beg the benefice from the King. "You have indeed ridden well," said the King, "but your intention is manifest. Therefore, since you are such a good horseman, ride back and announce that you have failed in your request."

[2] In *The Papyngo*, 656 sq., the Pie, as Canon Regular, says:
"My quhyte rocket my clene lyfe doith declare;
    The blak bene of the deith memoriall."

[3] Pp. 102 sqq.

[4] Page 107, auro insignes et murice refulgerent.

[5] Pp. 56, 83 sq.

they sleep at matins or come ill prepared. "I myself", says Richardinus, "knew one who brought himself to such a habit of drinking that he durst not go to sleep at night without having at his bed's head something to drink. Once it happened not to be there: he died of thirst."[1]

Pride, the enemy of obedience, is rife in monasteries. Eschew pride, says Richardinus, for it is the root of all sins; and destroys every advantage and every good quality a man possesses. Hear the well-known jingle:

> Si tibi copia
> Seu sapientia
>   Formaque detur,
> Sola superbia
> Destruit omnia
>   Si comitetur.[2]

All virtues, says Gregory, are ruined by pride, that deadly plague which sent the angels hurtling from heaven.[3]

The vow of chastity is again and again broken by monks. Richardinus expounds St Augustine's injunction not to fix one's eyes on a woman; and he elaborately describes the innate wickedness of women.[4] They should be altogether shut out from the abbey buildings. Do not let them enter even the outer gate; if you do, they will find a way also to the inner.[5] Monks who are guilty of any breach of the vow of chastity should be punished.[6] He mentions a bad custom prevailing in certain monasteries. Each brother has a special laundress, which leads

---

[1] Pp. 86 sq.   [2] Pp. 52 sq.   [3] Page 61.
[4] Pp. 111 sqq. One of his descriptions is: Estque mulier animal, animali leone brutorum ferocissimo atque superbissimo, superbius: symia lasciuius, aspide uenenosius, et syreneis monstris fallacius, et decipientius.
[5] P. 117.   [6] Pp. 117 sqq.

to unbecoming familiarities.[1] In their palatial houses
many superiors live sumptuously surrounded by everything that provokes lust.[2]

Since it was the paucity of learned men in the Abbey
of Cambuskenneth that influenced the Abbot to send
novices to Paris, Richardinus naturally speaks of monkish
ignorance. When he was censuring, as we saw, the keen-
ness of monks to gather riches, he wished that they
would show equal zeal in sacred studies.[3] Some of the
religious may be heard singing without knowing what
they sing, and bawling out psalms they do not compre-
hend. What is needed is not the chanting but the understanding of the psalm. The heart, as well as the lips, must
be there.[4] He calls to mind Jerome's saying that ignorance
of the Scriptures is ignorance of Christ. All religious,
not novices only but also abbots and seniors, should have
stated hours of study.[5] Ignorance, the mother of all vices,
is for monks the special cause of offences. There is grave
danger if, when we have the Bible containing the words
and works of God and his Christ, we neglect those for the
vain things of this world and its trivialities.[6]

The members of communities infamous for lack of
learning and for broken vows could not be expected to be
regular and devout in the daily services. Richardinus
accordingly urges that devotions at the stated hours
should be attended to, and that all monks, but especially
abbots and priors, should be present at monastic prayers.
There they should shake off all care and anxiety for things
temporal, and should not indulge in jesting, chattering,

---

[1] Page 137. Quot enim sunt fratres, tot habent distinctas mulieres
eorum lauantes uestes, cum quibus contrahunt familiaritates.
[2] Page 99.   [3] See above, p. 175.   [4] Pp. 28, 74 sq.
[5] Pp. 145 sq.   [6] Pp. 149, 152.

backbiting, foolish babbling or vain thoughts. Instead of worshipping humbly and sincerely, some will intersperse worldly matters. At vespers one addresses his neighbours: "And what is preparing in the kitchen? How many kinds of fish? In what way dressed? The wine is very much watered, and the beer is frothy." In the midst of supplications and confessions to God, others bandy jests with their comrades. During prayers they read books, or trim their nails with their penknives. They gaze about, and have hardly patience enough to hear one psalm to the end. For their stalls seem beds of nettles.[1]

Abbey churches are profaned when used for lawsuits or for reckoning of dues or of tithes at Easter. Crowded with men and women, they are scenes of quarrelling, swearing and of many other offences. Certain brothers are guilty of wrongdoing in their practice of buying linen from women in the church.[2]

Richardinus would have agreed with Archibald Hay, that the members of a religious house are what the head is;[3] and the deterioration of monasteries he ascribes in part to the bad example of superiors and their laxity of discipline.[4] Certain superiors are like one who is not the true shepherd: they enter the sheepfold not by the door but by other ways.[5] They choose entrants of the same type, not for chastity of life, mortification of the body, grieving for sins, but for the world's vainglory and mad

---

[1] Pp. 68 sqq.   [2] Pp. 73 sq.

[3] *Panegyricus*, folio XVI. See below, p. 190.

[4] Pp. 159 sqq., 171.

[5] Resembling those in Milton's *Lycidas*, who
> "for their bellies' sake,
> Creep, and intrude, and climb into the fold."

pleasure.[1] Such superiors spend their time with laymen and women in their hospices built like the strongest castles, where sumptuously and in most unseemly fashion they squander the patrimony of the Crucified One. How can these superiors rebuke their monks?[2] In secret they provide superfluities and delicacies for themselves and their intimates, while the brothers serving God day and night have hardly enough food to keep them alive.[3] Some superiors build splendid palaces in royal style to entertain nobles; but the abbey and the church go to ruin and waste away through age, not once restored by the superiors.[4]

Many superiors fail in the duty of looking after their monks. They pay more assiduous attention to their horses, dogs or hawks, and to their mistresses than to any of the brethren, even *in extremis*. How many of the huge throng of superiors are eager to visit and console the brethren entrusted to them, or to administer the eucharist or extreme unction? Yet a man is much worthier than a dog. Let them be warned, and remember the doom of those to whom it was said, "I was sick and ye visited me not."[5]

Hardly thrice a month do some superiors accompany the monks to the choir, nor do they examine their life and manners.[6]

Richardinus also notes the prevalence of nepotism. Abbots and prelates, as if induced by the motive of turning God's Sanctuary into a thing to be held by hereditary succession, intrude into monasteries their little nephews, who resist with tooth and nail, as the saying is. Those who

---

[1] Page 28.   [2] Page 30.   [3] Pp. 48, 86.
[4] Pp. 54 sq.   [5] Page 97.   [6] Page 30.

are placed in authority in this carnal manner cannot but live carnal lives themselves and allow others to do likewise.[1] This is not the only way in which unsuitable persons enter monasteries—sons of princes, barons, knights—simply for their own advantage.[2]

Towards the end of his book, Richardinus tabulates the causes of the ruin of all monasteries.[3] Some of these are

Indiscriminate admission of the unfit.
Neglect of training of novices.
No right intention on the part of entrants.
Omission of study.
Promotion of relatives and of unsuitable persons.
Excessive hankering after temporalities.
Concealment of faults and lack of due correction.
Negligent and ill-advised visitation.
Inexperience and greed of badly educated superiors.

This is supplemented by a catalogue[4] of obstacles to those who would advance in the monastic life. Among these hindrances he specially mentions excessive laxity of discipline, for monks may live as they choose;[5] failure of learning and training; want of good example;[6] and lack of wisdom and discretion.[7]

QUINTIN KENNEDY

Quintin Kennedy, Abbot of Crossraguel, published in 1558 *Ane Compendius Tractive*, in defence of Church Councils as representing the whole Church, which is the

---

[1] Page 157. [2] Page 46. See above, pp. 129 sq.
[3] Page 171. [4] Pp. 181 sqq.

[5] He adds: ubi disciplinae rigor, ibi et religionis uigor est.

[6] For: longum siquidem iter est (teste Seneca) per praecepta, sed breue et efficax per exempla.

[7] Discretio enim mater est uirtutum et sola uirtus principalis, quae omnium uirtutum radix, custos et consummatio extat, et omnibus ordinem ponit.

judge and interpreter of Scripture. Kennedy writes in a
clear and forcible manner, and puts his arguments well.
Only one part, however, concerns us now—the part
where he admits the faulty condition of the clergy, and
lays the blame on patrons of benefices eager to possess
the patrimony of the Church.[1]

Perhaps some zealous men, pitying the poor miserable
people, will ask what wonder it is if the simple people are
abused with errors, blinded in ignorance, drowned in vice.
Heresy is openly preached without punishment, while those
[the clergy of the old Church] who ought to preach the true
word of God, are like dumb dogs; they neither preach
themselves nor provide preaching suitable to resist errors.
The clergy who should guide the people are more ignorant
than the simple people themselves. "And if the blind lead
the blind, both shall fall into the ditch." Open shame is
brought on the Church by the most part of those who should
be mirrors of good life. All estates are declined from the way
and will of the Lord. It is an everyday occurrence that, if a
benefice is vacant, the great men of the realm[2] will have it
for temporal reward, else they will stir up sedition, be dis-
obedient contrary to God's command, serve as they think
good, with perpetual grudge and disdain. When they have
secured the benefice, if they have a brother, or a son—even
though he can neither sing nor say—nourished in vice all
his days, at once he shall be mounted on a mule, with a long
gown and a round bonnet, and then it is a question whether
he or his mule knows best how to do his duty. Perhaps
Balaam's ass knew more than both! When such counterfeit
persons are chosen to have Christ's flock in guiding, it is no
wonder that the simple people are wicked (as they are
indeed), thinking vice to be virtue and virtue to be vice.
Not only are such men crept into the Church, but one may
daily see a child, yes, a baby, to whom one would hardly
give a beautiful apple to keep, get perhaps five thousand

---

[1] Laing's Edition in *Wodrow Miscellany*, pp. 150 sqq.

[2] Quintin Kennedy was himself of noble descent, being a son of the
Earl of Cassilis.

souls to guide; and all for avarice, "the root of all vice", that the parents may obtain the profit of the benefice for their own special advantage, and the poor simple child scarcely receive enough to bring him up virtuously: the convent and place where God should be daily honoured and saved, goes completely to ruin; and yet the promoters of such monstrous farces in the Church are the chiefest criers out on the vices of the clergy. If the old liberty were restored, the bishop chosen by his chapter, the abbot and prior by the convent and from the convent, then qualified men would be in all estates of the Church; all heresies should be banished, and the people well taught. This would be to come in by the door to be a minister in the church of God, where now by tyranny and avarice, for the most part, as it were thieves or brigands, we creep in at windows and back-doors. Blinded in avarice, great men believe in this way to build up their houses by abuse of the patrimony and revenues of the Church....Meanwhile, the poor, simple people perish miserably; the Church is disgraced; God is dishonoured; all heresies, wickedness and vice reign.

Kennedy prays that patrons may provide properly qualified pastors, and that all clergymen, especially bishops, may remember the apostle's severe sentence: "Woe be unto me if I preach not"; and the prophet's words: "Woe be unto you pastors of Israel who feed yourselves and not my flock!" If pastors did their duty to the simple people committed to their charge, all heresies, wickedness and vice would be suppressed, the Church freed from slander, and God honoured.

NINIAN WINZET

Ninian Winzet was for a number of years Rector of Linlithgow Grammar School, and, after the Reformation, Abbot of the Benedictine Monastery of St James, Regensburg, in Bavaria. A man of independent mind, he was moved to speak out amid the troubles of the time, to declare himself

an unfeigned Christian; that is, stoutly to gainstand all abuse, negligence, licentious living, and pharisaical hypocrisy to me known, either of the former age or of the present; and similarly to show myself a manifest adversary to all schism, sedition, error and heresy.[1]

He writes to maintain the prestige and power of the old Church, but he is ready to point out its faults. Of his works we need examine only *The First Tractat*, one of those published at Edinburgh, 1562.

Addressing the Queen,[2] he likens (as regards religion) the state of the realm to that of a ship in a deadly storm, buffeted by contrary winds between dangerous sand banks on the right and terrible death-presenting rocks on the left; a ship which, guided these many years by slothful mariners and sleeping steersmen (the pastors of the Church and their patrons), is badly crashed on the shallows. Some [the Reformers] in fear of their own lives and the lives of others have seized the management of the ship from the former officers [the clergy of the old Church], for these many years most unworthy of that name.

He then turns to the bishops and other pastors of the Church, whose supremacy in the Church he calls "ruling misruled and misguided government"; time, however, is too short to lament that before God and to cry for redress before the world. Yet he must say something in praise of bishops and others; but he is doubtful if it is their holy lives or their sound doctrine he should first commend. Winzet accordingly proceeds to attack their

[1] *The Buke of Four Scoir Thre Questions*, i 54 (Scottish Text Society).
[2] *The First Tractat*, i 3 (Scottish Text Society).

lives and doctrine with ironical praise and straight-forward blame.

Since your godly living adorned with chastity, fasting, prayer and sobriety, by its noble fruits, is patent to every one, no more need be said! Who does not speak of your merchandise, your simony, your glorious estate, your solicitude about marriage, after bringing the barons to be scions of your posterity, and witnessing in future ages of your godliness? All countries and colleges deplore your liberality to the poor, your magnificent colleges of godly scholars in your company, your fostering of poor students of rich intellectual powers, able afterwards to rule the Church of God in sound teaching. Every Gentile, Turk and Jew may laugh at your godly and circumspect distribution of bene-fices to your babies, ignorant persons and filthy; that, O Scotland, being the special ground of all impiety and division among you. Your wise, sage and grave household servants, void of all vanity, bodily lusts, and heresy, are spoken of to your praise, God knows! All the world is acquainted with your dumb doctrine in exalting ceremonies only, without any declaration of them; and far more, keeping in silence the true word of God necessary to every man's salvation, and not resisting manifest errors! What part of the true religion is not corrupted and obscured by your slothful rule and princely estate? Have not many, through deficiency of teaching, in mad ignorance misapprehended their duty, which we all owe to our Lord God, and so have sorely stumbled in their perfect belief? Were not the sacraments of Christ Jesus profaned by ignorant and wicked persons, able to persuade to godliness neither by learning nor by living—of the which number we confess the most part of us of the Ecclesiastical State, in our ignorant and inexperienced youth, to have been unworthily admitted by you to the adminis-tration thereof. If those most important things are, through ignorance and avarice, brought from their purity, what marvel is it that matters of less esteem, as images, invocations of saints to pray for us, the prayer for the souls departed and many similar things, lawful in sobriety and learned simplicity, should by the same vices be corrupted and profaned from

the mind of your old forebears? Were you in vain commanded
by God, through the mouth of His Prophets and Apostles, to
watch attentively and continually over your flock and carefully know each one by face? Or did the princes of the earth
give you yearly revenues...to the end that every one of you
might spend them on his Lady Delilah and bastard brats?[1]

Winzet next accuses the nobles of Scotland because
through "the two infernal monsters, pride and avarice,"
they trafficked in benefices, and by this simony thrust
unqualified bishops and other pastors into the Church.
The nobles and their predecessors, blinded by carnal
affection for their babies, brothers or other relations,
or by avarice, destroyed the true religion and triumphant
kingdom of Christ, putting, in the place of godly ministers
the true successors of the Apostles, dumb dogs who not
only dare not bark, but even, when shamefully struck
with staff and pole, dare neither whimper nor whine.[2]

GEORGE CONN

George Conn, born at Auchry, near Turriff, in Aberdeen-
shire, of a Catholic family, was a man of learning, skilful
in diplomacy, charming in manners. From 1636 to 1639
he acted as papal agent in England, where he was a great
favourite with Queen Henrietta Maria and with King
Charles. Conn was just on the eve of attaining to the
rank of cardinal when he died. His book on the state of
religion in Scotland contains references to the sixteenth-
century Church.[3] His evidence is not contemporary
evidence; but it is interesting to find an important dignitary of the Roman Church in 1628 uttering the views of

---

[1] *The First Tractat*, 1 4 sqq.   [2] *Ibid.* 1 6 sqq.
[3] Georgii Conaei *de duplici statu Religionis apud Scotos libri duo*. Romae:
Typis Vaticanis. MDCXXVIII.

men like Archibald Hay, Quintin Kennedy and Ninian
Winzet, and not those of the apologists of the last decades of the sixteenth century. Through an idealizing
medium, the apologists saw pre-Reformation days as a
golden age with a Church possessing all excellences, intellectual and moral.[1]

In former days (Conn writes) the Church in Scotland
flourished greatly, but love began to grow cold in men's
breasts and the famous piety of their ancestors to languish.
Avarice seized on the minds of the nobles, who blamed their
fathers for extravagant liberality to God, and finally cast
greedy eyes on the revenues of the Church. Children, nothing
more than born, were nominated abbots and bishops. Anyone unfit, through weakness of body or mind, for secular
pursuits, was willy nilly consecrated to the service of God.
Those who, through the faults of the family, were cut off
from a sure hope of entering on the ancestral inheritance,
were, not adopted, but forcibly thrust, into the ranks of the
sons of God, so that they snatched from the altar what would
support them in a life of luxury.

Men of the lower classes wished to escape the necessity of
sowing and reaping for others; and, seeing nowhere a more
tranquil refuge than in monastic cloisters, they went into
retirement there. As soon as one from the dregs of the people
obtained a slight knowledge of letters, he began to canvass
for a benefice: he had no thought of any holy duty, he
merely sought to fill his belly, to enlarge his robes, to occupy
loftier seats. What else could be expected from one whose
call to the divine ministry came neither from zeal to serve
God nor from love of virtue nor from regard to what is
honourable or upright?

In addition, unbridled lust appeared, the most loathsome
plague of a consecrated life. The houses of many priests
were common brothels: the sacrilegious debauchery of some
clerics left unviolated neither the matron's honour nor the
virgin's purity. Consequently, reverence for the religious

[1] See T. G. Law, *Catholic Tractates*, 1573–1600, pp. xxviii sqq.
(Scottish Text Society).

turned to ridicule. Friars were no longer called "mendicantes" but were nicknamed "manducantes";[1] while all
kinds of opprobrious epithets and of vile charges were
hurled at religious houses and their inmates. The noble
piety of the upright, which always shone forth among our
countrymen, failed to close the mouths of calumniators.

Conn has nothing to relieve his sorrow but the thought
that everything has ebb and flow. "Est enim rerum
omnium occulta quaedam vicissitudo et periodus: et
suas, ut Respublica, ita religio conversiones experitur."[2]

ARCHIBALD HAY

One of the most valuable documents for first-hand information about the state of the Scottish Church in the
last years of James V's reign is Archibald Hay's *Panegyricus* upon his cousin, David Beaton, when elevated to
the dignity of Cardinal. A panegyric may appear a
strange place to find such information, but it is altogether
a strange panegyric.

Hay became M.A. of the University of Paris in 1533,
and was afterwards professor in Collège Montaigu. He
was presented to the Principalship of St Mary's College,[3]

[1] Gormandizers, gobblers. Buchanan (*Historia*, XVI xxviii) mentions
someone who shrewdly called the wealthy Dominicans "non fratres
mendicantes sed manducantes". [2] Pp. 89 sqq.

[3] St Mary's was the successor of the Paedagogium, which in the early
sixteenth century had not become a college. Archbishop Alexander
Stewart intended to endow the Paedagogium, but his death at Flodden
intervened. Archbishop James Beaton obtained a bull from Pope
Pius III, and in 1537 began to build, but died before much was done.
In honour of James Beaton's foundation, Hay, his nephew, composed an
oration, published in Paris, 1538; of which Kellas Johnstone says only
one copy exists, that in York Minster, originally belonging to Cardinal
Beaton. See McCrie, *Andrew Melville*, 452 sqq. (1856); Kellas Johnstone,
Bibliographia Aberdonensis, I 38 sq. (The Third Spalding Club); *Pane-
gyricus*, folios IIII, XII; *Register of the Privy Seal*, 29 June 1546; and A. F.
Mitchell, *The Scottish Reformation*, pp. 285 sqq.

St Andrews, on the twenty-ninth of June, 1546; but his tenure was brief; for he died before the first of October, 1547. McCrie praises Hay as pre-eminent above most of his Scottish contemporaries in learning and liberal views. He was a sincere and devout son of the Church, a man of upright life and of sound commonsense, a type unfortunately in the minority among Scottish clerics of that period. Hay tells us himself that his life-long determination had been to write, not what might please, but what ought to be written truly and piously. His address to the Christian Reader ends:

Haec scribo (Christiane lector) neminem cupiens perstringere, quum nulli malevelim: nec cuiusque auribus blandiens, quum a nemine commodum aut sperem aut ambiam.[1]

Panegyricus was written in 1539. *Epistola Nuncupatoria* is dated "Parisiis ex Monte Acuto Calendis Augusti 1539". The colophon runs:

Excusum Parisiis Anno redemptionis nostrae, 1540. Decimo tertio Calend. Iunii.[2]

Omitting the Epistle Nuncupatory, the Epistle to the Christian Reader, and two poems, I calculate that the Panegyric proper consists of about 60,000 words. Its sixty-six folios, however, are not all eulogy. That is mostly in folios IX to XXIII. At times Hay gives Beaton undeserved praise, manifestly on the principle that praise undeserved is one method of correction, by showing what the eulogized should be; or, as Hay puts it, "Eulogists

[1] Folio LXVI.

[2] Kellas Johnstone describes the Aberdeen University Library copy as the finest he had seen: *Bibliographia Aberdonensis*, I 40 sq. He catalogues other five copies: Blairs College; St Andrews University; Edinburgh University; National Library of Scotland; and British Museum.

often give praise to lead men to the practice of worthier deeds."[1]

Take one example of undeserved praise. Under Beaton, remarks Hay, the Abbey of Arbroath was renowned for the learning of the monks, for their piety, for their purity of life and for their moderation in eating and sleeping. And why? Because in Beaton they found a pattern of all the virtues: "fieri saepissime solet ut in domo bene instituta tales sint liberi qualis est paterfamilias."[2] Now in regard to one virtue, the virtue of chastity, what was the truth about Beaton? The *Register of the Privy Seal* (as we have noted)[3] records, under date 5 March 1530–31, the legitimation of one son and two daughters, bastards, natural children of David, Abbot of Arbroath; and under date 4 November 1539—while *Panegyricus* was printing—the legitimation of three natural sons of David, Archbishop of St Andrews. When we remember that, though Beaton was of outstanding ability in statesmanship, a man of resolution, a patriot, in the sense of being anti-English when England was acting harshly towards Scotland, he was proud, ambitious and intolerant, and that .his private life was a scandal to religion; when we remember this, much of Hay's eulogy sounds ironical, and the duty laid on Beaton to correct defaulting clergymen seems laid on the wrong shoulders. Hay's eulogy is perilously near exemplifying the poet's line:

> Praise undeserved is satire in disguise.

That Hay was not blind to Beaton's shortcomings is

---

[1] Folios VII sqq.   [2] Folio XVI.
[3] See above, p. 150.

evident in the beginning of the Epistle to the Christian Reader:

It ought not to seem surprising that I describe such a cardinal as, in these days, it is easier to long for than to behold, since it has been my determination to set forth not so much what they are as what they should be. For no other reason did I congratulate a man exalted by the dignity of cardinal than that I might show clearly that great honours are not without heavy burdens and that such a dignitary must not fall asleep in his endeavours strenuously to defend his sublime dignity with a mind buttressed by bulwarks of virtues, otherwise he will in vain claim to be in the eyes of men a great prelate who in the sight of God is much lower than the meanest type of cobbler.[1]

The greatest part, however, of *Panegyricus* consists of a picture of the degeneracy of the Scottish Church and of the ignorance and depravity of the clergy. In it we find neither outbursts of a fierce satirist nor sallies of a merry jester, but the serious statements of a reformer within the Church. His love of truth constrains him to speak out, to describe what he would rather conceal; and as a sincere churchman, he must, in his love of piety, religion and uprightness of life, bring to Beaton's notice those faults and vices of which his entourage for reasons of their own keep him in ignorance. Knowing the state of affairs, the Cardinal-Archbishop will, as head of the Scottish Church, be bound to take steps to remove all the abuses, and especially to show an example of upright life and conduct to all his ecclesiastics, as he shall render an account at the Last Day to the Judge of all.

Hay's strictures are not aimed at individuals, but at those ecclesiastics in general who deserve to be blamed. He could cite particular cases, but he prefers to give no

[1] Folio LXV.

names. For example, he refers to the prelate who boasts
of never handling the New Testament, but he does not
mention the Bishop of Dunkeld.[1] Nor, when speaking of
clerical immorality, does he name the prelates notorious
for their illegitimate children.[2] His account of the failings,
faults and vices of the clergy, while strong in substance,
is moderate in tone, and so is doubly effective. It comes
from a man of high character; and we have every reason
to accept it as a true picture of the almost universal degeneracy of the Church and of the degradation of very
many of the clergy. Hay's plain speaking is all the more
remarkable since he was manifestly eager to be head of
the college which he again and again prayed Beaton to
establish.[3] His outspokenness did him no harm, for
Beaton, not long before his murder, had arranged for his
appointment as principal.

Let us now hear what Hay has to tell about the condition of the Church affairs in Scotland in 1539, just
about the time when Sir David Lyndsay was busy with
his first version of *Ane Satyre*.

For a number of years past[4] religion has in Scotland,
and not in Scotland alone, been decreasing. Many people
have no fear of God, no love of their neighbours. Love
has yielded place to coldness and apathy, sound doctrine
to superstition. Heresies abound, schisms, strange be-
liefs, impostures, rebellions against the true dignity of
the Church, while clerics are generally held in contempt.

[1] See above, p. 95.
[2] Had he named Patrick Hepburn, Prior of St Andrews and then
Bishop of Moray, ten of whose children were at one time or other
legitimated under the Great Seal, he might have been asked why the
Cardinal himself should be omitted.
[3] Folios VIII, XII, LVIII sqq.
[4] Folios XXVII sqq., XXXII sq., XXXVI sq., XXXIX sqq., XLIV, XLIX.

The cause lies in the corrupt morals of the wicked clergy. For no one willingly listens to admonitions from such as are stained by grave vices.

Ecquis ab auaro liberalitatem, ab incontinente castitatem, ab impudente verecundiam, ab intemperante modestiam, discet? quis feret vitam suam ab eo reprehendi qui semper vixit moribus corruptissimis?[1]

This, which is not to be forgotten, must be proclaimed: that the infamous morals of churchmen have inflicted the greatest disaster on the whole of Christendom. Writers may keep silence, but the uneducated shout aloud.[2] There is a lack of good pastors to teach God's word and by the example of a blameless life lead men to meditate on heavenly things. Good pastors rebuke old and young, rich and poor, sparing none through hope of gain or fear of harm.[3]

Here is Hay's catalogue of the vices of churchmen: ambition, avarice, revenge, perjury, insolence, perfidy, baseness in deed, haughtiness in speech, fickleness in thought, craftiness in life. None could write the biographies of such men without shame, none read them without shuddering. Had clerics paid less attention to gain and more to godliness, things would not have been so much upset. Hay prophesies a bloody end to the tragedy caused by what are in his eyes "sceleratissimae pestes" of ecclesiastics, ambition and avarice. He warns them that, unless they understand their condition and reform themselves, they are sure to be cast out to make room for others whom it shall please God to call into His

[1] Folio xxviii.
[2] The uneducated said and sang such things as appear in *The Gude and Godlie Ballatis*. See also p. 147.
[3] One remembers Chaucer's Parish Priest.

sheepfold to drive off the wolves. If he were to recount the wickedness rampant in the breasts of churchmen, no one would believe that under the human face such savage monsters lie hid. If he had to speak of the terrible crimes of ecclesiastics falsely so called, his language would go beyond all bounds. If he were to detail the pretended miracles, the cunning words and deeds; if he were to proclaim the abuses of both sexes which have been devised, abuses surpassing in vileness the power of man's brain; he would, in consequence of speaking the truth, incur hatred more bitter than the scoundrel Vatinius did in Rome.[1] Hay contrasts the clergy with the beautiful and modest Spurinna, who gashed his fair countenance in order that neither maid nor matron might fall in love with his beauty. On the other hand, several of our well-fattened priests spare no expense or flattery to entice into their snare any woman of surpassing beauty, deterred from their infamous intention by no consideration of marriage, of religion, no, nor yet of kinship, so that most truly the name of father suits those clerics, not so much father in Christ—the name of honour that many claim for themselves—as father in the flesh, in whose service they are thoroughly exercised.[2]

As a lover of learning, Hay naturally denounces the prevailing ignorance of the clergy and their neglect of

[1] Folio XLVII: ex veritate conciliarem mihi odium plusquam vatinianum. Vatinius was a notorious character in the last years of the Roman Republic. Hay was thinking of Catullus, XIV 3, "odissem te odio Vatiniano".

[2] Folio XLVI. This irony has point given to it, unintentionally, by entries of legitimation in the *Register of the Privy Seal*. For example, under date 25 September 1542, we find "Preceptum legitimationis Johannis Stewart, thesaurarii Abirdonensis, bastardi, filii naturalis, reverendi in Christo patris, Willelmi, Abirdonensis Episcopi."

reading, even of the Holy Scriptures. Those who grope helplessly in broad daylight, do not fix the eyes of the mind on reading the Scriptures and so they fail to gather the sweetest fruit of learning; they also suspect anyone who is learned, who grieves that the blind cannot guide the blind, and who tries to expel ignorance in his desire to change things for the better. Hay is especially shocked that one is thought deserving of the amplest stipend and the most holy title of "vir ecclesiasticus", who boasts that he has never busied himself with the New Testament,[1] who by his example shows that the Sacred Books should be neglected and who passes his life in the foulest darkness of ignorance. Such as pride themselves on never reading the New Testament utter fearful threats against those who most diligently search the Holy Scriptures to find the mind of the Lord.[2] He accordingly urges Beaton to do all he can to promote higher learning among the clergy and to encourage those who show a turn for scholarship. Hay's zeal for learning culminates in the elaborate plan of a college.[3]

Hay falls foul of ecclesiastical hypocrites, with their outward show and their neglect of duties. The monk by his dress has renounced the world, but he carries it about with him in his heart. He assumed the "religious habit" not to live a better life but to live a life more free from care, under the cloak of poverty indulging his appetite

---

[1] See above, p. 192. [2] Folios XXXI, XXXVIII.

[3] Folios LVI sqq. The curriculum was to comprise Latin, Greek, Hebrew, and if possible Arabic and Chaldee, dialectic, moral philosophy, natural philosophy, canon law, civil law, medicine, arithmetic, geometry, astronomy, music. There was to be a well-stocked library, and also a printing-press. The principal must be carefully chosen; and, while nepotism must be avoided, if a relative of Beaton's should be found duly qualified (Hay means himself) he should be preferred to all others.

luxuriously. Such men, and there are many of them, are
the plagues of true religion.¹ One receives the pastoral
staff and thinks he has done his duty sufficiently if on the
chief holy days, crosier in hand, he pronounces in an in-
articulate voice certain formulas; while others, bishops
and abbots, receive stipends for many years and do not
even once perform any duty.² Many are the pseudo-
pastors who do not feed but flay their flocks, do not seek
the strayed, do not heal the ills of conscience, do not
console the afflicted, do not help the poor. Of each of
these it may be said: "pro pastore agit depastorem."³
Many clerics spend the best part of their lives in hunting,
hawking, dice-playing, elaborate banquets, and other
pleasures not to be named without a blush. They delight
to keep dogs, fools and apes, when their surplus money
should be used to relieve the needs of poor brothers.⁴

To explain how and why so many unworthy clerics are
found in the Church, Hay states that many unsuitable
persons are attracted by the expectation of wealth,
dignity and ease. Archdeacons also in examining candidates for the priesthood, patrons in presenting to benefices, and bishops in collating, are moved by nepotism,
by influence, by simony.⁵

St Paul wrote to Timothy:

qui Episcopatum desiderat, bonum opus desiderat.⁶

True; but not when one seeks a bishopric, as many do, in
order to live luxuriously, to enjoy greater leisure, to have

¹ Folios xv sq., xxiv sq., xxxiv, xli, xliii.
² Folios xxxvii, lii.
³ Folios xxx sq., xxxiii. "He acts the eater instead of the feeder."
⁴ Folios xxxv, xl, xlvi sq., li, liii.
⁵ Folios xxxiii, xxxv.
⁶ A slightly modified form of the Vulgate, I Timothy iii 1.

a larger revenue, to pass wakeful nights in dicing, to spend whole days in hawking, in hunting or in amatory talks. Such an one, in the eyes of all, is manifestly seeking "opes", not "opus".[1] The ample revenues of the Church cause much evil. Many a man, after spending years in lewdness, after wasting the flower of his age in the basest acts, receives a fat benefice in order to pass his old age in luxury. An arrant fool, born to excite laughter, will obtain a rich prebend without any trouble: a man of tried and true life and scholarship will not be admitted. One most fit for the plough-stilts will not be refused a benefice: a good man will be given nothing. Benefices are often bestowed not merely on the ignorant, but also on boys not yet capable of reasoning, so that they seem born to the benefice as to an inheritance. How repugnant this is to the pastor's duty, Hay will not proceed to describe offensively, lest he should appear not to be sufficiently just to dispensations—the crutch of these bestowals—or to be alone in deriding laws already accepted. The only excuse that Hay has heard is: "Take away the annual revenue, and I'll soon remove the burden of the benefice laid on the boy's shoulders." For what bishop, deeply concerned for his office, would entrust a benefice to a boy, unless spurred on to do so by ample gifts of money?[2]

Hay has no desire to reduce clerical incomes, provided they are properly used. Those who minister at the altar should live by the altar: only let them not misuse church funds in luxury and lust. After their own necessities are supplied, they should employ the surplus to help

[1] Folio LI. That is, seeking "wealth", not "work".
[2] Folios XXXII sq.

the poor and the aged, to provide dowries for girls, to
train in literary studies youths of good capacity. The
enormous wealth of the Church has been given not to be
hoarded in a treasure-house but to be bestowed on the
poor. Founders of monasteries intended the endowments
to be used to succour the needy and entertain travellers.
Far too many clerics are not "dispensatores" but "dis-
sipatores".[1] The money received for charitable purposes,
they do not bestow in alms but spend in ways contrary
to divine law.[2]

Hitherto I have summarized Hay's statements. The
following extracts are in a fairly close translation:

I am ashamed to view the life of ordinary priests, and also
of others, a life obscured on all sides by the darkness of
ignorance, so that I often wonder what in the world bishops
were thinking about when they admitted such men to
handle the Lord's sacred body—men who hardly know the
order of the letters of the alphabet. Priests come to serve
the holy table who have not slept off yesterday's drunkenness.
Priests prepare to perform the sacrifice who have not had
the faintest tincture of instruction. I know perfectly that
the morals of the celebrant are not prejudicial to the efficacy
of the sacrifice.[3] But it is expedient to amend these faults,
which to our extreme disgrace have held sway for so many
years....Ignorance on the part of priests is a very muddy
spring, from which flow the most of the calamities of the

---

[1] "Not stewards but scatterers", "not dispensers but dispersers".

[2] Folios XVI, XXIX sq., XLII, LVI.

[3] Archbishop Hamilton's *Catechism* states this doctrine in four passages:
Law's Edition, pp. 173, 182 sq., 192 sq. and 233 sq. Chaucer's Parish
Priest does not hold this view: "Soothly, the preest that haunteth deedly
Sinne, he may be lykned to the aungel of derknesse transformed in the
aungel of light; he semeth aungel of light, but for sothe he is aungel of
darknesse. Swiche preestes been the sones of Helie, as sheweth in the
book of Kinges, that they weren the sones of Belial, that is, the devel....
Thise preestes, as seith the book, ne conne nat the misterie of preesthode
to the peple, ne god ne knowe they nat." *The Parson's Tale*, 896 sqq.

Church. Bishops blame the examiners of candidates for the priesthood, but the bishop is responsible for the examiner, the archdeacon. The examiner is often a greater blockhead than the examinee, and admits candidates without selection, for fear he lose any part of his income, believing it enough to admit to ecclesiastical functions candidates not as learned as possible but as many as possible.[1]

Were the very wise writer of Ecclesiastes now alive, he would ascribe it to the height of vanity that brute beasts should be admitted to ecclesiastical benefices, sometimes even invited. The woeful upsetting of this order no man of piety sees without a groan, speaks of without fear, thinks of in his heart without sighs.[2]

I consider it intolerable that entrance to the Church should be open to all without selection. Some of those admitted bring with them pure ignorance; others come with a false reputation for knowledge; several have a mind corrupted by most shameful acts, trained to commit all kinds of horrible wickedness; certain intend to do harm, so that less danger is to be dreaded from the most noxious animals than from these offscourings of abandoned reprobates. Who will be found so shameless as to deny these most patent facts? What man of patriotic feelings would consider that they should be passed over in silence? What man trained in liberal studies would bear with equanimity the bestowal of honourable posts on wicked persons?[3]

If David Beaton laid to heart the counsels of his cousin, he was too busy with political matters in the years after 1540 to put the counsels into practice. Perhaps he had not much will. Yet in time the condition of the Church and the popular feeling against churchmen so influenced him that he called a Provincial Council to meet in Edinburgh, 13 January 1545–46, which should enact laws for the rooting out of heresy and for the reforming of the manners of the clergy. But nothing resulted. For

[1] Folio xxxiiii.   [2] Folio xl.   [3] Folio xlii.

news came that George Wishart was in East Lothian, at
the House of Ormiston. "More important to the best
interests of the Church, it seemed to Beaton, than the
reform of the lives of the clergy, was the capture of
Wishart."[1] The burning of Wishart and the murder of
the Cardinal followed. Let us remember, however, that
one of his last acts had been the nomination of Archibald
Hay as principal of St Mary's College.

[1] Herkless, *Cardinal Beaton*, pp. 286 sq.

CONCLUSION

I submit that the evidence in the foregoing pages amply and conclusively shows the substantial truth of Lyndsay's charges against the Scottish Church. It also justifies the strictures found elsewhere: in John Rowll's *Cursing*, for example; Glencairn's *Epistle direct fra the Holye Armite of Allarit*; Duncan Macgregor's *Testament*; *The Gude and Godlie Ballatis*; Alexander Scott's *New Yeir Gift to the Quene Mary*; George Buchanan's *Somnium, Palinodia* and *Franciscanus*; *Satirical Poems of the Reformation* (Scottish Text Society); John Knox's *History*; Pitscottie's *History*; and *The Beggars' Summons*.

It is manifest that, in the generation preceding 1560, the Church had degenerated seriously and, in a sense, irretrievably. The last Provincial Council, that of 1559, frankly admitted the accusations of the Church's bitterest enemies; but the admission came too late. In the fifteenth century the heads of the Church had been men of worth, patrons of learning, three of whom founded universities; but in the succeeding century leaders like Bishop Elphinstone became rare. There were, however, still a few good churchmen, such as Bishop Reid of Orkney, Abbot Mylne of Cambuskenneth, Friar Arth, Archibald Hay, Ninian Winzet, and the author (or authors) of Hamilton's *Catechism*. But the majority of the clergy, of all ranks, were neither good nor learned. They disobeyed the injunctions of the Councils that they should attend the universities. In morals they were mainly of the type of Cardinal Beaton, Archbishop Hamilton, and Bishop Hepburn. They refused to listen to Archibald Hay's warning[1] that, unless they reformed themselves, disaster would overtake them, and their inheritance would be given to others. Reform from within could not be effected by the few good clerics in the face of the many whose unworthiness of life, unfaithfulness to vows, and neglect of sacred duties proved the chief causes[2] of the collapse of the old Church as a moral and spiritual force.

P. F. Tytler, discussing ecclesiastical affairs about 1545, calls the churchmen

...those blind guides who were often remarkable for little else than their ignorance and licentiousness. The Romish Church in Scotland had, indeed, in former times been distinguished by some men who combined profound learning with a primitive simplicity of faith. Even in this age it could boast of its scholars and poets; but at the period of which we speak, its character for sanctity of manners, ecclesiastical learning, or zeal for the instruction of the people in the word of life, did not rank high; and the example of its head and ruler, Beaton, a prelate stained by open profligacy, and remarkable for nothing but his abilities as a statesman and politician, was fitted to produce the worst effects upon the great body of the inferior clergy.[3]

Consider the period from 1520 to 1560. In general, the buildings had long been uncared for, and were very unsightly: the vestments were ragged and dirty: the sacred vessels were tawdry and ill-kept. In general, the services were performed with little reverence; and latterly even the semblance of devotion had vanished.

[1] See above, p. 193.

[2] I do not forget other factors working against the old Church—the attraction that the superabundant wealth of the clergy had for nobles and gentry; the effect of foreign intervention, English and French; and the influence of John Knox.

[3] *History of Scotland*, v 411 sq.

Few parishioners attended Mass; and many of those who did, mocked and jeered, talking and laughing and singing wanton songs. Church buildings and precincts were profaned by games and secular business. Sundays and saints' days were held in contempt. Hamilton's *Catechism* traces the troubles of the time to the neglect of Sunday observance, and strictly enjoins the duty of keeping Sunday holy.[1]

Here, then, was a community which to a very great extent had lost all trust in priests and all respect for them because of their faithlessness, negligence, avarice, ignorance, immorality; a community maddened by the exaction of teinds as well as by other grievances, and grimly asking why these men should engross the wealth of the nation. To the community in this mood had come the polished wit of Buchanan's Latin, the piercing sarcasm and flashing mockery of Lyndsay's vernacular, besides the plain, pointed home-thrusts of songs and ballads, such as *The Gude and Godlie Ballatis*. Read the rollicking verses which begin:

> The Paip, that Pagane full of pryde,
>   He hes us blindit lang,
> For quhair the blind the blind dois gyde
>   Na wounder baith ga wrang;
> Lyke Prince and King, he led the Regne,
>   Of all Iniquite,
> Hay trix, tryme go trix, under the grenewod tre.

The outrageous fun of this ballad deals shrewd blows which miss hardly one of the failings of the churchmen.

Lyndsay's poetry and drama, overflowing with humour and satire, appealed to the eyes, the ears, the

[1] See Patrick's *Statutes*, lxiv sqq.; Law's Edition of Hamilton's *Catechism*, pp. xiii sqq.; and A. F. Mitchell's *Scottish Reformation*, pp. 7 sqq.

feelings of thousands whose minds remained cold and irresponsive to sermons and theological disquisitions. Naturally, then, he became one of the principal instruments in the downfall of the Church from which he never formally seceded; and Sir Walter Scott does not exaggerate when, describing Lyndsay, he speaks of

> The flash of that satiric rage,
> Which, bursting on the early stage,
> Branded the vices of the age
>   And broke the keys of Rome.

BIBLIOGRAPHY

Accounts of the Lord High Treasurer of Scotland. Record Series. 1877 sqq.

Aschenberg, H. *Sir David Lyndsays Leben und Werke.* 1891.

Bannatyne MS. Vol. III. Scottish Text Society. 1928.

Bellenden, John. *The History and Chronicles of Scotland.* 1821.

Bellesheim, Alphons. *History of the Catholic Church of Scotland.* Hunter Blair's translation. 1887 sqq.

Brown, P. Hume. *John Knox.* 1895.

Buchanan, George. *Rerum Scoticarum Historia.* 1582.

Calderwood, David. *The True History of the Kirk of Scotland.* Wodrow Society. 1842 sqq.

Cameron, Annie I. *The Apostolic Camera and Scottish Benefices.* 1935.

Chalmers, George. *The Poetical Works of Sir David Lyndsay.* 1806.

Chambers, E. K. *The Mediaeval Stage.* 1903.

Chambers's Cyclopaedia of English Literature. 1901.

Christie, George. *The Influence of Letters on the Scottish Reformation.* 1908.

Complaynt of Scotlande. E.E.T.S. 1872.

Conn, George. *De duplici statu Religionis apud Scotos.* 1628.

Coulton, G. G. *Scottish Abbeys and Social Life.* 1933.

Diurnal of Remarkable Occurrents. Bannatyne Club. 1833.

Dowden, John. *The Mediaeval Church in Scotland.* 1910.

—— *The Bishops of Scotland.* 1912.

Du Cange, C. D. *Glossarium in scriptores mediae et infimae Latinitatis.* Editions of various dates from 1678 to 1883 sqq.

Ecclesiae Scoticanae Statuta. Edited by Joseph Robertson. 1866. Translated by David Patrick. Scottish Historical Society. 1907.

Exchequer Rolls of Scotland. Record Series. 1878 sqq.

Eyre-Todd, George. *Scottish Poetry of the Sixteenth Century.* 1892.

Fleming, D. Hay. *The Reformation in Scotland.* 1910.

Geddie, William. *A Bibliography of Middle Scots Poets.* Scottish Text Society. 1912.

Gude and Godlie Ballatis. Scottish Text Society. 1897.

Hamer, Douglas. *The Works of Sir David Lindsay.* Scottish Text Society. 1931 sqq.

Hamilton, Archbishop. *Catechism.* Edited by T. G. Law. 1884.

Hay, Archibald. *Panegyricus.* 1540.

Henderson, T. F. *Scottish Vernacular Literature.* 1898.

—— *Sir David Lyndsay* in *Cambridge History of English Literature.* Vol. III. 1909.

Herkless, John. *Cardinal Beaton.* 1891.

—— and Hannay, R. K. *The Archbishops of St Andrews.* 1907 sqq.

Innes, Cosmo. *Sketches of Early Scottish History.* 1861.

—— *Scotland in the Middle Ages.* 1860.

Irving, David. *The Lives of the Scotish Poets.* 1804.

—— *The History of Scotish Poetry.* 1861.

Jusserand, J. J. *Histoire littéraire du peuple anglais.* English Translation. 1906.

Keith, Robert. *The History of the Affairs of Church and State in Scotland.* Spottiswoode Society. 1844 sqq.

Kennedy, Quintin. *Ane Compendius Tractive.* Wodrow Miscellany. 1844.

Knauff, Gustav. *Studien über Sir David Lyndsay.* 1885.

Laing, David. *The Poetical Works of Sir David Lyndsay.* 1879.

—— *The Works of John Knox.* Wodrow Society. 1846 sqq.

Leslie, John. *History of Scotland.* Bannatyne Club. 1830.

—— *De Origine, Moribus et Rebus Gestis Scotorum.* 1578. Dalrymple's translation (1596), edited for Scottish Text Society, 1888 sqq.

Lindesay of Pitscottie, Robert. *The Historie and Cronicles of Scotland.* Scottish Text Society. 1899 sqq.

Lindsay, Lord. *Lives of the Lindsays.* 1840 and 1849.

Lorimer, Peter. *Precursors of Knox.* 1860.

McCrie, Thomas. *The Life of John Knox.* 1855.

Mackay, A. J. G. *Lyndsay* in *D.N.B.* 1893.

Major, John. *Historia Majoris Britanniae.* 1521. Translated by Archibald Constable. Scottish Historical Society. 1892.

Medieval Latin Word-List (from British and Irish Sources). 1934.

Melville of Halhill, Sir James. *Memoirs.* Bannatyne Club. 1827.

Mill, Anna J. *Mediaeval Stage in Scotland.* St Andrews Publications. 1927.

—— "Influence of the Continental Drama on Lyndsay's Satyre." *Modern Language Review.* 1930.

Millar, J. H. *A Literary History of Scotland.* 1903.

Mitchell, A. F. *The Scottish Reformation.* 1900.

Nichol, John. *Sketch of Scottish Poetry* in Part V of E.E.T.S.'s *Lindesay.* 1871.

—— *Lyndesay* in Ward's *English Poetry*, Vol. I. 1880.

Paterson, James. *James the Fifth or the Gudeman of Ballangeich.* 1861.

Pollen, J. H. *Papal Negotiations with Mary Queen of Scots.* Scottish Historical Society. 1901.

Register of the Great Seal. Record Series. 1882 sqq.

Register of the Privy Seal. Record Series. 1908 sqq.

Richardinus, Robertus. *Commentary on the Rule of St Augustine.* Scottish Historical Society. 1935.

Ross, J. M. *Scottish History and Literature.* 1884.

Smith, Janet M. *The French Background of Middle Scots Literature.* 1934.

Spottiswoode, John. *History of the Church of Scotland.* Spottiswoode Society. 1847 sqq.

Theiner, Augustus. *Vetera Monumenta Hibernorum et Scotorum historiam illustrantia.* 1864.

Tytler, P. F. *Lives of Scottish Worthies.* 1831 sqq.

Veitch, John. *The Feeling for Nature in Scottish Poetry.* 1887.

Walker, Hugh. *Three Centuries of Scottish Literature.* 1893.

Walton, F. C. *Commissary Court* in *The Sources and Literature of Scots Law.* Stair Society. 1936.

Ward, A. W. *A History of English Dramatic Literature.* 1899.

Warton, Thomas. *The History of English Poetry.* 1774 sqq.

Winzet, Ninian. *Certain Tractates.* Scottish Text Society. 1888.

Other histories dealing with the Scottish Church are by George Cook, John Cunningham, George Grub, R. H. Story, and T. M. Lindsay.

GLOSSARY

The Glossary is not exhaustive. As a rule it does not give such forms as *ar*=are, *chaire*=chair, *maie*=may, *tawnie*=tawny, *bearyng*=bearing, *armes*=arms, *vapouris*=vapours, *orisoun*=orison, *obscurit*=obscured, *proces* = process, *humbill* = humble.

a', all
abesies, abbacies
abhominabyll, abominable
abowt, about
abufe, above
abyll, able
adew, adieu
ado, to do
aff, off
affore, before
againis, against
agane, at, for
aganis, by, at
aige, age
aill, ale
airly, early
al, all
alace, allace, alas
Alhallowmes, All Saints' Day
allanerly, only
allevin, eleven
als, also, as
amang, among
amland, ambling
amyable, lovable
an, and, if
ane, one, a
aneuch, enough
ane-uther, another
ansuert, answered
appellatiounis, appeals
appreve, prove
areir, backward, away
armoneis, harmonies

armyne, ermine
as, than
aucht, eight. *Auchtdayis* = a week
auen, own
aufull, awful
auld, old
aunciente, ancient
aungel, angel
awin, own
ay, aye, always

babis, babes, babies
babland, babbling
bairnis, children
baitand, feeding, grazing
baith, both
bak, back
bak, the bat
bakwart, backward
Baliell, Belial
ballants, ballads, poems
ban, curse
band, agreement
bane, bone
baneist, banished
barbour, barbarous, uncultured
bardyng, trappings
barnis, children
barras, barriers in lists
battellis, battles
baxters, bakers
be, by

beck, bow, courtesy
bed-fallow, bed-fellow
been, are
begouth, began
begynnis, begins
behuffit, behoved
beidis, beads, rosary
beir, bere
beis, is
belangis, belongs
beleve, belief
bene, been, is, are
benefyse, benefice
beris, bears, carries
beseik, beseech
besyd, beside
betuix, betwixt, between
bewtie, beauty
biddis, biddest
bischop, bishop. Plural forms are *bischopis, bischoppis, bischops*
blads, pieces, portions
blait, bleat
blak, black
blaud, piece, portion
blesfull, blissful, happy
blew, blue
blindit, blinded
blude, blood
blynd, blind
blyndid, blinded
blysfull, happy
blyssit, blessed
blyth, blyith, blithe, happy, merry
boith, both
boll, a Scottish dry measure of six bushels
bonats, bonnets, caps
bonis, bones
bony, bonny, bonnie
bordourit, bordered

borrowstoun, borough, burgh
bot, but, only, except
bow, see *boll*
bownis, make for, repair to
braid, broad
breikkis, breeches
brether, brothers
brewsters, brewers
Britaines, Britons
brocht, brought
browsters, brewers
bruke, use well
brycht, bright
buik, book
buir, bore, carried
buke, book
buller, bellow
bullis, papal bulls
burde, board, table
bure, bore, carried
bureit, buried
bus, bush
but, without
buttock-mail, fine (instead of penance) for fornication
by, buy
bynd, bind
byrdis, birds
byscheopis, bishop's
byschope, bishop. Plural *byschoppis*
byte, bite

cace, case
cair, care
cald, cold
callit, called
calsay, causeway
can crye, cried
candill, candle
Candilmes, Candlemas
cap out, in *play cap out*=drink out the cup

carle, man, fellow
cartis, cards
carvoure, carver
caryit, carried
catel, property
catyvis, rascals
cauld, cold
cawteill, crafty device, trickery
ceiss off, cease from. Plural *ceissis*
celsitude, highness
chaft blaid, jaw-bone
chaistytie, chastity
chalmer, chamber
chanoun, canon
chapman, pedlar
cheiffe, chief
cheik, cheek
circumstans, circumstance, details
Citandum, summoning, citing
claith, cloth
claithis, clothes
clark, clerk
clayis, clothes
cled, clad
cleikand, taking, seizing
cleikis, snatches, seizes
cleikit, clutched, seized
cleirly, plainly
cleith, clothe
clene, clean
clenelie, trimly
clerk, scholar
clerkit, wrote, composed
clethyng, clothing
clinck, clink
closter, cloister
clym, climb
clymmis, climbs
coattis, coats
coill, coal
coird, cord

coit, coat
come, came
commoditeis, advantages, profits
commonweill, commonwealth
commonyng, communing
commounis, commons, laymen
compairith, compares
compear, be present when cited
complexioun, temperament, nature
compt, account, attention
comptit, accounted, regarded
Concludendum, conclusion
concubeins, concubynis, concubines
conne, know, understand
constry, consistory
consydder, consider
contempnit, despised
contemptioun, contempt
continewalye, continually
contrar, against, the opposite
coppare, cup bearer
cordiners, cordwainers, shoemakers
cornecraik, corncrake, landrail
corruppit, corrupt
counsall, counsel
counsalours, counsellors
count, in *tak in my count* = hold my audit
counterfeicte, counterfeit
courchye, kerchief, nightcap
covatyce, covetousness
cowclink, courtesan
craftelly, ingeniously, neatly
crammosie, crimson
crawe, crow

creill, basket carried on back
croun, crown
crukit, crooked, not straight, lame
cryit, cried
cubiculare, groom of the bed-chamber
cuir, care
culd, culde, could
culum, buttock
cum, come
cumis, comes, come
cumming, coming
cunning, learned
cure, care, attention, charge
curiouslye, elaborately

dalyance, dalliance
dansand, dancing (verb)
dansing, dancing (noun)
dar, dare
dasyis, daisies
dayis, day's
dayis darling, day's darling, sweetheart
daylie, daily
dayntay, dainty
de, dee, die
debait, debate, contest, struggle
debaitit, contested
deceis, decease
dede, dead
deedly, deadly
defaltis, defaults
deid, dead
deidis, deids, deeds
deir, dear, loved, precious, high-priced
deit, died, dead
deith, deithe, death
delatouris, dilatory exceptions
delyte, delight

delyvering, delivering
demandis, questions
deneris, deneiris, denners, pennies, money
depairt, depart
dere, dear
derigeis, dirges
derknesse, darkness
despyte, despite
destroyit, destroyed
desyrith, desireth
devoit, devoitly, devout, devoutly
devysit, devised
dewitie, duty, dues, payment
deyand, dying
did, diddest
dillatoris, delays
din, dun, black
ding, beat, excel
ding, worthy, noble
diosies, dioceses
direct, directit, directed
dirke, dark
disdene, disdain
disfigurate, disfigured
disiune, breakfast
dispone, dispose of
dispyte, despite
dissagyist, disguised, dressed up
dissait, deceit
dochteris, dochtours, daughters
doe, dooe, do
dois, does, do
doith, do
done returne, returned
donkis, moistens, wets
doun, down
doung, knocked
doute, doubt
dowbyll, double

dreid, dread
drinkis, drink
droun, dround, drouns, drown, drowned, drowns
drynkand, drinking
drynkis, drink
dule, sorrow, grief
dulefullie, woefully
dum, dumb
dumisday, doomsday
Duplicandum, duplication, defendant's plea in answer to plaintiff's replication. See *Replicandum*
dyce, dice
dyke-lowparis, wall-jumpers, intruders, interlopers
dysche, dish

ecleped, called, named
efter, after
eis, eyes
eit, eitand, eat, eating
el, ellis, ell, ells
elf, goblin
ellis, else
empreour, empriour, emperor
enamilit, enamelled
ennimie, enemy
erlis, earls
eschaip, escape
estaitis, estates, rank, dignity
euer, evir, ever
euyn furtht, straight forward
evin, evening
exaultit, exalted
expreme, set forth in detail

fabils, fables
fact, deed
failyeit, failed
fairs, fare, are treated, are fed

fairweill, farewell
fallowis, fellows, equals
fangit, caught
farsis, farces, antics
fe, fee
febyll, feeble
feild, field
feind, fiend
feind a plak, devil a plack, none at all
feinzeing, feigning, pretending
feinzeit, feigned, pretended
feiralie, nimbly, cleverly
feirie, active
feist, feast
feit, feet
fenyeit, feigned
fenzeyng, feigning
feychtyn, fighting
feyned, feigned
fflattry, flattery
flang, flung, capered
fleich, wheedle, cajole
fleicheing, wheedling, flattering
fleis (*v.*), fly
flesche, flesh
flescher, flesher, butcher
flour, flower
flure, floor
foill, foal
follou, follow
fond, found
for'd, for it
forein, foreign
forlorne, forlorn, forsaken
foryet, forgot
fra, from
frahand, straightway
freindes, frendes, friends
freir, friar. Plural forms *freirs, freiris, freris*
frenyeis, fringes

freris, friar's
fresche, fresh
fruchtfull, fruitful, profitable
fude, food
fuill, fule, fool
furth, forth, out
fut, foot
futsteppis, footsteps
fyfe, five
fyftene, fifteen
fynd, find
fysche, fish

ga, go
gaille, cry like the cuckoo
gaine, gone, walked
gaist, ghost
gait, gaittis, way, ways
gait, gate
ganer, gander
gang, go, walk
garris, gars, makes, causes
gart, made, forced
gearking, showy, vain
geir, gear, property
genneris, beget, produce
gentyll, beautiful, noble
gett, gettis, get, gets
gette stone, jet
geve, gevin, give, given
geyre, gear
gie, give
gif, give
gif, if
givin, given
glaid, glad
gled, kite
Goddis, God's
goik, cuckoo
goodwyiff, goodwife
gormand, gormande, gluttonous, greedy
gossop, crony

gould, gold
gragit, cursed, excommunicated
graip, feel, handle
graunt, grant
grediness, greediness
greidie, greedy
greif, grief, umbrage
greislie, grisly
greit, cry, weep
grene, green
grenesyd, Greenside
grenewod, greenwood
gret, great
grice, gray fur
gruntill, snout
gryce, gryse, young pig
gud, gude, good. *Gude* (p. viii) = God
guddis, goods, possessions
gude-chaip, good-cheap, cheap
guse, goose
guyder, guider
gyde, guide
Gye, Guy of Warwick
gyf, give
gyf, if
Gyre Carlin, a gigantic witch of ghastly appearance

habitis, dress
hae, have
hag, notch
haif, haiff, have
haiffeing, having
haill, whole
haistelie, hastily
hait, haits, hate, hates
haldin, holden, held
halds, holds
halie, haly, holy
halines, holiness

hame, home
handill, handle, lay hands on
hangit, hanged
hapnis, happens
happinit, happened
happis, happit, covers, wraps, covered, wrapped
hard, heard
harlit, pulled by force, dragged
harlot, jade, rascal
harns, brains
hart, hartis, heart, hearts
hashes, dunderheads
hauld, hold
hauldin, holden, held
haunteth, practises, indulges in
haym-cumin, home-coming
hedde, head
heich, high
heid, head
heir, here
heir, heiris, hear, hears
heit, heat
helsum, wholesome
heremeit, hermit
herisie, heresy
hes, has, hast, have
heve, have
hevinlie, hevinly, hevinlye, heavenly
hie, hiest, high, highest
hir, her
Hodie ad octo, to-day week. See *aucht*. In Scots *eight days* is sometimes = a week
hog, a young sheep
hoilsum, wholesome
holynes, holiness
honestie, decency, worthiness, suitability
hoot awa, get away
howbeit, although, nevertheless
howlat, owl

hude, hood
huir, huirdomes, whore, whoredoms
hummill-bummill, a rhyming combination to echo unintelligible mumbling. Compare *hurry-scurry, hugger-mugger*, and others
huris, whores
hycht, height
hym, him
hyr, her
hyreild, heriot

Iapes, japes, jests
ilk, every
imagereis, images
impit, grafted
incontinent, at once
indure, continue
indyte, writing, composition
ingyne, talent
injure, injury
instant, present, current
Interloquendum, intermediate decree
in till, intill, in tyll, in
in to, into, in
iren, iron
ischare, usher
Iune, June
I wis, certainly

jugis, judges
justynis, joustings

ka, jackdaw
kaies, keys
keip, keipit, keep, kept
kekell, cackle
ken, kend, know, known
kene, sharp
kepis, kepith, keeps, keep

kirk, kirkis, church, churches
kirkmen, churchmen, clergy
kirtil, kirtle
knaw, knawin, know, known
kne, kneis, knee, knees
knicht, knyght, knychts, knight, knights
knowis, know
kow, cow
ky, kye, cows, cattle
kynd, kyndnes, kind, kindness
kyng, king

ladies, lady's
laird, lord, owner
lait, late
lamber, the amber
Lammes, Lammas
landwart, country
lang, langer, long, longer
larglie, largely, freely
lassis, lasses
lat, let
lauch, laugh
laverock, lark
lawe, low, lowly, humble
layik, laic, lay
ledder, ladder
leid, lead
leife, leifis, live, lives
leir, teach, learn
leit, let
lemand, shining, bright
lenth, length
lernand, learning
leve, live
levis, leaves
lewed man, layman
leyrn, learn
littill, little
livery, allowance of food or clothing to retainers and servants

loon, fellow, rascal
lorimers, saddlers
lufe, lufit, love, lovedst
luif, luiffis, love, lovest
luife, love
luik, look
lustis, lust's *or* lusts'
Lybellandum, the first plea or statement of a legal case
lychtleit, lychtlyit, made light of, disparaged
lyfe, lyfis, lyffis, lyvis, life, lives
lyis, lies
lyk, lyke, like
lykned, likened
lynnyng, linen
lyoun, lion
lyre, cheek, face
lytill, little

ma, more
maid, made
maiglet, mangled
maine, moan
mair, mare
mair, more
maist, most
maister, master
mak, make, do
makand, making, doing
makis, makes
maleson, curse
man, must
maneris, manners, morals, behaviour
mantyll, mantle
marchellit, marschellit, marshalled
mareguildis, marigolds
marie, marry
markit, market
marrowis, companions

martrik, marten
marye, maryit, marry, married
matenis, matins
mater, matter
mear, meir, mare
medicinar, physician
meikle, much, great
meinze, meinzie, company
meit, meat, food
meitis, meet
mekil, mekill, much, great
menever, miniver
menstrall, minstrel
merle, blackbird
mess, the Mass
me think, methinks, it seems to me
midding, midden
mirrie, merry
miscaryit, injured
misgydit, misled
misreule, misbehaviour
misterie, office, duty
mistoinit, out of tune, harsh
mither, mother
mo, more
moist, most
mon, must
moneth, monethis, month, months
monie, mony, many
monkrye, monkery
monstour, monster
month, mount
morne, next day, morrow
morow, morrow, morning
most, moste, must
mows, jests. *In mowis* = in fun
muill, mule
muk, muck
mummill, mummyll, mumble

murne, mourn
mute, utter
mycht, might
mylk, milk
mynd, mind
myne, mine
myrthfull, mirthful
mystie, misty

na, no
nae, no
naething, nothing
namit, named
nane, none
nat, not
nathing, nothing
natyvitie, nativity
naymis, names
ne, nor
neids (*v.*), needs
neids (*n.*), needs, necessities
nek, neck
new, newly, recently
nichtbour, neighbour
nixt, nearest
nocht, not
nochttheles, nevertheless
non-compearance, absence
nor, than
nuicket, cornered, with corners
nycht, night
nychtbour, neighbour
nychtlie, nightly
nychtyngaill, nightingale

obayit, obeyed
obscurit, obscured
observance, duty, reverence
occiane seis, ocean seas
occupyit, occupied
ocht, aught, anything
of, off

offerand, offering. Plural forms, *offerandis, offerands, offrands*

officiaris, officers

onder, under

onis, once

Opponendum, reply of opponent in law case

or, before

ordane, ordain, provide

ordinance, armament

oster-schellis, oyster shells

ouer, over, too

ouersene, overlooked, connived at

ouerthort, across, from side to side

ower, over, with

paine, pain, punishment, penalty

painfull, hard, laborious

Paip, Pape, Pope

pair, set

pak, pack

palyard, impostor, cheat

palyce, palace

panefull, painful

parisshens, parishioners

partan, crab

Pasche, Easter

pastyme, pastime

pat, did put

patent, licensed

pattryng, pattering

paven, pavin, a stately dance

payit, paid

peax, pece, peace

peirles, peerless

pelts, blows

peopill, pepill, peple, pepyll, people

perdition, destruction, ruin

peremptouris, peremptory decrees

perfyte, perfect

perisshens, parishioners

perle, pearl

perqueir, offhand

persewing, pursuing

persith, pierce

person, parson

pertene, pertain to, belong to

petuouslye, piteously

pew, cry like a kite

pietie, pity

pietuus, pious

pikestaff, staff with sharp iron point

placebo, sycophant

places, mansions

plaine, plainly, clearly

plainlie, openly

plak, plackis, plack, placks. The plack was worth four pennies Scots and equalled one-third English penny

platt, clapped, put

playand, playing

playis, pleas

playit, played

pleasand, plesand, pleasant

pleasandlye, plesandlie, pleasantly

pleinze, pleinzie, complain

plesance, delight

plesis, pleases

plesour, plesoure, pleasure

pleuch, plough

pleyis, pleas

poast, post, wooden pillar

pontifical, bishop's service-book

portuise, portable breviary. The variants in spelling of this word are over twenty

poure, poor
prayand, praying
precedand, preceding
preche, preich, preach
precheing, preicheing, preaching
preest, preestes, priest, priests
preesthode, priesthood
preist, preistis, priest, priests
preistheid, priesthood
prelattis, prelates'
prencis, princes
prenis, pins
prenteischip, apprenticeship
prepotent, puissant
prey, pray
profect, profeit, proffeit, profit
promovit, promoted
Pronunciandum, judgment
proportionat, proportioned
propre, own
provocand, provoking, inciting
publict, public
puir, poor
pulchritude, beauty
pullit, pulled
pundis, pounds
punitioun, punishment
pure, poor, shabby
purelye, poorly
puris, the poor
pyne, pain, distress, vexation

qualifeid, qualyfeit, qualified
queir, quire, choir
querrell hollis, holes full of water in disused quarries
quha, who
quhaill, whale

quhair, quhar, quhare, where. So in compounds, as quhairin
quhairfoir, for which
quhais, whose
quham, whom
quhat, what
quhen, when
quhilk, quhilkis, quhilks, which, who
quhill, quhyll, while, till
quhite, quhyte, white
quho, who
quhome, whom
quhose, whose
quhow, how
quhowbeit, although
quhy, why
quhyle, quhyll, a while
quod, said

raggit, ragged
raige, rage
raisit, raised
rak, matter
rang, ruled
raploch, rapploch, coarse undyed homespun woollen cloth, hodden
red, did read
redar, reader
Red Etin, Red Giant
redie, ready
regiment, rule, government
rehersis, relates
reid, advise, read
reiding, reading
reif, plundering
reiffis, steals, snatches
rejosit, rejoysit, rejoiced, delighted
relict, relic
religious, monastic, monk

relikes, relics
remede, remeid, remedy, reparation, amends
rent, revenue, income
renuncit, renounced
Replicandum, plaintiff's reply to the defendant's plea
repreuit, reproved
ressave, receive
ressett, received illegally. *Reset* means receive stolen property
retraited, retracted, reversed
reuin, rent, torn, destroyed
reverent, reverend
rew, have pity
rew, ruing, repentance
rewlaris, rulers
rewlis, rules
rewlit, adorned, ordered
richt, right, very, fully
rin, run
rocket, rochet
roploch. See *raploch*
roupit, croaked
rowte, rout, company
Rude, Rood, Cross
Rudmes, Rood Mass. May 3rd
ruiks, rooks
ruschit, rushed
ruse, praise
rute, root
ryche, rychelie, rich, richly
rycht, right
ryde, ride
rymis, rhymes
ryng, reign
ryngis, times of ruling
rysche, rush (the plant)

sa, so
sa, say

saif, safe
saik, sake
sair, sore, sorely, bitterly
sait, seat
sal, sall, shall
sallbe, shall be
samin, samyn, same
sanct, saint
sangis, songs
sauld, sold
saule, saulis, sauls, soul, souls
sax, six
say, tell, bid
schame, shame
schaw, schawis, schawin, show, show, shown
sche, she
sched, shed
scheif, sheaf
scheip, sheep
schene, bright
Schenis, Sciennes in Edinburgh, where was a nunnery of St Catherine of Siena
schir, sir
scho, she
schortlye, shortly
science, knowledge
scule, scuilis, school, schools
se, seis, see, seest
seald, sealed
seavin, seven
secreit, secret, confidential, privy
secretis, secrets
secund, second
see, seis, sea, seas
see, seat, place
seik, seek
Seinzie, Consistory Court
seith, saith

selit, sealed

sell, self, selves

selye, seilye, simple, poor

semestair, seamstress

semeth, seemeth

sen, since

sene, seen

Sentenciandum, sentence in court of law

ser, sir

sers, search

servyce, service, duty

Sessioun, Court of Session

seuer, sure, certain

sevin, seven

sevint, seventh

sevintene, seventeen

seware, sewer, attendant at table

seycht, sight

sic, such

sicker, sure, firm, certain

siclyke, similarly

sillabis, syllables

sillie, simple, harmless, defenceless

sindry, various

singulaire, singular, singulare, personal

sittith, sitteth

skaith, harm, injury

skaplarie, scapulary

skarlote, scarlet

slane, slain

sleip, sleep

sleit, sleet

sleuthfull, slothful

slidder, slippery

slummer, slumber

slyding, sliding

snell, sharp, terrible

snyp, snip

soir, sore, expensive

solysitatioun, solicitation

sonder, in phrase a sonder = asunder

sonsy, lucky

sorie, sad, gloomy

sors, source

sorye, sorry, sad

sothe, truth

souertie, surety

sould, should

soune, soon

soveraine, soverane, sovereign

soveranitie, sovereignty

spaice, space

sparit, spared, forbore

speik, speak

speir, ask

speirs, spears

spell, read

spendit, spent

splene, spleen, heart

spreit, spirit

spring, surprise

spryngis, lively tunes

spulye, spoil, pillage

spune, spoon

spurtill, a rod or stick for stirring porridge, broth, etc.

stait, state

staitly, stately

stanchit, stanched

steir, stir. The phrase on steir = in an uproar

sterris, stars

stirkie, diminutive of stirk, used of cattle between the ages of one and two

stollin, stolen

stottikin, contemptuous diminutive of stot, a young bull

stoup, flagon

strydlingis, astride
stryk, strike
stude, stood
stuiff, stuff
stylit, styled
subditis, subjects
suith, suthe, truth
suithlie, in truth
suld, should
sum, some
sumptuus, expensive
sumthing, something
sumtyme, sometimes
superflew, superfluous
supportatioun, support
sustene, sustain
sweir, sweiris, swear
sweit, sweet
sweitlie, sweetly
swich, such
swink, labour, toil
syd, side; *on syd*=sideways
syde, long
syllie, simple, harmless
symonie, simony
Symonis, Simon's, Simony's
syn, synnis, sin, sins
syne, then, next
syng, sing
Synthea, Cynthia, the Moon
syster, systeris, sister, sisters

tabillis, tables, backgammon
tailzeour, tailor
tailzie, entail
taine, taken
tak, take
takand, takkand, taking
takis, takes
taks, take
tarie, tarry
tasker, a piece-worker, often receiving his wages in kind

teche, teach
teicheing, teaching
teichouris, teichours, teachers
teind, tithe
teith, teeth
telling, counting
tent, attention, regard
terribill, terrible
tether, rope
thae, those
thair, thare (*pr.*), their
thair, thare (*adv.*), there
thairfoir, thairfor, therefore
thairto, thereto
thame, them
than, then
thay, they
theim, them
then, than
thesaurare, treasurer
thi, thy
thift, theft
thir, these, their
thise, these
tho, those
thocht, thought
thocht, thoucht, though
tholis, sufferest
thow, thou
thowsand, thousand
thre, thrie, three
thrid, third
thrissil, thistle
throuch, throw, through
thynk, think
till, to
togidder, togydder, together
toun, town
toung, tongue
towrnament, tournament
traine, artifice, trickery
traist, trust

tramalt nett, trammel net
transfigurate, transfigured
trappit, trapped, snared
trattyl, prattle
treassoun, treason
tree, wood
treis, trees
trentalls, services of thirty masses each for the dead
trew, trewly, true, truly
Triplicandum, triplication, plaintiff's reply to defendant's duplication. See *Duplicandum*
triwmphand, triumphal
trow, believe
trows, thinkest
trybulatioun, tribulation
trypartit, divided into three
tryumphantlie, tryumphantlye, triumphantly
Tueid, Tweed
tuik, tuk, tuke, took
tun, put into casks
turnements, tournaments
turnit, turned
twa, tway, two
twelf, twelve
tweye, two
twyse, twice
tydier, neater
tyll, till, to
tyme, time
tynt, lost
Tysday, Tuesday
tythes, tithes, teinds

umaist, umest, uppermost
umquhyle, formerly
unburyit, unburied
undefamit, undefamed
unfained, unfeigned
unhappy, shrewish

unhonestie, indecorum
unmaryit, unmarried
unpayit, unpaid
unsell, wretched, worthless
Upeland, upland, in the country. *Jhone Upeland* = a country fellow
uphauld, uphold, keep up
uther, other

vailyeand, valiant
vald, would
vane, vain
veray, very
verteous, virtuous
vertew, virtew, virtue, power
vickar, vicar
vicuus, vicious
vilipendit, thought of little value, despised
villanie, wrong, harm
vmquhile, the late, deceased
vp, vppon, up, upon
vpon lond, in the country
vs, us

wa (*n.*), woe
wa (*adj.*), sad
wad, would
waik, weak
wait, know
wald, would
walkers, fullers
walloway, alas
wan, won, gained
wander, bad luck
wantand, wanting
war, were
warkis, works
warldlie, worldly
warmis, warm
warst, worst
was, were

wat, know
waur, worse
we, wee
websters, weavers
wedderis, wedders, wether's
weddir, weather
wee, we
weicht, weight. *Gould of weicht* = gold of standard weight
weidis, weeds, clothes
weill, well
weir, war
welcum, welcome
weman, wemen, woman, women
wer, weren, were
werkis, works
wes, wast, was
whan, when
whaur, where
whilk, which
wicht, strong
wickit, wicked
widdie, withy, halter, gallows
widdiefows, gallows birds
wirk, work
wirkis, works
wist, knew
without, without, outside, beyond, unless
withouttin, without
witsone, whitsun
witt, wisdom
wolfis, wolves
woll, wool
wonder, wonderfully, excessively

wot, knew
wount, wont
wracheis, wretches'
wrang, wrong
wrangous, wrongful
wrights, carpenters
writtin, written
wryts, writes
ws, us
wyfe, wyfis, wyffis, wife, wives
wylbe, will be
wyll, will
wyre, wire
wyrschip, worship
wysdome, wysedome, wisdom
wyse (*adj.*), wise
wyse (*n.*), wise, way
wytles, witless
wyttin, known
wyvis, wives

yairnis, yearn for
yeir, year
yeirlie, yearly
yer, yere, yeris, year, years
yeven, give
yit, yet
yow, you
yowis, ewes
yschare, usher

zeid, went, walked
zong, young

ȝeir, ȝeiris, year, years
ȝow, you

INDEX

abbots and monks, 46, 48, 60, 63, 72, 80, 83, 84, 85, 91, 92, 93, 96, 97, 99, 122, 139, 141, 145, 147, 150, 160, 163, 165, 170, 173, 190, 196

amusements of clergy, 91, 99, 180, 196

Antwerp letter, vii note, 10

Arth, Friar, 145 note, 167 note, 201

Bannatyne MS., 38, 43, 66

beards, 137, 138

Beaton, Cardinal, 13, 32, 150, 188, 201, 202

Beaton, James (Cardinal's uncle), 162, 188 note

Beaton, James (Cardinal's nephew), 125

Bellenden, John, 6, 7 note, 168

Bellenden, Thomas, 38

bishops, 56, 60, 63, 66, 69, 80, 83, 86, 89, 91, 92, 93, 95, 100, 113, 127, 150, 162, 166, 170, 186, 196

Buchanan, George, 3 note, 4, 18 note, 95, 203

Bullein's *Dialogue*, ix

Catechism, Hamilton's, 125, 129, 131, 152, 203

celibacy, 81, 84

chaplains, 141, 150, 164

Charteris, Henrie, 44, 94

chastity, 81, 84, 174, 177, 185, 193

children admitted to benefices, 129, 161, 182, 185, 187, 197

church services neglected, 140, 178, 202

clergy, charges against: abuse of the confessional, 101, 156; ambition, 98, 172, 193; covetousness, 81, 85, 160, 171, 173, 183, 186, 193, 196; envy, 64,

173; extravagance in dress, in houses, in food and drink, 81, 91, 97, 99, 137, 138, 166, 170, 176, 178, 196; ignorance and incompetence, 92, 126, 129, 131, 161, 170, 174, 178, 182, 185, 187, 191, 194, 197; immorality, 81, 102, 121, 128, 147, 155, 160, 161, 168, 170, 174, 178, 180, 187, 192, 196; misbehaviour during services and at synods, 141, 178; misuse of the patrimony of the church, 91, 135, 139, 157, 159, 167, 170, 180, 185, 197; neglect of church buildings, 91, 139, 140, 157, 160, 161, 180, of the poor, 91, 138, 140, 157, 166, 168, 170, 196, 198, of preaching and other duties, 100, 127, 130, 153, 158, 162, 165, 168, 171, 178, 182, 185, 195, of study, 126, 172, 178, 185, 195; pride, 64, 81, 96, 173, 177, 186; sloth and idleness, 64, 168, 170, 172, 184; tenants ill-treated, 57, 134, 166, 172

Commentary on the Rule of St Augustine, 173

Complaynt of Scotlande, x note, 62 note, 171

concubinage, 121

Conn, George, 186

Consistory Court, 58, 109, 143

Constantine's Donation, 27

corpse-present, 88, 133

Douglas, Janet, 7, 15

Douglases, 7

Dunbar, Archbishop, 6, 7 note

Durie, Bishop, 147

Ecclesiae Scoticanae Statuta, 121

Elphinstone, 126, 201